GREAT LAKES
PASSENGER SHIP
DISASTERS

WAYNE LOUIS KADAR

Avery Color Studios, Inc.
Gwinn, Michigan

©2005 Avery Color Studios, Inc.

ISBN-13: 978-1-892384-29-4
ISBN-10: 1-892384-29-9

Library of Congress Control Number: 2004115507

First Edition–2005

10   9   8   7   6   5   4   3   2

Published by
Avery Color Studios, Inc.
Gwinn, Michigan 49841

Cover photos: *S. S. George M. Cox,* from the H.C. Inches Collection, Port Huron Museum; *Tashmoo,* Courtesy *The Detroit News*; *Pere Marquette No. 18,* from the Collection of the Michigan Maritime Museum, South Haven, Michigan; *City of Cleveland, III,* from the Harlow Meno Collection of the Port Huron Museum; 1929 Goodrich Fleet Brochure, the Library of Michigan, an agency of the Department of History, Arts and Libraries

I am proud to dedicate this book to my family. My wife Karen, who has been by my side supporting me for over thirty years. Our sons Brandon and Grant who share my love of most anything nautical and our daughter Kasie for her assistance in editing this book.

TABLE OF CONTENTS

INTRODUCTION

In the late 1600s Europeans arrived on the shores of the American continent; they built settlements on oceans, rivers and lakes. There were no roads. The waterways were the only means of transportation. The geographic locations of most of the larger or prominent cities around the Great Lakes are on one of the lakes or a tributary leading to one of them. Detroit, Chicago, Buffalo, Toronto, Green Bay, Milwaukee, Toledo and Cleveland are all examples of cities whose location was determined by their proximity to the lakes.

American and Canadian entrepreneurs were quick to realize there was money to be made in the transportation of people on the lakes and rivers. The canoes of the 1700s gave way to ferries to transfer passengers. As technology progressed, steam ferries were soon transporting passengers.

The simple ferry competing for passenger fares became larger and more elaborate. Simply getting across a

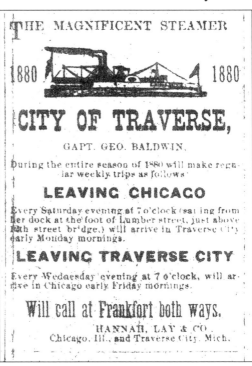

THE MAGNIFICENT STEAMER

1880   1880

CITY OF TRAVERSE,

GAPT. GEO. BALDWIN.

During the entire season of 1880 will make regular weekly trips as follows:

LEAVING CHICAGO

Every Saturday evening at 7 o'clock (sailing from her dock at the foot of Lumber street, just above 12th street bridge,) will arrive in Traverse City early Monday mornings.

LEAVING TRAVERSE CITY

Every Wednesday evening at 7 o'clock, will arrive in Chicago early Friday mornings.

Will call at Frankfort both ways.

HANNAH, LAY & CO.,
Chicago, Ill., and Traverse City, Mich.

1

river or getting from one town to another was no longer just a trip, it became an adventure. As Canada's and the United States' economies grew so did the income of the middle class. Travel became not just a necessary part of life for some, but a means of escape from those trapped in cramped city living.

A trip on a ship to playgrounds around the lakes was no longer reserved for the idle rich. Resorts catering to the middle class, as well as the rich, were growing in popularity. Destinations such as Lake Huron's Mackinac and Les Cheneaux Islands, Lake Ontario's Thousand Islands and Lake Erie's Put-In-Bay and Cedar Point were becoming very popular. In addition, Isle Royale on Lake Superior, Lake St. Clair's Harsens Island and many coastal resort towns on the Michigan and Wisconsin coasts were increasingly popular. The middle class could now afford passage on these ships. There were still ships and resorts which catered to the rich, but there was money to be made in transporting and housing the new money of the middle class.

Front and back cover of a 1929 Goodrich fleet brochure. Library of Michigan, an agency of the Department of History, Arts and Libraries

The passenger ships transported people but to maximize profits were also filled with cargo destined for lake ports. Yet to compete for the traffic, the ships continued to grow larger and more elegant. The passenger and excursion ships of the late 1800s and early 1900s became a destination in their own right. They had

A 1916 view of the main saloon of the Steamship Alabama. *From the collection of the Muskegon County Museum*

large dance floors and never sailed without at least one orchestra. Carpenters created beautiful interiors of exotic and domestic woods and windows were often beautiful stained glass objects of art. Dining halls rivaled the most luxurious restaurants and the state rooms were eloquently appointed. They were the Carnival Cruise Line of their day. And like today, the ship designers tried to out do each other with each new vessel launched.

As railroads were built to regions previously deemed too remote or unprofitable, the passenger ship traffic began to wane. Some tragic and very publicized passenger ship accidents also contributed to the demise of the industry. The luxury ships that carried thousands of passengers on carefree summer excursions to exclusive resorts were replaced by the railroad and improved roads for personal motorcars.

As the passenger ship market declined, the ships were scrapped or sold to foreign countries where the infrastructure of roads and rail had not yet been developed.

The era of steam passenger ships on the Great Lakes had come to a conclusion. Some ships held on as novelties, the *Columbia* and the *St. Clair* carried passengers to Bob-lo Island, an amusement park in the Detroit River well into the 1990s and a few vessels found life as ferries servicing remote locations. The classic old ships were burned, scrapped, sold or sent to back waters to rot. But,

A 1929 brochure of the Detroit & Cleveland Navigation Company.
Library of Michigan, an agency of the Department of History, Arts and Libraries

*A book passengers received on a cruise on the Detroit & Cleveland
steamer* Greater Buffalo. *From the collection of the Port Huron Museum*

as airline travel became more economical and highways were
paved to almost any location in America and Canada, passenger
travel on the Great Lakes all but disappeared. An era had passed.

The ship that holds the dubious distinction of the most deaths
on the Great Lakes, the *S. S. Eastland*, ended its career as a Navel
Reserve training vessel. The *Tashmoo* of Detroit, famed for her
1901 race with *City of Erie*, struck a rock, sank and was sold for
scrap. The *Put-In-Bay*, which provided luxury passage to the Lake
Erie resort of the same name, was burned to her iron hull as a
spectacle in Lake St. Clair before being sent to the scrap yard. The
two Bob-Lo boats, the *Columbia* and *St. Clair* were removed from
service and left to decay.

Many of the other ships that sailed the lakes and carried
passengers have met with a disastrous end. Some met an
unceremonious end by catching fire and burning to the waterline

One of the most unique Great Lake passenger ships, the Whale back design Christopher Columbus. *Library of Michigan, an agency of the Department of History, Arts and Libraries*

while they were tied to a dock during winter lay-up. Others were run aground by pilot error and broken apart by the force of the waves. Some ships, ripe with age, simply disappeared in Great Lake storms without a living soul to testify to the cause or the suffering of the passengers or crew.

This book explores the tragic tales of the ships designed to carry passengers, be it a ferry, a day or weekend excursion vessel, or a ship with cabins for extended cruises.

INTRODUCTION

A 1910 travel brochure from the Goodrich Steamship Lines. Library
of Michigan, an agency of the Department of History, Arts and Libraries

The day of the beautiful ships sailing the Great Lakes with
hundreds of passengers has passed, but there are a few
individuals looking to the past to preserve this piece of history.
Both Bob-Lo boats, the *St. Clair* and the *Columbia* are being
renovated to preserve a piece of history for future generations.
Other industrious individuals have worked hard to bring back the
Great Lake passenger cruise ship. I hope these ventures are
successful and are able to continue this small piece of Americana
for our children to enjoy.

THE COLLISION OF THE CITY OF CLEVELAND III

The excitement of the almost one hundred members of the Benton Harbor Chamber of Commerce was contagious on that late June day of 1950. They were going to see the Detroit Tigers play the New York Yankees in a double header. The Tigers were a rebuilt team in 1950. They had acquired future Hall of Fame player, George Kell and a group of young players developed in the farm club, they were maturing into a "Cracker Jack" team. The Tigers were in first place with a four game lead over the second place Yankees.

For the Benton Harbor Chamber of Commerce, getting to the game was going to be an adventure in its own. They would be making the fourth annual excursion to Detroit on the Detroit & Cleveland Navigation Company pas-
senger ship, *City of
Cleveland III*. The
*City of Cleveland
III* was considered
one of the most
luxurious liners on
the Great Lakes. At
425-feet, it was the

City of
Cleveland III

The City of Cleveland III. From the H. C. Inches collection of the Port Huron Museum

second largest ship in the D & C Fleet and capable of carrying 750 passengers and 160 crew.

The group climbed aboard the C & O train Thursday at Benton Harbor for the trip to Grand Haven where they would meet the ship. As they boarded the train, Chamber members wore the white "Skippers" caps they were all given. Alvin Boyd replaced his Police Chief's hat with the yachting hat and looked as distinguished as the ship's captain, while Tom Dewhirst with his thick full beard looked more like a pirate.

As soon as they boarded the ship the group, in a festive mood, began to celebrate in anticipation of a sunny, fun-filled cruise. The itinerary included a stop at beautiful and historic Mackinac Island and a trip up the St. Marys River to Michigan's oldest city, Sault St. Marie, where they would cruise through the Soo Locks. The trip would then take them back down the St. Marys River into Lake Huron, passing such historic maritime ports as Cheboygan, Alpena and the harbor of refuge at Harbor Beach. They would then leave Lake Huron, heading south into the St. Clair River at Port Huron and through Lake St. Clair. The final leg of the journey was

The Chamber members leaving the train in preparation of boarding the City of Cleveland III. Benton Harbor Palladium

into the Detroit River and finally disembarking for the baseball game. From there, the ship would continue on to Buffalo, New York and the Benton Harbor Chamber of Commerce would return home via train.

The journey was well organized, every detail addressed. The trip was billed as better than the previous three trips. However, even the best laid plans sometimes crumble when Mother Nature is involved. Almost as soon as the ship had departed Grand Haven, the party goers were forced to stay inside their cabins and other interior areas. A summer storm bore down across Lake Michigan onto the *City of Cleveland III*.

The storm didn't seem to hamper the spirits of the Chamber members. They couldn't walk sun drenched decks, so they simply moved the party inside. A little rain wouldn't ruin their trip, it was just a minor setback.

That evening Berrien County Circuit Judge E. A. Westin was selected to preside as "King Neptune" in the "Crossing the Line" extravaganza, part of the onboard entertainment. "King Neptune" stood proudly center stage surrounded by various other passengers, dressed as "His Highnesses Polliwogs."

The passengers enjoyed ship life, until the storm churned the tranquil rolling sea into violent storm-tossed waves. That evening the ship rolled, pitched and pounded on the waves. The passengers partying in the ballroom soon looked more like patients in a hospital flu ward. The dream trip of fun, became a nightmare of seasickness. But as bad as it had become, the voyage was going to get worse.

The skies darkened with night, the seas subsided but a fog rolled in, encapsulating the ship in a shroud of white. The ship's fog signal blasted and whistles and horns of other ships could be heard coming from all directions. Most of the passengers turned in early. The Benton Harbor Chamber of Commerce members retired to the block of cabins reserved for them, most located on "B" deck on the port side, aft of midship. They fell asleep as best they could, with hopes for better weather.

The passengers awoke to find the ship still in a blanket of fog. Becalmed in Lake Michigan at first was a somewhat unique, albeit a frightening experience, but faced with another day of becalmed boredom the passengers' mood became depressed. A mood even the creations of the ship's bar couldn't lift, although not for trying. For over thirty-six hours, The *City of Cleveland lll* was fog bound, she crawled through the fog, stopping several times out of fear of other ships in her immediate area.

Rumors began to fly through the ship: the radar wasn't working; they were going to turn around and head back to Grand

The City of Cleveland III *awaits at the dock for her passengers.*
From the collection of the Michigan Maritime Museum, South Haven, Michigan

Haven; they were on a collision course with another ship. Passengers listened to the rumors and to ships' fog signals all around them. Fearing collision, most prayed for their safety.

Saturday night, the ship still in dense fog, slowly found its way into the port of Harbor Springs, Michigan on a non-scheduled stop. Thomas O'Hara and Edward Brown, both of the Benton Harbor Chamber of Commerce, elected to leave the ship. O'Hara, pale and weak, had not handled the rough seas well and his seasickness persisted. Brown later recounted that he had heard the crew say the stop at Mackinac Island and the tour of the Soo Locks had been cancelled due to the delay caused by the storm and fog. Based on his calculations, Ed figured the ship had been delayed to the extent that they could not possibly make Detroit in time for the baseball game. Several other passengers also left the ship in disgust. That evening the ship steamed out of the harbor to continue around the tip of Michigan's mitten into Lake Huron.

Most passengers turned in early, hoping sleep might bring relief from the fog and their fear. In the night air the fog lifted a little, allowing the ship to pour on the coal, trying to make up some of the time they had lost fog bound on Lake Michigan. The top speed of the *City of Cleveland III* was eighteen MPH, on this evening they were running at sixteen MPH trying to make up lost time. Through the night the ship raced around the top of Michigan's mitten and south through Lake Huron.

Mervyn Stouck had served as mayor of Benton Harbor for four terms and it was his custom to awake early and walk. This Sunday morning was no different. He woke up about 5:30 a.m. and looked out his cabin window to see the fog had persisted. Determined to make the best of this cruise, he dressed and went out on deck for a stroll. He briskly walked around "B" deck in a blanket of thick, pea soup, fog.

Most passengers elected to sleep in while the *City of Cleveland III* steamed south through the fog. Tom Spooner said he woke up early to the sound of a foghorn and looked out the window, but seeing nothing but fog, he returned to bed and slept until he found himself… underwater. Arms stretching out in a desperate attempt to reach the surface, his mind tried to make sense of the situation.

Dick Cronin rose early that morning, as was his habit. He stood before the cabin mirror, his Gillette twin blade safety razor removing stubble and Burma Shave cream, when a large plank of wood crashed through his cabin window, flew through the room, embedding into the cabin wall… narrowly missing his head.

Out on the deck, Benton Harbor city commissioner Jim Bowen absentmindedly stared out into the fog, listening to the foghorn. He heard a rumbling sound and thought the *Cleveland* might have run aground. Then he realized the ship had struck something.

Mervyn Stouck's stroll around "B" deck brought him back in front of his cabin, number 134. There he stood listening to another ship's fog signal when suddenly a large gray ship's bow cut through the fog and ripped into the port side of the *City of Cleveland lll*, right where Mr. Stouck was standing. He was thrown into the lake.

Dr. Ozeran, a Benton Harbor physician, held a stateroom on "D" Deck, the uppermost deck, away from the crowd. He was sleeping when a wrenching sound woke him up, he then realized that the man yelling in his dream was in fact, in the hall.

"Get to the lifeboats, get to the lifeboats!"

Dr. Ozeran opened his door asking the crewman yelling and pounding on doors, what was the need of the commotion.

The man yelled from down the hall, "We've been hit… I think we are going to sink!"

Police Chief Alvin Boyd never woke up, he was killed as he slept in his stateroom.

Nelson Foulkes a reporter for the *Benton Harbor Palladium* and *St. Joseph Herald* shared a stateroom with George Culverhouse on "C" deck. They awoke at 6:15 a.m. when the ship jarred, shaking their beds. While slumber still clouded their heads, the ship's alarm bell began to sound. They concluded it must be a drill and thought 6:15 a.m. was a damn poor time for a drill.

They quickly dressed, hearing the voice of a crew woman in the hall telling passengers to put on their life jackets.

Still thinking this was a drill, the men casually walked to the open deck. There, they found crew scurrying about to their lifeboat stations. The two men were directed to lifeboat station number two, where crew were at the davits readying to launch the lifeboat.

The fog was so thick visibility beyond ten feet was impossible. The men on deck were deafened by the blast of the *Cleveland's* foghorn, answered by a ship somewhere in the fog off the *Cleveland's* port. Several Chamber members gathered, joking about the drill until one of them noticed through the fog that the *Cleveland* had sustained damage towards the stern. They moved closer for a look and suddenly realized the seriousness of the situation.

Chief Boatswain's Mate, Kenneth Call, of Coast Guard Station Harbor Beach, was on ship to shore radio communicating with Captain Rolf Thorson of the Norwegian freighter, *S. S. Ravnefjeel*. The freighter was north bound on Lake Huron in the upbound shipping lane about four miles offshore. The captain reported that fog limited visibility to no more than a few feet; he was concerned that his radar showed a ship in their vicinity.

Chief Call instructed the captain to keep sounding his fog signal and to proceed slowly.

The *Ravnefjeel's* radar indicated the other ship was downbound, about four miles off shore and moving at a fast rate of speed. Then the ship disappeared from the radar screen, indicating it was too close for the *Ravnefjeel's* radar to pick it up.

"Starboard!" Captain Thorson ordered, realizing the *Ravnefjeel* was on a collision course with the other ship.

On the bridge of the *City of Cleveland lll*, Captain Kiessling, heard a fog signal close to his position. He stepped out, listened and surmised it came from a ship which was also on a downbound heading. However, he could not verify the direction of the other ship because the radar on the *Cleveland* was inoperable.

The hulk of a freighter suddenly came into view. Realizing a collision was imminent Captain Kiessling ordered the wheel to starboard to veer away from the freighter. The freighter rammed the passenger ship on the port side just astern of midship. The collision was a glancing blow from fore to aft. One survivor described it as if a huge spoon had scooped out a section of the side of the ship.

The damaged City of Cleveland III *while the ship that rammed her, the* S. S. Ravnefjeel *remains nearby. From the collection of the Michigan Maritime Museum, South Haven, Michigan*

The spoon scooped out a section more than sixty-feet long and extending from the first deck to the fourth.

Captain Kiessling, on the bridge of the *Cleveland* ordered a distress signal be sent out, which was picked up by the Harbor Beach Coast Guard station. Chief Call and his men quickly launched the motor lifeboat and sped to the scene, some four miles south and east of the Harbor Beach Coast Guard Station. Upon reaching the collision site, the lifeboat had to work its way through floating wreckage. "There were pillows, bedding and other furnishings cluttering the area." Call said.

After the collision, the *Ravnefjeel* immediately backed off and stopped. Two lifeboats were lowered. Rowing towards the

The City of Cleveland III *as she departed Grand Haven. The circled portion indicates the location of the damage.* Benton Harbor Palladium

Cleveland, one stopped to retrieve something floating on the water...a body. The other lifeboat moved toward the damaged section of the *Cleveland*, towards voices of men screaming for help. They cautiously maneuvered around the debris towards the cries of men obviously in pain.

Passengers on deck watched as the crew poked at the damage with pike poles, pulling wreckage away until two men were uncovered. The men were in the water, tangled in wreckage. Pulled aboard the lifeboat, the men lay motionless.

The observers on the upper deck watched the lifeboat as it turned towards the stern; the crew began rowing hurriedly. The lifeboat disappeared behind the damage for a while, then reappeared as it moved towards a forward freight companionway of the *Cleveland*.

Someone from the group on deck watching the rescue saw a third man in the lifeboat. The man was large with a full beard.

"That's Dewhirst in the bow, I can see his whiskers!" It was Tom Dewhirst, badly injured, but alive.

Dewhirst had suffered leg and chest injuries, including several painful broken ribs. From his Harbor Beach Hospital bed, he later recounted that one moment he was in his cabin and the next he was in the cold water with wreckage falling on him.

"It kept falling on me. Every side of me, it fell on me and smashed my whole body. I had to keep swimming deeper to get away from it. I swam about twenty minutes and when I found some wreckage I climbed onto it. I don't remember where I was but I saw the *Cleveland* drifting away."

The other two men in the lifeboat with Dewhirst were Mervyn Stouck and Tom Spooner. Stouck had been walking on "B" deck when the collision occurred. He had leg and internal injuries. Spooner had received a deep gash to the head and damage to his internal organs. Spooner would eventually recover from his injuries. Mervyn Stouck died in the Harbor Beach Hospital just hours after the collision.

Passengers watch in horror as bodies of their friends are recovered from Lake Huron. From the collection of the Michigan Maritime Museum, South Haven, Michigan

The group on deck looked about in amazement. The fog slowly lifted allowing them to see the full extent of the damage. Robert Cannell, of Benton Harbor, stared down from the top deck in disbelief. Scanning the destruction, he hesitated, had he seen what he thought? His eyes darted about the wreckage until he saw it again... a hand protruding from the wreckage. The hand belonged to fifty-six-year-old Dick Lybrook, Sales Manager of a Chevrolet dealership in the Benton Harbor area. Lybrook, with a severe injury to his chest, was rushed to the hospital at Harbor Beach for immediate surgery.

The other life boat retrieved the lifeless body of Police Chief Alvin Boyd. Asleep in his stateroom when the collision occurred, his legs were nearly torn from his body and he suffered considerable loss of blood. He was given the last rites by the Reverend O'Neil when his body was returned to the *Cleveland*.

A check of the ship's cabin assignments revealed that two men were not accounted for and a search of the ship could not find them among the survivors. The missing were Fred Skelley, forty-three, a Benton Harbor Automobile dealer and Louis Patitucci,

Damage sustained by the City of Cleveland III. *From the collection of the Michigan Maritime Museum, South Haven, Michigan*

From the Harlow Meno collection of the Port Huron Museum

forty, a frozen food salesman from South Bend, Indiana who accompanied the Chamber.

The *City of Cleveland lll* was built as most passenger ships of that time. The deckwork, all structure above the hull, extended out beyond the width of the hull. On the *Cleveland* the deck and cabins extended out beyond the hull by twenty-two-feet. When the slow moving freighter struck the passenger ship, the damage was confined to the deckwork, while the hull remained intact. The large passenger ship was not taking on water and not in jeopardy of sinking.

The wood deckwork of the *City of Cleveland lll*, however was no match for the steel hull of the *Ravnefjeel*. The *Ravnefjeel* was not badly damaged in the collision. She backed off the *Cleveland* with one of the *Cleveland's* lifeboats stuck on her deck at the bow.

A lifeboat from the *Cleveland*, two from the *Ravnefjeel* and the Coast Guard motor vessel continued to search the waters for Fred Skelley and Louis Patitucci. The Coast Guard found Patitucci's body, badly broken, floating on wreckage and covered with debris… twelve hours after the collision. After a thorough search the Coast Guard also located Fred Skelley's body.

The damage to the City of Cleveland III. This photograph was taken as part of the investigation.
From the Harlow Meno collection of the Port Huron Museum

After several hours the *Ravnefjeel*, proven to have only superficial damage, was allowed to proceed north. Chief Ken Call ordered the *City of Cleveland lll* to the harbor at Harbor Beach. There the ship was inspected to determine its sea worthiness. The following day the *Cleveland* was found to be damaged but in no immediate danger of floundering. The *Cleveland* was allowed to proceed to Detroit but ordered not to exceed eight MPH.

The injured and dead remained in Harbor Beach under the care of the ship's doctor, Dr. Ozeran and Dr. Oakes of Harbor Beach. They were later transported back to Benton Harbor.

George Kolowich, President of the D & C Line, publicly charged that the freighter had rammed the passenger ship and demanded the Coast Guard seize the foreign ship before it left the territorial waters of the United States.

Inspectors boarded the *City of Cleveland lll* as it passed through the St. Clair River at Port Huron, more investigators boarded as the ship arrived in Detroit. The *Ravnefjeel* was boarded as well, it's captain and crew interviewed when the ship docked at Chicago.

A Federal Board of Inquiry was immediately assembled to look into the accident which claimed four lives and injured twenty others. Captain Kiessling testified he did not consider the fog severe enough to merit checking the speed of his vessel and also surmised the fog signal he heard was from a ship heading south, as was his ship. He admitted the *Cleveland* was indeed six miles east of the downbound shipping lane, but justified it by saying, since his ship moved faster than freighters it was less dangerous for the *Cleveland* to take the shorter route, closer to shore, than to dodge other slower downbound traffic. The captain did confirm that the *Cleveland's* radar and direction finder were not operational.

The Board of Inquiry found that the *Ravnefjeel* was not at fault in the collision of the two ships. It was traveling in its assigned shipping lane with its speed checked as the conditions dictated. The *Cleveland*, although, had elected to leave the downbound lane, trying to make up lost time by traveling the shorter course closer to shore. Also the captain of the *Cleveland* was admonished for not following Pilot Rule thirteen, which requires a vessel on fog signal to reduce speed to bare steerage and navigate with caution.

The crash ended the run of the D & C Navigation Company's record of ninety-eight years without a fatal accident.

The Tigers lost the first game in the double header 4-1 and won the second game 10-9, maintaining its four game lead over the Yankees.

The lives of the passengers and crew were forever changed and four passengers on the *City of Cleveland III* died that day.

WHEN SHIPS COLLIDE: THE STORY OF THE LADY ELGIN

J. C. Herbert leaned on the railing of the *Lady Elgin* looking out into the night, listening to the splash, splash, splash sound of the paddle wheel turning in Lake Michigan. It was late or early in the morning, whichever 2:00 a.m. is considered. He had been dancing and celebrating with the others in the salon, but he left to cool off on deck. It was a warm night, but the open deck was still cooler than it was on the dance floor in the forward salon.

He reflected on the events of the day, a day which had already lasted some twenty hours. The Milwaukee Union Guard, one of Wisconsin's State Militia companies, left on the sidewheeler *Lady Elgin* during the early morning hours on September 7, 1860, arriving in Chicago at dawn. The hours were filled with a parade through the streets of Chicago, a tour of the city, a dinner dance and a rousing speech from presidential candidate, senior Illinois Senator

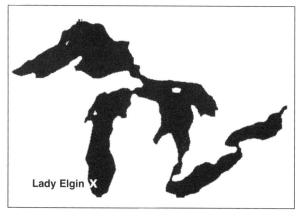

Lady Elgin X

25

The Lady Elgin at dock. From the H. C. Inches collection of the Port Huron Museum

Steven Douglas, who opposed a young lawyer also from Illinois, Abraham Lincoln.

Remembering the parade, J. C. thought to himself, what a site we must have made. The Milwaukee City Band led the way, the brass and drums announcing their arrival, followed by a procession of members of the Union Guard and guests. Next, the Milwaukee City council, representatives of several of the cities' fire companies and a large number of Milwaukee Policemen proudly waved to the gathered crowd. Wrapping up the spectacle was the Milwaukee Light Guard Drum Corps, always a favorite wherever they play.

He enjoyed the dinner and dance that followed, but his favorite memory of the evening was listening to Steven Douglas. J.C. and the Milwaukee Union Guard shared the beliefs of Senator Douglas. While they did not support slavery, they felt that it was the right of each state to determine if they wanted slavery. The Governor of Wisconsin did not share this belief and revoked the Milwaukee Union Guard's charter and took back the Guard's weapons. The Governor was so upset that one of the state's Militia would defy him that he ordered them to disband.

The Union Guard was determined to fight the Governor. They organized several fund raising events to purchase new weapons, including an excursion aboard the passenger ship *Lady Elgin* to Chicago. They vowed they would remain a Wisconsin militia. They would sell tickets for the boat excursion to listen to Senator Douglas and a portion of each ticket sold would be returned to the Union Guard.

The excursion was such a success, the ship was filled. The 252-foot long by 33.7-foot wide *Lady Elgin* was rated for 200 cabin and one hundred deck passengers, but for this momentous trip there were many more than that. The ship sailed with those supporting the Union Guard and the *Lady Elgin's* passengers on her normal route. The decks were lined with people, young and old, standing, sitting and sleeping wherever space could be found. The actual count of passengers on board the *Lady Elgin* that evening isn't known, yet the estimate is about 385, many more than the ship's capacity.

The *Lady Elgin* had been built just nine years earlier at Buffalo, New York. Her steam engine turned two paddle wheels, thirty two-feet in diameter, one on each side of the vessel. Known as a luxurious ship, she originally made the run from the eastern ports on Lake Ontario to Chicago; but during the 1860 season, she ran primarily as a passenger and general freight boat up Lake Michigan to the Soo Locks, into Lake Superior and back.

J.C., staring absentmindedly, was suddenly brought back to reality as the first flash of lightening lit the sky. Within seconds, a terrific crash of thunder followed. The seas were running high and the wind had been freshening, but the ship was still making good time. The wind shifted to the northeast and the rain came so hard it obscured visibility for but a few feet and the waves grew, assaulting the starboard bow of the ship.

That morning the *Lady Elgin* had traveled sixteen miles north of Chicago on the first leg of her normal route up Lake Michigan stopping at various ports. The first stop would be Milwaukee where the Union Guard would disembark. Her position was ten miles off Winnetka, Illinois.

An 1860 drawing of the Lady Elgin. *Courtesy of the Wisconsin Marine Historical Society*

The deck passengers, already pressed for space, scurried to find shelter from the rain. Mothers with babies in their arms, elderly and youth all trying to keep out of the rain and the wind. The main salon was filled with the Milwaukee Union Guard and guests. Although many had retired to their cabins, several still danced and reveled in the success of their day while the deck passengers huddled together attempting to stay dry.

Captain Wilson of the *Lady Elgin* had retired to his cabin. He felt his ship being pounded by the seas and heard the wind mounting. He prepared to return to the bridge, thinking he may not be needed, but he felt more comfortable there. Before he could leave his cabin, he was knocked to the floor. The *Lady Elgin* had struck something or something had struck it.

People dancing in the salon were thrown to the floor. Several were crushed against the wall by their friends as the ship took a sudden and severe list to port. Those asleep in the cabins were awakened as their belongings flew from tables and they were thrown from their beds.

Young Kenneth Cole, with his mother and a party of fifteen others returning from eastern ports, was walking to his cabin when the ship took a tremendous lurch. He was thrown against the cabin wall, bouncing off a lady who had fallen. Blood ran down his face from the gash above his right eye.

Passengers on the decks, already panicked by the rain, thunder, lightening and heavy seas, now questioned the mysterious shutter and severe list to port.

On the bridge of the *Lady Elgin*, the wheelman held the wheel tight, his knuckles white as he fought the force of wind and waves. Scanning the horizon through the rain and spray, he saw something off the port bow. It disappeared in the rain, but then suddenly reappeared; it was a schooner sailing towards them. The schooner with its sails mostly tattered, with a severe list, was being blown by the storm on a collision course with the *Lady Elgin*!

Captain Darius Malott of the 128-foot, two masted schooner *Augusta* stood near the helm. The wheelsman held tight to the wheel. The ship was blown before the wind, not responding to the wheel. The suddenness of the squall had not allowed the crew time to decrease sails. She was caught with a full head of sail with a gale force wind blowing down on her and her deck load of lumber had shifted causing her to list drastically. Her canvas was being ripped to shreds as she was pushed with the wind. Her foresail was blown out, removing her ability to maneuver, making her sail out of control. With no way to decrease the remaining sail area or to realign the deck load, the wind pushed her almost on her starboard rail. The storm was having its way with the schooner. She was sailing directly at the *Lady Elgin* and there was nothing Captain Malott could do about it.

The first mate saw the *Lady Elgin* appear out of the wind driven rain on a collision course with the *Augusta* and screamed to the wheelsman, "Port the wheel, port the wheel!" trying to pass the *Lady Elgin* at her bow, rather than port to port as was the rule.

Veins on his neck and muscles in his arms bulged as the *Augusta's* wheelsman fought the wind and seas to bring the ship to port. The mate prayed his ship would turn and avoid a collision with the large steel vessel.

The wheelsman and mate were violently thrown to the deck as the *Augusta* smashed into the port side of the *Lady Elgin*. The schooner's bow struck the side of the passenger ship just aft of the sidewheel, near the wheel box.

The schooner had penetrated the *Lady Elgin* to the extent that its bowsprit penetrated deep into the *Elgin's* cabin work and was embedded into her side.

The *Augusta*, for several minutes, was dragged across the lake with her bow buried in the side of the *Lady Elgin*. The forward motion of the *Lady Elgin* dislodged the *Augusta*, its bowsprit prying the port paddle wheel off of the passenger ship.

Panicking passengers onboard the over-crowded *Lady Elgin* ran in all directions, not knowing in which direction safety laid. Adults, small children and the elderly unable to keep up were pushed down and trampled by the scared passengers. People cried

The Lady Elgin *at dock. Courtesy of the Wisconsin Marine Historical Society*

for life preservers. Unfortunately, there were just a few canvas vests with wood sewn into pockets and passengers fought over them. The panicked lot screamed, cried and prayed. Some injured lay moaning in pain. Others yelled for loved ones separated in the chaos. Above the human wailing could be heard the clanging of the ship's bell and the steam whistle sounding a distress signal into the night.

The frightened crowd on the *Lady Elgin* watched the schooner as it slowly broke away. A loud cracking of heavy timbers could be heard as the port paddle wheel was ripped away. The schooner, what was left of her sails, still set, caught the wind and the ship began to be blown away. Passengers on the *Lady Elgin* stared in disbelief, they screamed for the schooner to stay and take them aboard, lower a small boat or at least throw over some of its deck load of lumber for them to use as floats. Despite the cries from the *Lady Elgin*, the ship sailed off, disappearing into the rain and the dark of night.

Captain Wilson ran below to the engine room to survey the damage. His ship had sustained a large breach extending from just above the main deck to below the waterline. Lake Michigan was pouring into the ship.

Captain Wilson ordered the ship be lightened by herding the cargo of fifty head of cattle off the ship. The cargo of heavy cast iron cook stoves were moved to starboard hoping to create enough of a list to bring the port side gash above the waterline.

Crew in the engine room yelled to the panicking passengers above them to throw mattresses and other bedding down. They stuffed the breach in the hull hoping to slow the incoming water.

A ship's yawl was lowered with crew aboard to survey the damage and assist with filling the breach. The seas were so rough that the small boat was tossed about as if it were a cork. As it approached the sinking *Lady Elgin*, the yawl was smashed against the hull. Crew attempted to fend the yawl off the ship with their oars, but as the waves pushed the small boat into the ship the oars were snapped like twigs. The *Lady Elgin*, still under power, pulled away from the yawl, leaving the crew to fend for themselves.

Returning to the bridge, Captain Wilson ordered the *Lady Elgin* towards shore. As long as the boilers produced steam, they would try to make it to the shallow water near shore. He turned to his first mate and confided, "Prepare yourself son, we won't make it to shore."

Aboard the *Augusta*, Captain Malott picked himself off the deck, where he had fallen as a result of the collision. He found his wood ship being dragged broadside by the large passenger ship. He knew his wood schooner would not fare well in a collision with an iron hull vessel. As his ship dislodged from the *Lady Elgin* he heard the cracking and splintering of timbers and feared the *Augusta* was breaking apart. Although, what he heard was not his ship breaking apart, it was the *Lady Elgin* being torn apart by the *Augusta*, ripping away the *Lady Elgin's* paddle wheel.

As the *Augusta* dislodged from the passenger ship, Captain Malott was amazed his ship was still afloat. Fearing the *Augusta* would soon sink and the iron hull of the other ship should remain afloat, Captain Malott ordered his ship to sail toward Chicago.

Onboard the *Lady Elgin*, John Crilley and Charles Everts were asleep when the *Augusta* smashed into the *Lady Elgin*. They had retired to their cabin and quickly fallen asleep after celebrating the success of the day by dancing and indulging in merriment. The crash jarred them awake, almost throwing them to the floor. In their bedclothes, they left their cabin to see what had occurred. The ship had taken on such a list they had to climb uphill to get out of their cabin doorway.

"The ship is sinking!" came a cry from aft. Crilley froze in fright…he couldn't swim.

Charles, running towards the cabin, yelled for John, "Come on, we need to find life jackets and get off the ship!" John couldn't move, "No, I'll stay on the ship."

Charles ran back and grabbed John by the arm and pulled him into the cabin. "The ship is sinking. You'll die if you stay!" Charles yelled at John.

No life preservers were found, so Charles began to remove the cabin doors. "We can float on these," he reassured John.

John, in a state of shock, took the door Charles handed him, holding on to it so tightly his knuckles whitened from his grip. He watched and listened to passengers on deck, running about and screaming. One woman clutching her baby to her breast screamed hysterically, "My baby, my baby!" While a man, face pale and eyes wide with fright slowly walked calling for his wife.

The two men, carrying their doors, joined the other panicked passengers in the main cabin. Captain Wilson came in and shouted over the wailing crowd, "Get to the other side!" in an effort to cause the ship to list on its starboard side, still attempting to raise the gash in the port side of the vessel above the waterline.

The *Lady Elgin*, black smoke bellowing from her stacks, headed towards shore. However, battling the seas, the wind, the water pouring into her hull and with the port side paddle wheel missing, the ship made very slow headway. The water pouring through the rupture in her hull caused the ship to sink lower in the lake. Women screamed, babies cried and men huddled in panic in

A sketch of the Lady Elgin *slipping below at the stern with victims of the collision scattered about on the lake. Courtesy of the Wisconsin Marine Historical Society*

the main cabin, where they had earlier danced. Gaiety was replaced with fear. John, scared of the watery death which he was sure awaited, clutched his door and prayed. Charles reassured him that they could make it to shore. "I'll carry you to shore on my back if I have to," he promised John.

Above the moaning and screams of the passengers, Captain Wilson ordered everyone to quickly go to the hurricane deck. There the crew was throwing overboard planks, doors, deck chairs and anything else which might float. Passengers reluctantly began to jump from the deck after the floats.

Charles yelled to John, "Follow me!" as he threw his door over and jumped in after it. Buoyed by the support of Charles, John held tight to the door as he jumped, fearing he would lose it if he threw it in. The door landed flat on the surface, John's face smashing into it on impact, breaking his nose and opening a gash in his forehead.

The damaged ship, creaking and twisting in the seas, was starting to break up. A metal strap supporting one of the smoke stacks broke in a metallic crack. The smoke stack crashed to the deck crushing several people huddled below. Panicked all the more, mothers threw their children into the lake as people jumped from every deck of the ship. Moments later, the ship broke apart. The hull, filling with water, couldn't support the additional weight; and the *Lady Elgin* slipped below the waves at the stern, as her bow remained at the surface.

Hundreds of people still onboard were cast into the lake, some with life preservers, some with something to float on, many others with nothing. The screams of the victims, the howling wind and the thunder filled the night.

As the ship sank, some of the wood cabin structure of the ship broke off and floated to the surface. A large section of the hurricane deck surfaced. Scared men, women and children climbed on and laid across it, praying the raft would not break up in the heavy seas. Reaching out from the raft, others were pulled onto it. Women called out their husband's and children's names, while searching the lake and praying they were safe.

The hurricane deck raft floated by Captain Wilson who was hanging onto a timber with one arm and holding an infant in the other. He handed the child aboard and climbed on. By this time, the large piece of decking held over forty people. He settled and reached for the child.

Waves washed the raft, knocking people off. They frantically swam back to the raft and climbed on. Some weakened by the regular assaults of the lake, couldn't regain the raft and slipped below the lake.

Captain Wilson handed the infant to a woman and stood to look for signs of the shore. He talked to those on the raft trying to reassure them that they would safely reach the beach. A large wave broke down on the raft knocking the captain flat. The woman holding the baby was washed off, she and the infant were lost in the churning lake.

John Crilley laid on his door, paddling as blood ran down his face. He yelled for Charles, who had given him the strength to jump into the raging sea, but Charles was nowhere to be found. The door Charles had thrown over was there, but Charles was gone.

John paddled towards the sounds of people. He saw a large amount of people on a makeshift raft. He climbed on and hugged friends he found for support and warmth.

One of the yawls lowered by the *Lady Elgin* drifted towards shore, picking up men and women as they floated by them. With eighteen aboard, the crew heard the surf breaking on shore. They knew the worst wasn't over. The small boat would be tossed and thrown in the heavy surf breaking on the rocks along the shore. Within sight of land, the boat was thrown end over end in the wild waves. The human cargo was cast into the lake, some washed up on shore, others were killed as their bodies were pounded on the rocks.

The few that made it to shore found a cottage and woke the sleeping family. Those who had survived the wild yawl ride were made warm by the fire and fed breakfast.

Captain Wilson heard the breaking surf and knew their raft would be broken apart as it entered the shallow water. He prepared his fellow passengers for the peril which lay ahead of them. By this time the number on the raft had been decreased by the constant assault of the waves washing the tired and cold away.

The raft and its occupants rose up on the crest of a wave then slipped back only for the following wave to crash down on it washing all souls into the angry water. The waves smashed the raft into splinters. The human cargo, cast into the water, were thrown about by the seas breaking on the rocky coast. Some people, trying to keep their heads above the surface, were speared by the splinters of the raft. Some were picked up by the waves and thrown above the rocks only to land on the beach. Others were smashed into the near shore rocks, their bodies broken and bloodied, while still others were pulled below, never to return alive.

Captain Wilson,who so bravely buoyed the spirits of those on the raft, never made it to shore. His battered body was recovered days later.

That night the *Lady Elgin* carried an estimated 385 passengers and crew. Only ninety-eight lived through the night of horror, making it the worst disaster to occur to date on the Great Lakes.

"The *Lady Elgin*"
Music and words by Henry C. Work
1861

Up from the poor man's cottage, up from the mansions door
Sweeping across the waters, echoing along the shore
Caught by the morning breezes, borne on the evening gale
Cometh the voice of mourning, a sad and solemn wail

Chorus:
Lost on the Lady Elgin, *sleeping to wake no more*
Numbered with three hundred who failed to reach the shore

Staunch was the noble steamer, precious the freight she bore
Gaily she loosed her cables a few short hours before
Grandly she swept the harbor, joyfully rang her bell
Little thought we are ere morning 'twould toll so sad a knell

Chorus:
Lost on the Lady Elgin, *sleeping to wake no more*
Numbered with three hundred who failed to reach the shore

Oh hear the cry of children weeping for parents gone
Children slept that morning, but orphans woke at dawn
Sisters for brothers weeping, husbands for missing wives
Such were the ties dissevered by those three hundred lives

Chorus:
Lost on the Lady Elgin, *sleeping to wake no more*
Numbered with three hundred who failed to reach the shore

THE PASSENGER SHIP HAMONIC BURNS IN THE RIVER

Dr. Green, his wife and niece, Susan, sat having breakfast in the dining room of the passenger liner, *Hamonic*. They had left Detroit just the day before, July 16, 1945, aboard the 349-foot ship with over 200 other passengers. Their journey would take them from Detroit up through Lake St. Clair and the St. Clair River, over the length of Lake Huron, then up the St. Marys River, through the famous Soo Locks into Lake Superior. Then they would return by the same course.

The *Hamonic*, now in her thirty-sixth season, was still a beautiful ship. In demand for a summer cruise, the Greens had to purchase the tickets more than four months early to reserve a cabin. The cabins were of a generous size. The dining room could rival any of the luxury ships sailing the Atlantic and the ship offered many forms of shipboard entertainment.

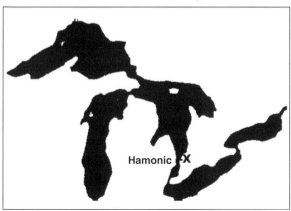

Hamonic ✦X

The Hamonic in 1915. From the collection of the Port Huron Museum

An artists rendition of the Grand Saloon of the Steamer Hamonic. *The Library of Michigan, an agency of the Department of History, Arts and Libraries*

The ship, having completed its first leg of the cruise was now tied up at the Point Edward wharf of the Canadian Steamship Lines just north of Sarnia, Ontario, across from Port Huron, Michigan.

The Green family looked out the port side window at the United States side of the river and Port Huron. The river was busy with vessels of all sizes: kids in small home-built row boats, commercial fishing boats heading out into Lake Huron for their catch and the huge freighters passing with their loads of iron ore, wheat or coal. There were also the beautiful sailboats making practice runs in preparation for the Port Huron to Mackinaw race.

Susan, a typical ten-year-old, picked at her eggs and ham while watching the excitement on the river. Soon she went to the starboard windows to watch the stevedores loading supplies into the hold of the *Hamonic*.

"Look Uncle, there's some smoke coming from the dock. It looks like a fire." Looking out the window, they could see flames leaping from the top of one of the sheds on the dock.

The family went forward to the bow to better see the small fire, but within minutes, the fire jumped to other buildings and soon all of the sheds on the dock were ablaze.

A drawing from the 1910 Northern Navigation Co. travel brochure.
The Library of Michigan, an agency of the Department of History, Arts and Libraries

The officers on the bridge watched as the blaze grew. The First Officer signaled the engine room for power. He wanted to move the ship away from the wharf so fire and Coast Guard boats could get near to spray the flames and to prevent an errant ember or flames blown by the wind from igniting the *Hamonic*.

The report came back that the boilers were down and it would take some time to develop steam to move the ship. They would make haste in bringing up steam.

Susan, her aunt and uncle watched the building on the dock burn and collapse, thick black smoke rising above the dock, the slight wind blowing it towards the ship.

Rail cars, filled with supplies for the ship's week long cruise, were afire and several other box cars nearby were in jeopardy of igniting.

Susan turned towards her uncle to ask a question, but her jaw dropped open as she stared over his shoulder in disbelief. "The boat is on fire!" she screamed.

Dr. Green turned to see flames leaping from the upper deck of the ship.

The ships of the day were constructed with steel hulls and main bulkheads, but most of the deckwork was made of wood. The

Hamonic's wood deckwork, coated with highly flammable paint, ignited, supporting the flame and the fire quickly spread.

Passenger ships with long narrow hallways and many stairwells act as channels for the flames to spread. Within minutes the *Hamonic* was fully engulfed.

Captain Beaton raced for the bridge, pushing his way through groups of panicking passengers. The boilers had developed sufficient power to move the ship from the wharf, away from the fully engulfed dock. He yelled to deckhands to release the cables holding the ship to the wharf. Deckhands on the dock braved the heat of the fire as they pulled the heavy steel cables off of the bollards and dropped them over the side. They ran for the bow, but the heat was too great for them to get near enough to release the ship.

The captain ordered the ship's telegraph to reverse full and hollered into the phone to the engine room to give it all they had. The huge propeller started to turn, churning the river into a frothing foam. The *Hamonic* backed off, ripping loose the mooring lines at the bow.

The crowds lining the Port Huron riverbank watched as the burning ship was backed into the middle of the St. Clair River.

The Hamonic *burns out of control in the St. Clair River.* From the *H. C. Inches collection of the Port Huron Museum*

"Full ahead!" Captain Beaton ordered the wheelsman. "But, captain…?" the First Officer began in protest. Full ahead would run the ship into the river bank.

"The passengers have a better chance to survive if the ship is closer to shore," the captain responded, not waiting for the First Mate to finish his question.

The current of the St. Clair River is about seven miles per hour. The captain knew many passengers jumping into the river would be swept downstream only to perish.

The telegraph clanged with the order, the big ship slowed its backward movement and began to move forward slowly, gradually gaining speed in the narrow river. With a jolt, the *Hamonic's* bow plowed almost twelve feet into the river's bank.

Doctor Green grabbed a life preserver and tied it around Susan. He looked for a way to escape. They ran to the nearest stairway leading below to the gangway but were met by a screaming group running up. "We can't get down! The smoke is too thick!" a passenger yelled to them.

They ran aft, but heat, smoke and fire blocked any chance for their escape. Dr. Green looked over the rail, thinking of jumping. He saw a small rowboat below. He lifted Susan over the rail and dropped her into the St. Clair River near the rowboat. He watched as Susan was pulled aboard the boat.

Dr. Green, content that his niece was safe, looked for an escape route for he and his wife, as did the other 200 passengers. Some were able to leave the vessel from the gangways before the fire grew too intense. Others elected to jump from the burning ship into the river, choosing the several story fall into the rapidly moving current of the river, where small craft rushing to their aid, picked them from the water.

Dr. Green and his wife saw people sliding down the heavy steel cables that once held the ship to the dock. It was their only chance for survival; they got in line to slide to safety.

The cables were hot from the intense heat of the fire, but burned hands were a small price to pay for their lives. They slid down the cable until the pain was too great and let go, falling into the river near

The Hamonic was grounded into the river bank to save the passengers. The coal shovel can be seen off the port bow. From the H. C. Inches collection of the Port Huron Museum

the riverbank where they were pulled to shore and taken to Sarnia General Hospital for care of their burns and smoke inhalation.

The ship lay almost perpendicular to the shore near the Century Coal Company docks. A quick thinking crane operator swung his bucket over to the bow of the ship. Passengers trapped on board ran for the bucket. Passengers climbed into the bucket, black with coal dust, for a ride to safety. Once his load was onshore, the crane operator raised the bucket up and quickly swung it over to the screaming people on the bow of the burning ship. The operator removed over one hundred frantic passengers from the ship eight to ten at a time in the coal bucket.

Vessels of all types worked the water around the burning *Hamonic*. Fishing boats, rowboats, race boats, anything that could be employed were used to pull the scared passengers from the river.

Harold Simpson, manager of the J. Wescott Marine Reporting Service, observed the ship catch fire from his office on the river. He

The Hamonic *burns while passengers watch from the safety of shore. The coal shovel which saved the lives of so many is seen removing passengers from the bow of the burning ship. From the archives of the* Sarnia Observer

and another man went to one of the company boats to help. While underway for the ship, they watched frightened passengers jump from the ship, a fall of thirty or more feet.

They came near a woman who held out her baby to them to be saved. Mr. Simpson found a towel to dry and bundle the baby, while the mother was lifted aboard. They continued picking passengers from the river. His boat full with survivors, backed away to the screams of those still in the river. He begged them to move away from his boat so he could take his human cargo to shore. He promised to return.

Onlookers and other survivors of the ship ran to help unload Simpson's boat. "The river is alive with screaming people," Simpson said as they turned back for more.

A thick blanket of smoke hung over the surface of the river, adding to the panic of those floating in life preservers or hugging debris floating around the wreck. Screams of men, women and children haunted Simpson as the frantic passengers disappeared in the smoke. True to his word Simpson returned. In all he made four trips, taking more than fifty people to safety.

The ship's nurse, Dorothy Dure, was on the main deck helping frantic passengers over the rail to slide down one of the mooring cables. She spoke calmly to the frightened passengers, although finding it sometimes necessary to raise her voice to keep the evacuation orderly. Standing not too far away she noticed a young boy looking all around and crying. He had become separated from his parents.

Dorothy went to him and reassured him that his parents were safe and that she would make sure he got to shore as well. She searched for a life preserver for him but all were taken. He stood by Dorothy until the last passenger had gone down the cable. Knowing the boy was not strong enough to hold onto the cable she had him climb onto her back for a piggy back ride. She stepped over the railing, tightly grasping the cable and they began sliding down the cable to the water. The boy lost his grip on Dorothy and fell fifteen to twenty-feet to the river below. Dorothy splashed into the river and quickly swam to the surface to find the little boy. He was

The ship Hamonic *burns while frantic passengers try to escape the flames. Coast Guard and fireboats were on the scene to assist with the fire and evacuation of the ship* A Port Huron Times Herald *photograph*

nowhere in site. Dorothy enlisted the boats who went to her assistance to look for the boy. They looked but could not find him.

"Maybe he was picked up by another boat and is already on shore," one of the rescuers said. Dorothy, now frantic, searched the dock area but didn't find the boy. She reluctantly got in a car to be taken to the hospital. The boy was later found wandering the wharf, crying and looking for his parents and the lady who helped him escape the fire.

In the following days, the extent of the damage became apparent. The fire was started by a faulty generator in the machine shop at the Canadian Steamship Lines' dock. All buildings at the wharf were destroyed as well as thirty railroad cars and their contents. The *Hamonic*, valued at $1,500,000, was beyond repair and salvage of the steel in her hull and machinery the only recourse.

Through the bravery and heroics of many, the 220 passengers and 130 member crew were removed from the burning *Hamonic*, averting an almost certain catastrophe. One hundred and fifty people were taken to the hospital for burns, mostly to their hands and faces. Twenty-three were hospitalized, thirteen in critical condition. Through the holocaust there was only one fatality, a dockhand who was killed as he fought to help others.

THE RISE AND FALL OF
THE FAMOUS TASHMOO

The decades before and after the year 1900 were a time when travel by water was both for commercial and recreational purposes. Passenger ships of all types plied the Great Lakes carrying passengers to ports around the lakes. For some, the ships were the only means of transportation for passengers and freight to isolated ports, but for others the ships were excursion boats giving people an opportunity to enjoy a beautiful summer day and escape the heat inland.

The ships of the time from the Detroit area included the *City of Mackinaw*, which carried passengers from Detroit to Mackinaw, for the round trip price of $12.50, meals and a cabin included. The *City of Detroit III* was the most luxurious ferry to ever cross a river. The ship carried passengers across the Detroit River between Detroit and Windsor and on excursions into Lake St. Clair and

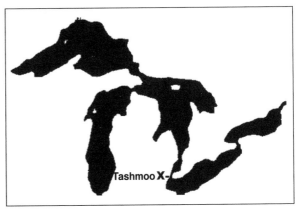

Tashmoo **X**

The Tashmoo. From the H. C. Inches collection of the Port Huron Museum

THE RISE AND FALL OF THE FAMOUS TASHMOO

Lake Erie. The *Put-In-Bay*, the 240-foot "dancing ship," so named for its large dance floor, carried passengers to and from the island of Put-In-Bay, Ohio in Lake Erie and the *Columbia* carried fun-seekers to the playground of Bob-Lo Island.

A discussion of the turn-of-the-century passenger ships would not be complete without including the steamship, *Tashmoo*. The *Tashmoo* was one of the most luxurious and popular passenger ships of its time. She was built in 1900 to carry passengers between Detroit and Port Huron, with stops at various playgrounds of the time, such as Belle Isle in the Detroit River and Harsens Island in the Lake St. Clair Flats. She was a beautiful sidewheel paddle boat with two decks above her steel hull, all painted white. She quickly was dubbed the "White Flyer."

Shortly after the *Tashmoo* had been launched, she was heralded as the fastest ship on the lakes. The two-year-old *City of Erie* took offense to the bragging of the new ship. The *City of Erie* was a passenger ship with the nickname "Honeymoon Ship," for its route from Cleveland, Ohio and Erie, Pennsylvania to Niagara Falls, New York. At the turn of the century, the *City of Erie* was widely

The City of Erie, *known as the "Honeymoon Ship" was the fastest ship on the Lakes. When the* Tashmoo *began billing itself as the fastest, a race was inevitable. From the H. C. Inches collection of the Port Huron Museum*

An advertisement of the "Great Race" between the Tashmoo *and the* City of Erie.

regarded as the fastest ship on the Great Lakes. A challenge to race was made by the brash upstart *Tashmoo* and quickly accepted by the veteran vessel.

The race was billed as the Greatest Steamship Race on fresh or salt water. One thousand dollars was put up as a wager from the owner of each ship, the money to go to a charity in the winning ship's home port. However, hundreds of thousands more dollars were unofficially wagered on the race.

Every available excursion ship was chartered to follow the racing ships.

The course was the ninety-four miles from Cleveland, Ohio to Erie, Pennsylvania. Tens of thousands of onlookers lined the Cleveland harbor to watch the start of the race. The *Tashmoo* crept away to a three length lead, but the *City of Erie* overtook the new ship on a course change. The wheelsman of the *City of Erie* was familiar with the waters and knew every trick. It was quickly noticed that the *City of Erie* had been stripped of all unnecessary weight. Even the ship's lifeboats were removed for the race. The *Tashmoo* was running in her normal condition.

A problem with its condenser caused the *Tashmoo* to drop behind by up to six lengths, but it was quickly fixed and she began to make up the distance. Black smoke bellowing from her stack, firemen were pouring coal into her firebox and the *Tashmoo* slowly made up the difference between the two ships. Nearing the finish line, the *City of Erie* was less than a ship length ahead. The *Tashmoo* had made an amazing recovery, with unmatched speed to catch up to the *Erie*. The two ships, leaving a trail of smoke on the horizon and their bows throwing spray, were too close to tell who would be the victor. But, at the finish line, it was the *City of Erie* barely beating out the *Tashmoo*!

Backers of the *Tashmoo* cried for a rematch. The *City of Erie* had too much of an advantage! The race was on her route, they knew the winds and currents, and she was stripped of weight! But the owners of the *City of Erie* had seen the speed of the *Tashmoo* as she made up the six length deficit and almost beat them at the finish line. They knew their ship could not beat the speed of the *Tashmoo* and politely declined the rematch.

The *Tashmoo* had a long and illustrious career, but she had met with some adversity as well. During the 1927 winter layup, the *Tashmoo* was secured to shore by fourteen steel cables. On the morning of December 8, a winter storm blew in. The temperature dropped and visibility was almost totally obscured by the snow. The wind steadily grew, reaching speeds in excess of sixty miles an hour.

"She's gone!" Robert McCrumb, the *Tashmoo* watchman said, "Gone up the river." He later reported that he remained near the ship during the storm. "Then the cables started snapping. They went one after the other, like they were grocery string." The storm had blown the *Tashmoo* upriver without a soul aboard. On her wild journey she first smashed into the ferry, *Promise*, where three men aboard the ferry were readying for that day's first crossing. They jumped to the dock after the *Tashmoo* struck, fearing the *Promise* might be smashed to bits by the larger vessel.

The ship insisted to continue on her northerly voyage. When word got out that the big ship was leaving a trail of damage on her solo trip up river, people lined the riverbank to watch. Some came out of concern, some interested and some to cheer the ship on.

The "White Flyer" continued upriver, pounding into anything in its path. But there was one thing that might stop her… the Belle Isle Bridge. The 2000 plus feet steel and concrete bridge crossing from Detroit to the city-owned park on Belle Isle. Blindly drifting in the storm, the large ship crashed into the bridge and careened off only for the wind to blow her back into the bridge again.

The snow was blowing so hard that long before the ship could be seen crashing into the bridge, onlookers heard the sound of the wood decks and cabin work cracking and splintering as the ship smashed into the concrete abutment of the bridge. The ship would surely break up if it was not soon pulled away from the bridge and possibly take the bridge with her as well. If the *Tashmoo* were blown beyond the bridge, what damage would she wreak upriver? What could stop her?

Two tugs responded to calls to stop the wild vessel. They cautiously approached the *Tashmoo*, watching the depths, the waves, the winds and the wildly bucking passenger ship. The tug captains carefully came close enough for two men to board the *Tashmoo* and get two hawsers secured to the ship. The tugs poured on the coal and slowly, defiantly, the *Tashmoo* was pulled from the bridge. Pulling the big excursion ship into the wind required all the tugs could give. The hawsers were pulled tight as smoke bellowed from the tugboat's stacks.

The Tashmoo *slamming into the Belle Isle Bridge after her wild ride upriver. Courtesy of the* Detroit News

After several miles, the *Tashmoo* decided she wasn't ready to go to port quite yet. One hawser snapped and then the other, the big ship was again on her wild ride heading upriver towards the Belle Isle Bridge.

The tugs came about and raced to regain the ship and the men on board. Lines were thrown, only to be blown astray. Several attempts later, one hawser was made fast and then the other, the tugs again poured on the coal trying to stop the drifting ship. The hawsers snapped tight, the tugs pulled and once again stopped the ship's northerly voyage, just ten yards from the Belle Isle Bridge!

Throughout the remainder of the 1927 winter layup, repairs were made to the decks and cabins. The *Tashmoo* had pounded on the bridge with such force that her steel hull was stove in at several places from beating on the concrete abutments of the bridge. But the excursion ship was ready for spring and her popularity only increased after her wild ride of December 8, 1927.

In 1934 the *Tashmoo* had run aground at Algonac, Michigan during a storm. The *Tashmoo* was running south from Port Huron with 150 passengers aboard. At Harsens Island they were to take on 1,200 more passengers when the storm struck, blowing the high profile ship into shoal water. The Coast Guard and local small craft assisted with transporting the 150 *Tashmoo* passengers to safety. The next day the ship was pulled free. The hull was intact, but one of the ship's paddle wheels was damaged. Repairs were promptly made and soon the ship was back on its normal run.

In 1936, thirty-six years since her launch, the *Tashmoo* remained a very popular excursion to escape the heat during the Michigan summer. The ship still cruised between the ports of Detroit and Port Huron and made day excursions on the river. On the warm evening of June 18, 1936, the *Tashmoo* had been chartered by the PAL's Club, a young men's organization. One thousand, four hundred passengers filed on board for that evening's "Moonlight cruise" on the Detroit River.

The passengers enjoyed the trip as the *Tashmoo* steamed south along the United States shore of the river to the mouth of Lake Erie. The Jean Calloway Orchestra from Baltimore played the popular big band tunes of the day. Passengers danced in the ballroom and walked the deck, enjoying the cool night air. Groups gathered along the ship's two decks, waving to passing ships and watching the skylines of Detroit and Windsor, Ontario disappear behind them, while others watched the colorful amusement park lights of Bob-Lo Island appear ahead.

The gaiety of the passengers continued as the ship rounded Grosse Isle at the mouth of Lake Erie, entered the Sugar Island channel and began on her return trip upriver. The band played on as the passengers danced, children ran on the decks and a general atmosphere of merriment prevailed.

As the *Tashmoo* cleared the Sugar Island channel, the ship seemed to momentarily shudder. The slight tremor was barely felt by the frolicking passengers, but the crew knew something wasn't right. Captain McAlpine was in the pilot house when he felt the shudder. "It was hardly more than a slight trembling…" he recalled afterwards, but a skipper knows every shake, shudder and sound his ship makes. This one was unfamiliar. He rang the engine room to inquire as to the cause of the shudder.

The chief engineer's voice answered frantically, "A hole has been stove in the hull!" he yelled above the roar of the engines. "It's in the bottom just aft of the boiler room."

"Start the pumps!" ordered the captain.

"Already done sir," came the reply from the engineer.

The captain turned to the first mate and told him to make for the nearest dock. "There is a Canadian coal wharf ahead about a mile," he replied.

A distress call was sent out by radio that the *Tashmoo's* hull had been holed and was taking on water. A Coast Guard patrol boat and a tug from Amherstburg, Ontario were in the vicinity and joined the "White Flyer." The *Tashmoo* was again in a race, a race against time, and the water raising in her hull.

The one hundred member crew of the *Tashmoo* remained calm as the ship sped at full speed, smoke bellowing from her stacks, towards the safety of the dock. The 1,400 passengers were told that the ship was experiencing some engine trouble but that there was nothing to worry about. The band continued playing, while passengers danced and had a great time. But below decks in the engine room, men labored in ever increasing water, trying to keep the ship's pumps working.

Captain McAlpine rang the engine room again to check on the damage. "Water's rising, captain," he was told. "The engine is running full, the pumps are working at full as well. I hope we can make dock before the water puts out the fire."

Survivors and the curious look at the Tashmoo *sunk in the Detroit River.* Courtesy of the Dossin Great Lakes Museum, Detroit, Michigan

Detroit River water was rushing into the ship faster than the pumps could send it out. If the water rose high enough to put out the fire, the steam pumps would quit and the ship would fill and settle to the bottom, sending 1,400 passengers into the river, many of which would not leave the river until their lifeless bodies floated to the surface and washed up on shore. The lifeboats and flotation vests would help, but Captain McAlpine knew this catastrophe had the potential to surpass Chicago's 815 person death toll of the *Eastland* disaster, making it the worst loss of life on the Great Lakes. "Not on my watch," he muttered.

"The waters getting deep!" The chief engineer reported to the bridge. "The boys are working in waist deep water trying to keep 'er fired."

"Almost there," came the reply.

As the injured ship hurriedly steamed up to the dock, Captain McAlpine ordered her to reverse. The paddle wheel was thrown into reverse, churning the water into white froth as hawsers were thrown and quickly made fast to the bollards.

Courtesy of the Dossin Great Lakes Museum, Detroit, Michigan

Gangways were lowered as crew began telling passengers that they had to leave the ship. Many left confused as to why they had not returned to Detroit, while others were having such a good time they wanted to stay aboard and keep dancing. The crew, without panicking the passengers, ushered all to the dock.

Water continued to rise in the ship's hull, eventually seeping into the boiler's firebox and extinguishing the fire. Without a fire, there was no steam. Without steam, the pumps didn't function. Without pumps the thirty-six-year-old ship filled with water. Within a half hour of arriving at the Brunner-Mond Co. coal dock, the "White Flyer" slowly sank to the bottom in eighteen-feet of water. The once proud ship lay submerged, only her upper decks above the river's surface.

But, all passengers and crew were safely ashore.

There was much speculation as to the fate of the ship. Could she be raised and sail again or was the damage too much for the old "White Flyer"? Later that season, the decision was made. The *Tashmoo* was raised to float again, but her next trip was to the scrap yard. The once proud Queen of the excursion trade was stripped of anything of value and then cut up, never to sail again.

THE COLLISION OF THE PEWABIC AND THE METEOR

James Buchan had been gone most of the summer of 1865, spending time with relatives in Michigan's Upper Peninsula. He was happy to be returning to Cleveland. He and about 175 other passengers were onboard the 200-foot steam propeller passenger ship, *Pewabic*. They had been sailing for days. Having left Lake Superior and passed through the Soo Locks, they were now southbound on Lake Huron.

The *Pewabic* carried a variety of cargo from the mineral rich Upper Peninsula of Michigan: barrels of iron ore, 170-tons of Copper, a mixture of ingots, barrels of copper pieces and large masses of raw copper, some weighing several tons. In 1865, it was very valuable cargo.

The passengers onboard the two-year-old *Pewabic* were some of the fortunate of the day, for she was a grand ship which catered to the wealthy. The ship offered lavish cabins and was

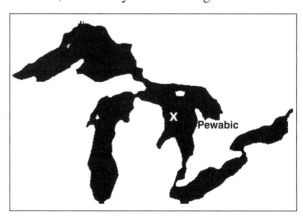

Historical Collections of the Great Lakes
Bowling Green State University

The Pewabic. From the Historical Collection of the Great Lakes Bowling Green State University

complete with stained glass and handcrafted woodwork. The ship was also equipped with a large dance floor and orchestra in the main salon for the entertainment of the passengers.

On the evening of August 9, 1865, the ship was sailing south on Lake Huron about seven miles off Thunder Bay. The seas were relatively calm and the weather was clear and warm. The day's earlier rain had blown east and the evening brought a gentle breeze, cooling the hot August night.

Word spread amongst those aboard that another ship was ahead and it might be the *Meteor*. The *Meteor* was the sister ship of the *Pewabic*, also running the route from Lake Superior to ports in the lower lakes. Many of the *Pewabic* passengers had friends and relatives aboard the *Meteor*, it would be a delight to see them, if only in passing. Seeing a familiar face or ship was a nice escape from the boredom of the long lake trip. Passengers began gathering on the decks of both ships as they approached one another.

The sister ships would pass to port with the *Pewabic* on the west, closest to shore. They could pass with miles between them, but the two ships altered their courses to pass closely.

About 8:30 in the evening Buchan and several friends gathered at the port bow in anticipation of the passing. The sun was low in the western sky and the weather clear. They could easily see the ship approaching. Conversations on the deck were jovial, the passengers in an excited mood.

GRAND PLEASURE EXCURSIONS

TO LAKE SUPERIOR.
OLD PIONEER LINE.

The new fast and magnificent steamers,

METEOR,   **PEWABIC,**
Thos. Wilson, Master,   George McKay, Master

Will Leave Detroit at 2 P. M.

TUESDAYS,   TUESDAYS,
June 13th, 27th.   June 20.
July 11th, 25th.   July 4th, 18th.
August 8th, 22d.   August 1st, 15th, 29th

The above justly favorite steamers will leave as above during the season of 1865, touching at all points of interest each way. For speed and comfort the METEOR and PEWABIC are not excelled by any boats now running. Their officers, well known as men of long experience, will be found at all times careful and attentive to the wants of their passengers.

For further particulars, and to secure rooms for part of or a "round trip," apply by letter or in person, to WHITING & O'GRADY,
J. T. WHITING & CO.,
Je14-40t   Foot of First street

James fell silent as he watched the *Meteor* approach; others stopped talking and began to stare in disbelief. The ships looked like they were on a course to collide. Passengers aboard the *Pewabic* ran to the starboard side for protection while others ran into the main salon. The decks of the *Meteor* were alive with passengers running and screaming as well.

Captain McKay, in the pilothouse of the *Pewabic*, looked in amazement as he realized the ships would collide if evasive maneuvers were not taken. He blew a warning whistle and ordered the wheel to starboard, taking his ship towards shore, out of the path of the *Meteor*.

Whether in confusion or in an enormous mistake, the wheelsman aboard the *Meteor* ported the wheel sending the *Meteor* on a direct course for the port side of the *Pewabic*.

With the sound of wood splintering and breaking, the bow of the *Meteor* smashed into the port side of the *Pewabic*. The *Pewabic* immediately began taking on water through a huge gash which extended from just below the wheelhouse to below the waterline.

Passengers huddled in the main salon, seeking shelter from the possible collision. When the ships collided, they struck with such force the *Meteor's* bow rammed deep into the side of the *Pewabic*. Passengers in the main salon were crushed by the massive bow of the *Meteor*.

Frantic passengers and crew jumped from the upper decks of the *Pewabic* onto the deck of the *Meteor*, fearing the *Pewabic* would sink and hoping that *Meteor* would remain afloat.

James yelled to his companions to get their cork jackets, as he ran to his stateroom for his. When he returned on deck, he could see the ship was going down. The deck at the bow was almost submerged. Within moments, it seemed, the ship sank and James found himself in the water being taken down by the suction of the sinking ship. He swam frantically for the surface, afraid he would strike debris at the surface and render himself unconscious. He was fortunate to surface between the debris and quickly grab onto a large section of the wooden hurricane deck.

THE COLLISION OF THE PEWABIC AND METEOR

He and others, equally as fortunate to find the floating debris, climbed onto the wreckage and reached for others still in the water. He watched as many of his fellow passengers succumbed to injury or exhaustion and slipped below the surface of Lake Huron. The screams lessened.

One of the heroes of the day was Mrs. McKnight, a passenger onboard the *Pewabic*. She treaded water after the *Pewabic* slipped from beneath her feet. Hearing the screams of a woman in the distance, she began to swim to her. Mrs. McKnight swam by a splintered section of the hurricane deck from the *Pewabic* and pushed it towards the woman. Just as she was about to succumb to the lake the woman grabbed the wood. Mrs. McKnight swam, pulling the raft behind her to a life raft. Mrs. McKnight is credited with saving several passengers that would have surely drown that night.

Captain Wilson of the *Meteor*, ran to the wheelhouse. He ordered the yawls lowered to pick up survivors. There were two sailboats in the area which raced to assist. The *Meteor* remained on the site until all survivors and bodies were taken aboard and nothing more could be done. The *Meteor*, the steam pumps

APPALLING CALAMITY.

FRIGHTFUL COLLISION BE-
TWEEN TWO STEAMERS.

The Pewabic run into by
The Meteor in Thun-
der Bay.

HEART-RENDING LOSS
OF LIFE.

The Pewabic Sunk in Four
Minutes.

From 70 to 100 Lives Lost.

Terrible Scenes During the
Catastrophe.

NOBLE HEROISM OF A LADY.

The Mohawk Comes to the Rescue.

Statement of Passengers.

Excitement in the City.

A headline from the August 12, 1865 Detroit Free Press.

65

holding off the water leaking into her hull, steamed north towards the St. Marys River and the locks.

It has been estimated that 125 lives were lost on that evening on Lake Huron. The exact number will never be known; the passenger list went down with the ship. The ship sank so quickly, due to the weight of her cargo of copper and iron ore, that most of the crew from below decks never made it out, while many of the passengers in their cabins were taken down with the ship as well. The *Pewabic* reached her final resting place in 180-feet of water. She became the mausoleum for the many dead entombed within her hull.

The ships probably altered their courses at the insistence of the passengers or possibly the captains needed to communicate. Although, another theory exists, one which has persisted through the years. While it was against company rules and an unsafe practice, it was common for ships passing to exchange packages and newspapers from ports they had called on. Ships passed on to oncoming ships, the newspapers of the ports where they were heading. Passengers and crew alike yearned for news. While it was adamantly denied, many feel this practice might have been the case with the *Meteor* and *Pewabic*.

Late in the day following the accident, the *Meteor* arrived at Sault St. Marie, docking for the night to allow some passengers and *Pewabic* survivors to disembark. The next day the ship steamed into the lock to rise the twenty-two-feet to the level of Lake Superior.

"Fire!" came a scream from the engine room of the *Meteor*. "There's fire in the hold!" The cargo of lime had ignited and was burning.

The ship passed through the lock into the north basin. Captain Wilson ordered the pumps to fill the hull. Another steamer, the *Ontonagon*, came abreast the burning vessel and directed its pumps at the *Meteor*. The hold filled to the level of the main deck, extinguishing the fire before the entire ship became completely engulfed in a blaze.

Had the fire been discovered a half hour later after the ship had passed through the locks and was in the open water of Lake

Superior, the entire ship and probably most of her passengers and crew would have drown or been burned alive, doubling the tragedy of the voyage.

The *Meteor* would be repaired to continue with her career until 1927 when she was intentionally sunk off Cleveland, Ohio. Her service ran an amazing sixty-four-years, unlike her sister ship, *Pewabic*, which sunk when she was only in her second season on the lakes.

THE BURNING OF THE "QUEEN OF THE LAKES" THE NORONIC

On September 17, 1949, Cabin 462, near the cocktail lounge near the aft of the 362-foot *Noronic*, was the site of a late-night party. The lounges were packed and the celebrating crowds spilled over into nearby cabins, like Cabin 462.

The party started when the ship departed Detroit three days earlier, headed south on the Detroit River, into Lake Erie to Cleveland. There, more passengers boarded. In fact, most of the 512 passengers onboard were either from Michigan or Ohio. The next leg of the festive adventure took the ship the length of Lake Erie to Buffalo, New York and then up into Lake Ontario to Toronto, Ontario.

At Toronto, the ship tied up to the Canadian Steamship Lines wharf, taking on supplies for the next leg of the journey, the 160 plus miles across the length of Lake Ontario to the

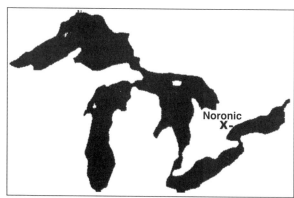

Canadian resort area of the Thousand Island Region.

The Noronic. From the Collections of the Michigan Maritime Museum, South Haven

The weather was predicted to be sunny and warm and those onboard were eager in anticipation of several days at sea onboard the "Queen of the Great Lakes," the Canadian Steamship Lines passenger ship, *Noronic*.

The ship was widely regarded as the most luxurious of the passenger ships which plied the inland seas. Valued at an amazing $4,000,000, the *Noronic* was complete with beautiful salons, large staterooms and eloquent dining rooms.

Whatever form of entertainment the passengers wanted, the crew tried to accommodate. They could jog or march around the promenade deck, dance under the stars or lounge on deck chairs.

A favorite with many was the Mile March. Passengers marched six times, approximately one mile, around the deck to peppy music played by the band, a sort of shipboard exercise program to combat the excessive eating and drinking at the onboard restaurants and lounges. Another highlight was the King Neptune's masquerade ball.

The Noronic *locking through in years past.* From the collections of the Michigan Maritime Museum, South Haven, Michigan

On the night of September 17, 1949, many passengers had retired to their cabins early, but some still frolicked on the dance floor in the main salon, socializing and drinking in the lounges and partying in private cabins. Ada Roberts and Bernice McCellan walked through the passageway returning from the aft lounge. They giggled, talking of young men they had met. Ada noticed it first, then Bernice asked, "Do you smell smoke?" They were outside Cabin 462.

A night watchman at the docks can sometimes be a boring job. Staying awake for the length of the shift is often the biggest challenge. But on that night, Dan Harper's shift was anything but boring. He listened to the band playing and watched the passengers dance and walk the decks. Around 1:38 a.m., he spotted a faint glimmer through a cabin window near the lounge at the aft of the liner. It looked like it might be a fire in a cabin. It was Cabin 462.

Within minutes, flames climbed up the next deck and shot through the roof at the upper deck. Dan stared in disbelief for a moment, then raced to call in the alarm. As he ran back to the ship to render any assistance, he could see the

Have *YOU* Made Your Reservation Yet?

"*Noronic*" Excursion Sept. 13

Spend this Week-End in Cleveland

Too busy all summer for a boat-trip? Make's a week-end cruise that every one can take

On the "Noronic," too, the finest ship that sails the Great Lakes. Come with us to Cleveland. Resume leaves Port Huron at 7.45 p. m. on Saturday, and returns in time for business Monday, at 7.45 a m.

You'll enjoy the delightful sail down St. Clair River in the early evening, the dance on the wonderful ball room floor. All day Sunday in Cleveland, visiting and sight-seeing, and the return ship Sunday night to Sarnia.

SCHEDULE
"Noronic" leaves Sarnia at 7 p. m.; leaves Port Huron at 7.45 p. m., Saturday, Sept. 13. Arrives Cleveland at 8 a. m. Sunday, Sept. 14. Leaves Cleveland at 8 p. m. Sunday, and arrives Sarnia at 6 a. m. and Port Huron at 7.45 a. m. Monday, Sept. 15.

One meal only served to passengers, dinner leaving Cleveland, $1.50.

$2.50 Berth Extra

RATES FOR BERTHS PER NIGHT
Inside Room—Upper $1.00, Lower $1.50.
Outside Room—Upper $1.50, Lower $2.00.
Grand Saloon Room—Upper $2.00, Lower $2.50.
Parlors—$10 per night for either one or two persons. If occupied by one person must hold two tickets.

Reservations at Sylvester's Drug Store Port Huron

Northern Navigation Co.

flames race the length of the ship, her wood upper structure almost completely ablaze. "It was like a torch extending from one end to the other. It went up like gasoline," he later reported.

Edward Johnson and his wife Nan decided to get a good nights sleep. They had turned in early that night.

Edward, on the top bunk fell asleep almost as soon as his head hit the pillow. Nan had been reading a book and wanted to finish the chapter before she slept. Absorbed in her book and annoyed with Ed's snoring, Nan heard something in the passageway. Noise at all hours of the night on the ship was nothing new on this cruise, but this was a different sound, sort of a crackling.

It was about 1:30 a.m. and dressed in bedclothes, Nan went to the door to see the source of the noise. Opening the door, she stared not comprehending what she saw, then screamed. The corridor was on fire! Flames raced along the ceiling. Pieces of burning ceiling trim fell to the floor igniting the carpet and walls. Somewhere down the smoke-filled hall a frantic voice screamed, "The ship's on fire!"

Edward awakened, looked at the blaze in the hall and slammed the door. Thinking the crew would soon extinguish the fire, he told Nan, "Let's get over by the porthole and if need be, we can jump through there and swim to the dock. It's only about thirty-feet."

However, Ed opened the port and found it did not open wide enough for them to fit through. Their only way out was through the burning passageway. Ed in flannel pajamas and black dress shoes and Nan in her nightdress and slippers, opened the door and ran towards the stairs.

The crew had arrived in the passageway and were directing a stream from a hose in the hall. Ed and Nan raced down the hall towards the stairwell that would take them down to the gangway and to safety. The Johnsons grabbed the hot metal railing as they ran down the stairs, scorching the flesh of their hands.

Many others on the same deck were asleep and didn't awaken until their only exit was completely engulfed in flames. They died of heat, burns or smoke inhalation, despite the heroic efforts of the crew.

The S. S. Noronic *burns at the dock in the early morning hours. An* Associated Press *photograph from the* Port Huron Times Herald

The *Noronic* was a steel hulled ship but most of the upper deckwork was built of wood. The combination of long interior halls with wood walls covered with flammable paint resulted in a conflagration which quickly spread despite all efforts to stop it. The long narrow corridors of the ship were responsible for the rapid movement of the fire. They acted as a channel for the heat, smoke and flames to spread unabated the length of the ship. Unfortunately, the corridors were also the only way for many passengers to escape. Many passengers were trapped in the long carpeted corridors where they drew their last smoke-filled breath.

Disaster had again struck the Canadian Steamship Lines. Just four years earlier the 349-foot *Hamonic*, sister ship to the *Noronic*, burned while tied up at a wharf on the St. Clair River. Fortunately, in the *Hamonic* disaster only one man, a dock worker was killed.

Passengers on the *Noronic* began to panic as they searched for a way off the burning ship. Some escaped by walking hand over hand down the steel cables holding the ship to the bollards on the wharf. The cables, heated from the fire, burned the flesh from their hands. Many, the pain in their hands too great, let go and fell into the water or to the concrete of the dock.

Groups of passengers searched for a way off the ship while trying to avoid flames and burning debris falling all around them. Some screamed and sobbed. Some in shock just looked wide eyed at the destruction. Lucille Roberts, burns on her arms and face, heard the pleading cries of a man on the upper deck. She looked up and saw a man surrounded by flames. The fire crept nearer to him, he had nowhere to go. She screamed, "Jump! Jump over the rail!"

Confused, scared or in shock, the man just stood there, his head turning side to side looking for an escape, screaming. Lucille watched as the flames encompassed the man. His last pained scream echoes in her mind.

Many frightened passengers, unable to find an escape, chose to jump the thirty to sixty-feet from the decks of the ship into the waters of Lake Ontario. To some it was a calculated risk, die an almost certain, painful death by fire or risk the possibility of broken bones, hypothermia or drowning. Many, wrapped in a life jacket, chose to jump into the black water, illuminated only by the ominous orange glow of the burning ship. They found the water hot, warmed by the fire, they made frantic swimming motions towards shore, fearing they would be scalded. Some made it the short distance to shore, but many died and floated on the lake's surface.

Eighteen fire trucks and two fireboats responded to the fire at the wharf, training their hoses from different angles on the flames. Heroic firefighters risked their own lives and entered the ship, helping passengers to escape.

Ross Leich, a taxi harbor boatman, ran to his boat and sped through the darkness towards the light of the burning *Noronic*. He could hear through the night air screams of both men and women and the splashes of people who jumped from the ship. As he grew closer to the eerie glow of the fire, he saw bobbing heads and bodies floating in the surface.

He slowly maneuvered his boat towards a large group of people floating near the hull, screaming and frantically waving to him.

Nearing the ship, watching the victims in the water, he was startled by a huge crash in his boat. As soon as he came near the *Noronic*, passengers on the deck jumped in panic from the ship. They jumped into his boat, smashing in the cabin roof, landing in the cockpit breaking the seats, bouncing off the deck and sliding into the lake. He heard the wood of his boat and the bones of the people breaking on impact. Men, women and children lay about his boat, crying, moaning, broken and bloodied. He headed towards shore with his cargo of human tragedy and then returned for more.

Sylvia Carpenter, an operator with Detroit Bell and several co-workers had saved for this cruise and looked forward to it for months. Sylvia and friends searched with others for a way to avoid the flames and leave the ship. They followed other passengers through passageways only to be turned back by fire or smoke. On the top deck Sylvia found a rope. She tied it to a stanchion and threw the rope over the rail. While assisting one of her screaming friends over the rail she was grabbed from behind and thrown to the deck. Three panicked men pushed their way to the rail and climbed down Sylvia's rope.

Many survivors reported cowardly behavior by some of the men onboard. To some, it was a self preservation situation. "Women and children first" was not their motto. Yet, there was nothing but praise for the crew and Captain Taylor.

Upon notification of the fire by crew, sixty-five-year-old Captain Taylor was quick to grab a fire hose and train the stream on flames near passengers, saving them from a painful death. Realizing the lateness of the hour and that many passengers were sleeping, he ran through the passageways pounding on, sometimes smashing in, cabin doors and windows to alert them of the fire. Captain Taylor was credited with saving the life of one woman by carrying her to safety. Still later, the captain stood at the bow helping people down the hawsers and other lines thrown over the side.

The captain, having helped all passengers off the bow, tried to move aft to assist passengers who might be trapped there, but was turned back by the flames. The crew pleaded with him to save himself and leave the ship. Only after all of his crew had climbed down the firemen's ladder, extending from shore to the ship, did Captain Taylor slowly step over the rail onto the ladder. He paused to take one last look at his ship, what was left of her anyway, then started down the ladder. He carefully climbed down one step at a

The Noronic, *still smoldering, the day following the tragic fire.*
From the H.C. Inches Collection at the Port Huron Museum

time until the ladder broke and the captain in a free fall, fell about fifty-feet to the lake. He, in the tradition of maritime ventures, was the last to leave his ship, his once beautiful ship.

A very distressed, Captain Taylor, his hand bandaged and his face still burned red, later said, "I had hoped to end my career without loss of life."

As with any disaster, there were many heroes. The captain of the ship *Kingston*, came to the side of the burning *Noronic* and remained next to her to allow frightened passengers to jump to the safety of his ship. The crew of the *Kingston* fought fires on their own ship caused by embers blown from the *Noronic*. The *Cayuga*, a sister ship to the *Noronic*, was pulled away from the dock into open water out of harms way, but her crew in lifeboats were lowered to pick up victims and survivors. Detective Cyril Cole was also one of the heroes. He dove repeatedly below the lakes surface grabbing onto people and bringing them to the surface. Some were alive, some not. One person that Detective Cole brought to the surface was Captain Taylor.

Passengers ran, jumped and climbed to safety, while many others were trapped in the conflagration and died. Firemen, volunteers and crew fought the flames of the *Noronic* for over five hours before the blaze had subsided. The ship, most of her deckwork gone and her hull buckled by heat in many places, had sunk twenty-eight-feet to the lake's bottom, trapping passengers and crew not killed by the fire, below decks in a watery tomb.

Divers were brought in to remove the dead from the hull of the ship. But, it wasn't until late the following day that the fire was out and the water cooled enough for the divers to enter the hull of the ship. There many victims were found in their cabins, some in groups and others in pairs or by themselves drowned or burned.

The Toronto coroner's office set up a temporary morgue at the nearby Canadian Horticulture building. Just weeks before, the building housed beautiful fauna, now it housed rows of tables with the burnt, blackened and charred remains of over one hundred people. Red Cross personnel searched through the remains looking

The burned out shell of the once beautiful S. S. Noronic. From the Michigan Maritime Museum, South Haven, Michigan

for jewelry, scraps of clothing, or anything else which could help identify the unrecognizable corpses. The bodies wrapped in tarps were often in pairs, couples locked in an eternal embrace.

The tragic fire aboard the Canadian Steamship Line's, *Noronic* is the most deadly maritime accidents on the Great Lakes in modern times. The number of lives lost on the ship is reported to be 112, with hundreds more injured. Another loss with the burning of the *Noronic* was the end of the large passenger ships on the Great Lakes. After the *Noronic* was raised and its hull sold for scrap, no large luxurious passenger ships were built for lake use. It was the end of an era.

THE TRAGIC TALE OF THE
S. S. EASTLAND

On the morning of July 24, 1915, Mrs. Grochwska, her daughter Kitty and Kitty's friend, Rose Moldt, were standing in a mass of people waiting to board the huge white steamship, *S. S. Eastland*. Kitty, eighteen years-old and Rose, nineteen, were excited, looking forward to a fun day at Western Electric's employee picnic.

The girls giggled as they pointed out good-looking young men they saw in line. Mrs. Grochwska playfully scolded the girls, then pointed out a man off to their left. The girls were giddy with anticipation of what the day would bring. They didn't know that in just a short time they would become victims of the worst ship disaster ever to occur on the Great Lakes.

The *S. S. Eastland*, a 265-foot long excursion ship, was docked on the Chicago River amid thousands of people anxious to board

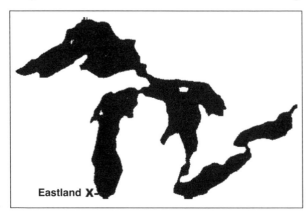

Eastland X-

The Eastland as she looked in years before her accident. From the collection of the Eastland Disaster Historical Society

the excursion boats. Of the five ships chartered by the Western Electric Company for their annual employee picnic, the *Eastland* was the first to board. Over seven thousand tickets had been sold for the event and the crowd assembled on the wharf early.

The trip aboard the *Eastland* to Michigan City's Washington Park would depart at 7:30 a.m. Passengers began lining up long before that in hopes of being on the *Eastland*. It would be the first ship to load and depart and it was the fastest of the five ships hired for the day.

Passengers poured through the gangways and most ran up the grand stairway to the top decks where they could line the starboard rail to wave and yell to their friends still on the dock. The ship began to take on a slight list to starboard, which is normal when passengers gather dockside prior to departure.

An order was given from the bridge

Passengers lined the wharf waiting to board one of the five ships chartered by the Western Electric Company for their annual employee picnic. From the collection of the Eastland *Disaster Historical Society*

to the engine room to steady the ship. Valves were turned and river water began to flow into the port ballast tanks. The ship righted as the water's weight countered the weight of the passengers at the starboard rail.

Listing while loading was nothing unusual for a passenger ship. On a freighter the cargo is carefully loaded and positioned to prevent the ship from becoming unstable. Yet on a passenger ship the human cargo does not evenly distribute their weight on the ship, in fact the people are a mobile cargo which results in the ship constantly being trimmed. Typically as they board, large groups of passengers gather along one side and the ship needs to take on or pump out ballast to compensate.

Kitty and Rose on the top deck of the *Eastland*, waved their handkerchiefs and shouted to friends on the dock, feeling special that they were lucky enough to board the first ship, the luxurious and fast *Eastland*. They would be the first to depart and first to arrive at the picnic.

A ship's officer walked by asking passengers to move to the other side, but the girls, like the rest of the passengers, stayed by the dockside rail.

Before long, the *Eastland* began to list to port, even though the largest congregation of passengers lined the starboard rail.

Again, the captain called the engine room with orders to take measures to compensate for the list. Below decks, ballast water was pumped from the port tanks and the ship slowly shifted back to an even keel.

Twenty-five hundred passengers, the maximum amount the *Eastland* was certified to carry in 1915, had boarded the ship. Those waiting on the dock were diverted to the next ships, the *Theodore Roosevelt* and the *Petoskey*.

The *Eastland* began to again list to port.

Captain Pedersen gave the order to prepare for immediate departure even though the ship remained unstable with a very noticeable list to port.

Kitty and Rose heard the Bradfield's Orchestra begin to play on the deck below them. They looked at one another, a wide eyed smile came across their faces and without a word, they ran from the rail and raced below decks towards the music.

The *Eastland* continued with a list to port. Some passengers noticed the angle of the ship as they walked, but few were

The S. S. Eastland *before gaining fame as the ship which killed more people on the Great Lakes than any other.* From the H. C. Inches Collection of the Port Huron Museum

concerned. Yet the crew, more experienced, were very concerned. In the engine room, men frantically worked the valves to the ballast system, trying to right the ship. As the stern line was released, the aft end of the ship drifted out into the river. The listing grew worse. Water began to pour in through the port gangways and scuppers. The bilge pumps were started.

Captain Pedersen felt if he could get the ship out of the river into the open water of Lake Michigan, he could better deal with the problem. He called for a tug to escort the *Eastland* and asked for the drawbridge to be opened. The bridge master refused to open the bridge fearing the ship was too unsteady to get underway.

The list to port of the ship dramatically increased as its stern floated free and the bow remained tied to the dock. Passengers began to scream as they could no longer ignore the list and began to slide across the decks towards the port side. Dishes could be heard breaking in the kitchen as they tumbled from the shelves.

Kitty and Rose had pushed their way into the main salon towards the music but could not reach the dance floor due to the huge crowd already there. They leaned against the port cabin wall

The tug Kenosha *forms a bridge for survivors to evacuate the* Eastland *just after the accident. From the H. C. Inches Collection of the Port Huron Museum*

as the list increased. Passengers in the main salon began to scream. The fun of the day turned to terror as Rose began to cry. They reached for one another and hugged trying to fight off fear.

Passengers ran as best they could to the deck in panic. Kitty screamed as she saw the piano rolling across the dance floor increasing in speed as it rolled on the inclined surface of the floor. The piano narrowly missed hitting several passengers as it crashed into the port wall.

Tables and chairs slid towards the port wall, pinning people. Kitty and Rose both screamed at the sound of the bar refrigerator crashing to the floor. The large, heavy refrigerator then slid across the floor. Passengers frantically tried to escape it until it crashed against the cabin wall, crushing Kitty and Rose.

Water poured in port gangways while the boiler stokers, in a panic, climbed the ladder to escape a certain death as the water rose in the bilge. The bilge pump, already working, struggled with the incoming water.

The orchestra had braced themselves as best they could and played, trying to calm the passengers, until their chairs slid out from under them. The music stopped and was replaced with the shrieks of the frightened and panicked aboard. Passengers above and below deck clung to the starboard rail or anything nearby to prevent themselves from sliding to port.

On the main deck, passengers crawled toward the stairwells attempting to save themselves. Others on the main deck jumped from the ship off the starboard side. Some made the leap to the dock some landed in the river.

As more water poured in through the gangways, the list worsened. Suddenly without hesitation... the list became too great for the ballast tanks to compensate. The *Eastland* rolled onto her port side, coming to rest on the river bottom, her starboard hull exposed.

Those on the open decks were thrown from the ship into the air to land in the river. A survivor of the disaster, Harlan Babcock,

The Eastland *lies near the wharf while hundreds of dead are brought from the interior of the ship. From the collection of the* Eastland *Disaster Historical Society*

described the scene: "In an instant, the surface of the river was black with struggling, crying, frightened, drowning humanity. Infants floated about like corks."

The ship, almost forty-feet in beam, settled to the bottom of the twenty-foot deep river. The river's surface became alive with hundreds of bobbing heads screaming for help. Many unable to swim or too scared, succumbed quickly to the river. Others looked to the thousands still lining the docks and screamed for help.

Passengers aboard the other ships still tied to the docks looked on in horror as their friends, just moments before happy and gay with the anticipation of the day's events, died before their eyes. A lifeboat and life rafts from the *Eastland* floated free but floated empty in the sea of drowning passengers and crew.

Life preservers, deck chairs and anything that could float was thrown to the screaming throngs in the water. Lifeboats were hurriedly lowered from nearby ships. Many victims were taken aboard, but the immensity of the disaster was so great that many of the passengers cast into the river were overcome by panic and shock and died in the water.

The Eastland *lies on her portside resting on the river bottom. Rescue vessels are seen assisting in the recovery of the hundreds of souls who died that morning.* From the collection of the Eastland *Disaster Historical Society*

A fireman holds the lifeless body of a child pulled from the wreckage. His expression speaks of the horror of the day. From the collection of the Eastland *Disaster Historical Society*

Harlan Babcock continued, "I shall also never forget the way those wailing, shrieking women, and some men, clung to the upper railings of the capsized boat. In mad desperation they grasped the rail, knowing that to let go meant possible death."

Those on the open decks who were cast into the river were the lucky ones. Many passengers were trapped below decks. Those in cabins on the port side were drowned as the ship rolled over and filled with river water. The unfortunate souls who were along the port cabin walls were crushed by the weight of others thrown against them as the ship overturned. Cries came from the mass of humanity stacked several deep. Some tried to claw out of the mass of carnage. Several bodies were later found to be scratched and gouged with torn clothing. The water crept up, slowly drowning those not killed by the weight of the others. Soon the screams and cries for help subsided as the passengers drowned within the confines of the ship.

Passengers trying to climb the grand stairway were crushed when the stairway collapsed under the weight of the crowd. Those who were not killed in the fall were trapped, their means of escape lay in a tangled heap of wood, metal, flesh and blood.

Many others were trapped in cabins, passageways, or other areas with no means of escape, screaming for help as the water slowly rose. They drew in a deep breath as the water neared their heads, only to involuntarily exhale and suck in river water, filling their lungs to die an agonizing death.

Families huddled together, nowhere to go, as water crept up around them. Fathers and mothers held their children high as the water rose, to no avail. The families died together. Many children, mothers and fathers were later found locked in a deadly embrace. Twenty-two entire families were killed on that fateful morning.

Some, trapped below decks, had to step on the bodies of their dead friends as they tried to find a way to escape death. Portholes on the starboard side were opened and those small enough to fit through climbed out

From the collection of the Eastland *Disaster* *Historical Society*

From the collection of the Eastland *Disaster Historical Society*

to join the several hundred passengers and crew who had made it to safety.

Several passengers who had staterooms onboard the ship were trapped when the ship overturned. They were killed when they were unable to exit though the damaged or blocked cabin doors. Groups of the dead were later found floating, trapped in their cabins.

Some passengers lucky enough to be close to a starboard gangway door, were able to climb or be pulled to the side of the vessel lying above the river's surface. Rescuers reached down into the gangways to the mass of people climbing on one another, trying to escape the ship. Many were pulled to safety while others were crushed by the panicked. Hundreds stood on the starboard side of the ship, shaken, many in shock, but alive.

The Chicago Police and Fire Departments were quick to respond to the capsizing. Tugs and other boats nearby steamed to the area. Dead bodies were pushed aside to gain access to those still alive, floundering in the river. Several people from the crowd on the wharf dove into the river to rescue those in the screaming mass.

Some victims reached out for anything that could save them, life preservers and furniture thrown from the other ships and wood ripped from the wharf. Some of the panicked grabbed other passengers and drown them in an attempt to save themselves.

The *Kenosha* was now pulling passengers from the river. "Save those who can be saved!" cried the captain as dead were ignored and only those showing movement were pulled to safety. Some men openly cried as they used pike poles to push away floating bodies to reach those showing life.

Pounding from inside the hull could be heard by rescuers and survivors standing on the starboard hull. The trapped pounded and scratched at the hull, hoping someone would hear their signal and rescue them. Firemen, on the starboard side of the ship used their axes on the wood cabin structure to release passengers trapped inside. Soon men arrived with cutting torches to cut holes in the *Eastland's* steel side. Captain Pedersen and his first mate ran to them, demanding they stop. He didn't want anything done to harm the integrity of the ship's hull. Several of his men tried to help the captain prevent holes being cut into the hull but they were arrested. The torches cut large holes in the starboard hull, allowing many to escape. Rescue workers jumped in through the holes and pulled the injured to safety. Later, as the water increased, the rescue workers in the hull waded in chest high water, feeling with their feet for the bodies of the dead.

Hard hat divers were summoned. They dove in the water and then in the ship with the grim task of bringing out the bodies of those trapped below decks.

The dead, by the hundreds, were brought out of the ship and river during the day and into the night. A temporary morgue was set up in the nearby Second Regiment Armory. Bodies covered with sheets were carried on stretchers to the Armory. The stretchers were quickly emptied and rushed back to the scene of horror to be filled again.

"A woman who was one of those rescued from the upper railing stood weeping at the top of the pier," Harlan Babcock continued.

The bodies of the hundreds of passengers killed on the Eastland *were taken to the Second Regiment Armory and lined up for identification by the next of kin. From the H. C. Inches collection of the Port Huron Museum*

"When she stepped onto the *Eastland* an hour before, she had her husband and little boy."

"Whenever a child's body would be brought to the street, she would wildly demand to see the face. Finally, a tiny form was brought up and before police could stop her, she grabbed the body and pulled the blanket away from the cold white face of the child. It was her baby and she fainted."

Rescue workers and the hundreds of people lining the river's edge watching the catastrophe unfold before their eyes were haunted by the painful screams of the people trapped below decks. Soon they were haunted by the silence when the screams stopped.

The screams of joy, as the passengers boarded, were replaced with cries for help, then tears for the dead. On that fateful morning of July 24, 1915, 815 people died as the *Eastland* rolled to port.

In the days that followed, the capsizing of the *Eastland* an investigation into the cause of the greatest marine disaster ever to occur in the Great Lakes began. Sailors, familiar with the vessel, recounted she was widely known as a "tender" ship, meaning she was prone to listing.

The investigation revealed that in her first year, just months after her maiden voyage, the *Eastland* took on such a list that lake water poured in through her gangways. The following year, while returning from South Haven, Michigan with a cargo of over 3000 passengers, the ship began to take a precarious list to port. The engineers over-compensated and the ship then listed precariously to starboard before she was brought steady.

The listing was of such concern that the passenger capacity of the *Eastland* was reduced from 3,300 to 2,800. In 1906 after another listing scare, the capacity was lowered yet again to 2,400.

The Eastland *lies on the bottom of the river as the wrecking tug* Favorite *prepares to right her. From the H. C. Inches collection of the Port Huron Museum*

CHICAGO RIVER~CLARK ST. BRIDGE.
S.S. EASTLAND, RAISED,
THREE WEEKS AFTER DISASTER.

The S. S. Eastland *is righted after over two weeks of lying on her side.* From the collection of the Eastland *Disaster Historical Society*

However, the capacity was later raised to 2,570, the amount of passengers and crew aboard the *Eastland* on July 24, 1915.

The *Eastland*, launched in 1903, was designed to transport passengers and cargo on the lucrative route between Chicago and South Haven and other west Michigan resort areas. The cargo she hauled was fruit grown in the South Haven area to the ready market of Chicago. The specific cargo and ports of call required the ship be built to certain specifications. The Black River at South Haven was only about twelve-feet deep, so the ship had to have a shallow draft and the ship needed to be fast. These two requirements would be found to have an effect on the stability of the ship. Simply stated, there was too much weight above the water line and not enough below. The ship was top heavy.

To counter the listing, the ship was equipped with a ballast system to take on lake water into either port or starboard tanks to help stabilize the ship, but the system proved to be inadequate. The tanks could not be filled nor emptied quickly. Another problem was the ballast intake port was the same used to pump the ballast water out, making it impossible to empty one tank while the tanks on the other side were filling. The way the ballast system was designed, water from one tank could not be shifted to the other.

The newspapers of the day, through either sensationalism or a lack of facts, projected that over 1,800 deaths would result of this tragedy. It was later lowered to just over 900, but most modern day projections agree that 815 souls met their death that day.

The dead were not the only to suffer. Thousands of Chicago residents lost relatives. Thousands more on the dock, on other excursion ships and the rescue workers had to live the rest of their lives with the screams echoing in their dreams.

In the days and months that followed the tragedy, many allegations of wrong-doing against the captain, officers and the ship's management were made. Indictments were made, grand juries were called and civil suits were brought.

The *Eastland* remained lying on the bottom of the Chicago River for over two weeks while salvage crews made repairs to the

The S. S. Eastland *once again afloat. The ship is still wearing a coat of Chicago River bottom mud. From the H. C. Inches collection of the Port Huron Museum*

The Eastland *after the accident was sold and renamed the* Wilmette. *From the collection of the Michigan Maritime Museum*

ship in preparation of righting her. On August 14, 1915, the ship was righted and moved to a nearby shipyard for repairs. The ship never sailed again under the name of the *Eastland*. She was sold at auction for $46,000 and eventually retrofitted as the *Wilmette*, an Illinois Naval Reserve training ship. The ship served until 1947 when it was cut up for its scrap value. No other shipwreck on the Great Lakes has come near to the level of human loss as the *Eastland* disaster. Ironically, the ship was still tied to the dock.

Authors note: Special thanks to the:
Eastland Disaster Historical Society
PO Box 2013
Arlington Heights, IL 60006-2013
1-877-865-6295
http://www.eastlanddisaster.org

THE FERRY OMAR D. CONGER MAKES ITS MARK ON PORT HURON

66 Life is a fragile thing. The Lord giveth and the Lord taketh it away," the Reverend Tredinnick told the mourners at the funeral of Henry Biddlecomb.

"We never know when the end will come. You could be walking down the street, asleep in your bed or sitting here in church when the Lord calls."

The congregation screamed as a huge explosion shook the church. Seconds later a large object crashed through the window at the back of the church, spraying shards of glass and debris on the congregation. Mrs. Biddlecomb was seriously cut on her head and Mrs. Carson was struck by glass, blinding her eye. Several others were badly cut. Panic ensued and some of the congregation was trampled as they ran from the sanctuary.

The object that flew through the window was a 200 pound radiator.

Sunday, March 26, 1922

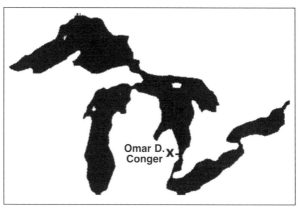

Omar D. Conger X

The Omar D. Conger as she looked for most of her 40 year career. From the collection of the Port Huron Museum

was a sunny spring day. A boy in a small rowboat played on the St. Clair River. He looked upriver when he heard the explosion. Soon debris began to float downstream. The youngster plucked life jackets and a wooden clock case from the water. The hands of the clock had stopped at 2:20.

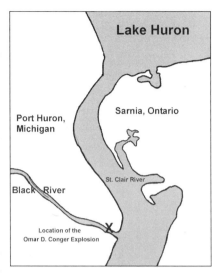

Destruction in the Port Huron downtown area was devastating. Plate glass windows in more than twenty-five businesses on Huron Avenue, Military, Quay and Water Streets were shattered. A twenty-five-pound valve crashed through the roof of the Higer Store, coming to rest on the counter as if it were a piece of merchandise displayed for sale.

A ship's lifeboat davit was thrust through a wall of Peg's Tire Store, sticking out the front wall. The owner claimed he would use it to hang a tire on to promote business.

A 1918 postcard showing the ferry boats tied to the dock on the Black River near the intersection of the St. Clair River. The Omar D. Conger *is the larger of the two ships at the dock.* Authors Collection

Harvey and Norma Davis, taking a leisurely Sunday stroll several blocks from the ferry docks, were knocked to the ground by the concussion. A shower of debris began to fall around them, pieces of timber, shards of glass, missiles of metal and even a lifeboat. They quickly regained their feet and ran for the protection of a nearby hardware store.

Mr. and Mrs. William Smith, their son and his wife were taking a drive north of Port Huron in their new car. Mrs. Smith had prepared a chicken and planned dinner at 2:00 upon their return home. The car became stuck in the muddy country roads and they wouldn't get home until almost 3:00. The dinner would be ruined. Little did they know that getting stuck was a fortunate accident.

The Smith family lived on Quay Street, just 300-feet from the ferry docks. While they were stuck in the mud, a twenty-five-ton steam boiler fell from the sky onto the Smith home. Their home was smashed and the red hot boiler set the wreckage ablaze. Firefighters could only fight to save the house next door.

The Port Huron Fire Department fights the William Smith home fire caused by the explosion of the Conger. *From the collection of the Port Huron Museum*

The 25-ton boiler from the Conger *lies in the shattered and burned remains of the Smith house.* From the collection of the Port Huron Museum

The residents of Port Huron and Sarnia, Ontario heard the explosion and most knew what had happened, a steamship's boiler had exploded.

A crowd of hundreds of people gathered on the Military Street Bridge crossing the Black River to look down upon what remained of the ferry, *Omar D. Conger*.

The *Conger* had been built in 1882 at the Muir Shipyard on the north side of the Black River. Ironically, the ferry now lay on the bottom, a torn and twisted hulk, just 150-feet from the spot she had slid down the ways forty years earlier.

The *Omar D. Conger*, named for a long time congressman from the Port Huron area, was a ninety-two-foot-long wood passenger ferry. The ship was built specifically to transport passengers and freight between Port Huron on the west side of the St. Clair River and Sarnia, Ontario on the east. There was no bridge, the ferry was the only way to cross.

The *Conger*, known as one of the most graceful and stable vessels on the river, made several crossings daily. The ferry worked long into the winter, until the Black River froze. The little ship was usually the first out in the spring.

Over its forty year career, the ferry had been repaired and rebuilt with very little of the original vessel remaining. In 1902, the ship had caught fire and partially burned. In 1904, a new boiler was installed. Just months before the explosion, the *Conger* had undergone another major overhaul, having most of the decks replaced and a new engine installed. The vessel was back in service in February 1922, in fine operating condition.

"I heard the explosion and looked up and saw a cloud of smoke and dust where the *Conger* had been." Captain Waugh said from the deck of the passenger ferry *Cheboygan*.

The *Cheboygan* had just made the crossing of the St. Clair River and was heading up the Black River towards the ferry docks with about 200 passengers onboard when the *Conger* blew up less than 200-feet away.

"My first thought was, anyone on her was gone." Then he looked about his ship for damage and injuries. No one was hurt. "If the explosion had occurred five minutes later, some of my passengers would have been killed or injured. They would have been walking out of the ferry house where the debris had fallen."

"It looked like the explosion blew the boiler right through the hull," Captain Waugh continued, "The boat sank almost in an instant."

Four men were onboard the *Conger* at 2:20 p.m. that Sunday afternoon. They were preparing the ship for the 3:00 p.m. crossing, its first of the day. Two deckhands were onboard, Tom Buckner and Ken Crandall. The explosion blew them off the ship and they were found on a coal pile several hundred feet way. Mr. Buckner was dead when he was found and Crandall died on the way to the hospital.

Chief Engineer Ramsome A. Cambell, sixty-years-old, was below in the engine room with fireman Clifford Althouse. They would have been the first to know there was a problem on the *Conger*. After the explosion, they were missing and believed to be entombed in the wreckage at the bottom of the river.

The remains of the Conger *after the boiler explosion which destroyed the ship.* From the collection of the Port Huron Museum

Firemen and volunteers were fast to get to the ferry docks. They climbed aboard the hurricane deck of the *Conger*, all that remained above the river. The lightener barge, *Atmosphere* , was brought alongside the wreck. The steam crane on the barge lifted wreckage from the hull, trying to find the bodies of the missing men. Although a diver was brought in to search the hull, the river water was still much too murky from the explosion, limiting his visibility.

The cause of the *Conger* explosion was the source of much speculation among the mariners of the area. Low water in the boiler is suspected to be the cause of the explosion, but no one lived to tell what actually happened prior to the blast.

A Marine Inquiry Board was assembled to investigate the cause of the explosion. Since no witnesses survived the blast, they can only theorize the steps which led to the disaster based on evidence found, such as discolored boiler tubes blown several blocks from the ferry docks. The discoloring indicates that the tubes had been heated red hot without any water in them for cooling.

The Inquiry Board determined that most likely the boiler was fired up with little or no water in it. Probably one of the men in the engine room noticed the boiler was heating dry and opened a valve to allow cool river water to fill the hot boiler creating a recipe for explosion.

The *Conger* plied the waters of the St. Clair River for forty years, providing necessary transportation for many citizens of the area. Prior to the explosion, the ferry was sometimes employed for picnic cruises on warm summer afternoons. Many residents remembered those excursions fondly. Unfortunately, the *Omar D. Conger* would now forever be remembered as the ship that killed four, injured many and caused much destruction to its home port of Port Huron, Michigan.

THE ALPENA SAILS
INTO THE STORM

In the 1880s the windmill was a common sight, their wood towers and spinning blades dotted the horizon across the country. The windmill was the nineteenth century answer to converting the power of the wind into mechanical energy. The mechanical energy was primarily used in rural America to pump water.

Montgomery Crossman of Grand Haven, Michigan, while still in his twenties, was a mechanical engineer and manager of the Sterns Manufacturing Company and widely known throughout the Midwest for his inventions to improve the windmill.

On October 15, 1880, he was sitting at the dock at Grand Haven, Michigan, waiting to board the Goodrich Transportation Company's side-wheel passenger ship, *Alpena*. He raised his coat collar against the wind. The *Alpena* was preparing to take on passengers and cargo destined for Chicago. The 110-mile voyage

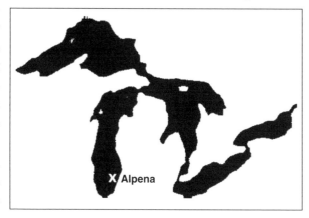

X Alpena

Michigan Maritime Museum

The Alpena. *From the collection of the Michigan Maritime Museum*

across lower Lake Michigan was to be the *Alpena's* last trip of the season.

It was a typical late October day on the Great Lakes, gray skies, a day long drizzle with periods of showers and occasional snow. As a first class passenger, Montgomery was one of the first to board. He ran up the gangway to the deck, his bag carried to his stateroom.

Captain Nelson Napier, long respected by Great Lake sailors, stood on the bridge looking out on the lake, scanning the dark and ominous sky. The wind had been blowing from the west and northwest most of the day, freshening as storms moved through. He watched the ships tie up to docks on either side of the river, seeking shelter from an angry Lake Michigan.

First Officer Kelly told the captain that the cargo had been loaded and the ship was prepared to depart. The cargo consisted of at least twenty-five passengers, 700 barrels of apples and other assorted cargo. The first officer looked out at the lake and asked if it be prudent to wait and leave at daybreak. Captain Napier, confident in his ship and crew, with a tight schedule to keep, ordered the *Alpena* to cast off.

As the ship slowly made its way through the confines of the river, sailors on other ships looked on in surprise that a ship would leave the safety of the river at 9:00 in the evening, heading into open water in a fall storm. With snow blowing from the northwest, the seas pounded the starboard bow of the *Alpena* as it left the safety of the river.

For Chicago.

Goodrich Transportation Co.'s ELEGANT SIDEWHEEL PASSENGER STEAMERS ALPENA and MUSKEGON.

In connection with D. & M. R. R. will leave GRAND HAVEN daily, excepting Saturdays, at 8 p. m.
ARRIVE IN CHICAGO next morning in time to connect with all early outgoing trains.
RETURNING, every evening, excepting Sundays, at 7 p. m.
Fare, Grand Rapids to Chicago, berth included.

$3.45.

Round Trip Tickets, Good for the Season

$6.00.

TICKETS for sale at D., G. H. & M. R. R. office, Rathbun House block, by J. W. Drew, City Pass. Agent, and at D., G. H. & M. R. R. Depot, Grand Rapids, and also tickets for sale at all stations on the Grand Rapids & Indiana Railroad north of Grand Rapids.

Montgomery Crossman left his stateroom on the port side, protected from the wind and rain, and made his way to the main salon where many of the first class passengers had gathered. As he looked around, he saw several familiar Grand Haven residents. He waved to a table of eloquently dressed individuals seated in the center of the room. They were Mr. Benham, editor of the *Grand Haven Herald* and his wife. They had been joined by Mrs. Curtes, the wife of a prominent Grand Haven attorney.

A woman and two young girls sat at a port side table. The girls giggled and played. The woman wore a very attractive Native American shawl. Although he did not know her, he had seen her in Grand Haven. She and her daughters were on holiday and returning to their home in New Mexico.

Montgomery turned when he heard his name called. It was Heb Squires, an old friend from Grand Haven. The two discussed the weather. They also talked about their daughters, Monte was the father of a three year-old-girl and Heb was traveling to Chicago to join his wife and three young daughters.

The ship followed the course across the lake towards Chicago making fair time with the conditions of the sea and weather. The passengers in the main salon passed time talking. Most conversations revolved around the weather.

The ship made slow headway in the storm. Three hours into the voyage the ship began to roll as the wind and waves increased. Most passengers passing time in the salon retired to their staterooms preferring to ride out the storm in bed.

Captain Napier braced himself against the motions of the ship while Second Officer Alvin Patten stood at the wheel. Alvin rocked side to side as the *Alpena* rolled with the waves assaulting the ship on its starboard bow.

Five hours into the trip another ship was sighted off to port. Waves were running ten to fifteen-feet and the wind was gusting. Both ships were struggling in the seas.

On October 16 and 17 of 1880, the unusually severe winter storm swept down the length of Lake Michigan. The storm formed

An artists concept of the Alpena *tossed about on a stormy Lake Michigan.* From the collection of the Muskegon County Museum

in northern Minnesota and raced down across Wisconsin and the lake. Snow came down heavily and quickly, blown by extreme winds. Passenger and freight railroad trains in Wisconsin were trapped by snow drifts ten to fifteen-feet deep.

The storm was called the worst storm ever to hit southern Minnesota. Winds reaching speeds up to seventy-miles-per-hour raced down Lake Michigan unabated, pushing huge waves in their path. At all ports on Lake Michigan, signals were flown warning vessels to seek shelter and not to venture out on open water. Despite the warnings, several captains put their ships in harms way, many never to be heard from again.

The schooner *Granada* was blown ashore north of Muskegon. Five of the seven crew members were killed. Two ships, the *Ebenezer* and the *Contest*, were aground. The *Ebenezer* was listed as a total wreck. In all, eighty-six ships were reported missing, sunk, or ashore along the east and west coasts of Lake Michigan and in eastern Lake Superior during the weekend storm.

On Saturday a telegraph to Grand Haven from the Goodrich Transportation's Chicago office reported the *Alpena* was late in arriving. There was no alarm, the ship may have sought shelter in an uninhabited cove or bay and was not able to communicate its location. Captain Smallman of the *Alpena's* sister ship, *Muskegon*, of the

LOST ON THE LAKE.

The Steamer Alpena Supposed to be Wrecked on Lake Michigan.

Seventy Passengers and the Crew Still Unheard From.

A headline from the October 19, 1880 Daily Times, *Grand Rapids, Michigan.*

Goodrich Transportation Company, arrived at Grand Haven and talked about the terrible night his ship had endured. He reported seeing the *Alpena* about 1:00 a.m. At that time, the *Alpena* was on course for Chicago in rough weather.

The barge, *City of Grand Haven*, arrived at Milwaukee after battling the seas. Captain Boomsteter, master of the *City of Grand Haven*, reported he had seen the *Alpena* around 4:00 a.m. Saturday morning. At that time, the sidewheeler was about thirty-five miles into the lake. The seas were breaking heavily on the *Alpena* and the storm blew white with snow. Captain Boomsteter said the *Alpena* was on course, but due to the adverse conditions, she was making little or no headway.

TELEGRAPHIC NEWS.

For Additional Telegraphic Matter See Inside.

THE ALPENA.

Nothing Definite Yet Known as to Her Fate.

She Was Seen Saturday Morning Thirty Miles from Chicago.

She Has Not Been Seen at the Manitou Islands.

The Missing Vessel.

Sunday morning the *Alpena* still had not arrived. Worried families and friends of passengers and crew began to gather in Chicago and Grand Haven asking for news of the *Alpena*. Each employee arriving or leaving the Goodrich Transportation office were besieged by the families pleading for information of their loved ones.

Fifty miles south of Grand Haven is the Michigan port of South Haven. Late Monday debris of a ship began to float ashore south of the entrance to the Black River. Beachcombers reported finding barrels of apples and boxes of shoes on the beach. The surf was still high and breaking in the shoals, smashing the barrels and boxes on the rocks near shore.

A beachcomber found a shawl washed up on the shore. It was a colorful Native American design, like the one Mrs. Brady wore. Nearby her lifeless body, was found, bruised and bloodied from being beaten on the rocks by the huge storm generated surf.

TELEGRAPHIC NEWS.

WILD WAVES.

Portions of the Wrecked Alpena Coming Ashore at Holland City.

One Body Picked Up on the Beach Yesterday.

Seventeen Wrecks Between Muskegon and Ludington.

Five Vessels Ashore at South Manitou Harbor.

Other Marine Mishaps.

The Lost Alpena.

A headline from the October 20, 1880 Daily Times, *Grand Rapids, Michigan.*

A large piece of the ship's foredeck washed ashore near the Black River. Although, the wreckage could not be identified, most theorized it was from the long overdue *Alpena*.

More wreckage came ashore in the following hours, furniture some say they recognized from the *Alpena*, a skylight and sections of a cabin wall. Yet, nothing that could point directly to the *Alpena*, until circular pieces of wood painted with the letters "G", "O", "C" floated ashore. The round pieces of wood were a trademark of the Line, spelling Goodrich on the port and starboard wheelhouse cover. There was no longer any doubt, the debris washing ashore was from the *Alpena*.

The *Alpena* proved to be no match to the storm which lashed the midwest on October 15/16, 1880.

THE S. S. GEORGE M. COX IS ON THE ROCKS

George M. Cox, owner of the Pabst Brewing Company of Milwaukee, Wisconsin, was a vivacious man who enjoyed a challenge. He owned a very successful Milwaukee brewery, a shipyard in New Orleans and in 1932, his newest venture was a Great Lake passenger ship service, the Isle Royale Transit Company.

He had purchased two vessels for his company, the largest was the 310-foot *Isle Royale*, formerly named the *Manitou*. The *Isle Royale* was certified to carry 400 passengers on a route from Chicago up Lake Michigan, through the Soo Locks across Lake Superior to the ship's namesake, Isle Royale, a rocky island in western Lake Superior.

The ship was very elaborate. She had a thirty by eighty-foot dance floor, a large elegant lounge and a sports deck for the adventuresome passenger. The *Isle Royale* also

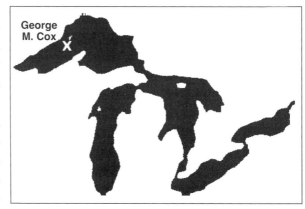

George M. Cox

The George M. Cox as she looked when she left Chicago on her first voyage. From the H. C. Inches collection, Port Huron Museum

provided first class entertainment with a complete orchestra and stage show.

The smaller of the two ships was the *George M. Cox*. At 307-feet the *Cox* was a thirty-year-old vessel initially launched as the *Puritan*. The *Cox* had been completely remodeled before she started service under the ownership of the Isle Royale Transit Company. Repainted a gleaming white, cabins upgraded and new staterooms added on her upper decks, the *Cox* was sure to become a Great Lakes' favorite.

In May of 1933, the ship would make its maiden voyage from Chicago to Port Arthur, Ontario. Aboard the *Cox* for her first trip was a small group of management personnel for the new transit company and friends of Mr. Cox. The trip would take them from Chicago to Houghton, Michigan in Michigan's Keweenaw Peninsula. There they would pick up passengers and continue on to Port Arthur, Ontario where 250 passengers waited. The return trip would travel to Chicago where the passengers would attend the Century of Progress Exposition.

Always the marketer, Mr. Cox took advantage of every opportunity to promote his latest venture. The ship was rechristened with many Chicago notables in attendance.

The Puritan *years before she was renamed the* George M. Cox. *From the collection of the Michigan Maritime Museum, South Haven, Michigan*

The *Cox* departed Chicago amid much fanfare, with flags waving and horns bellowing, the ship was escorted through the river to the open waters of Lake Michigan.

The select few onboard, only a small fraction of the capacity of the ship, were treated to the best of everything: fine dining, premier entertainment and elegant accommodations. The ship was certified to carry 400 passengers and a crew of 120, yet on this inaugural cruise the thirty-two guests were pampered by a crew of eighty-six. Their every desire was satisfied.

The *Cox* made a stop at Mackinac Island in Lake Huron. The ship was opened for anyone who wanted to see what it had to offer and the passengers were able to enjoy all that the island offered before they departed heading north in the St. Marys River towards the world famous Soo Locks. The Locks were, as they remain, an attraction tourists travel hours to see. The passengers waved and shouted greetings to the onlookers lining the sides of the concrete locks. The ship raised to the level of Lake Superior and steamed out of the lock into the Lake.

The next stop was Marquette, Michigan, some 115 miles east on the south shore of Lake Superior. Marquette was to be a stop on the regular schedule, so it was an opportunity for Mr. Cox to again show off his vessel to a public which might in the future use his services.

At Marquette the *Cox* was met with much excitement. Almost as soon as she was at dock, the gangways were opened to the curious and potential customers. In the time the ship remained in Marquette over 2000 people toured the *George M. Cox*. Leaving Marquette on Saturday morning, the ship set a course to Houghton, Michigan on the Keweenaw Peninsula.

On May 27, 1933 the *Cox* steamed up the Portage River into Portage Lake and docked at the Peninsula Wholesale Company dock. The ship was met with the same exuberance it had encountered at all other stops. The beautiful freshly painted white hull shined bright in the morning sun and attracted hundreds of residents from Houghton and her sister city of Hancock. They lined up for a chance to tour the ship. Dignitaries from both cities welcomed the ship and its passengers, knowing the passenger ship service was going to be an economic boom for the area.

George Cox stood proudly on the promenade deck welcoming and talking to the visitors.

He announced, "We are greatly pleased with the greeting given to us here in the Copper Country. I want people to know that our company is prepared to give its patrons the most attractive schedule of Great Lakes cruises that ever has been offered. Our boats are seaworthy, in first class condition and we have spared no effort to provide the last word in comfort, luxury, service and entertainment." Mr. Cox also eagerly pointed out that not only would the ship carry passengers but freight as well.

Captain Johnson, of Traverse City, ordered the *Cox* to cast off and set a course for Fort William, Ontario some sixty miles northwest. The ship cleared the Portage Lake ship canal, passing the upper entrance light. Captain Johnson ordered First Mate, Arthur Kronk, to follow a north by northwest course, the recommended chart course to Fort William from the ship canal.

Captain Johnson, tired from the day's festivities, retired to his cabin. The First Mate was experienced and was reminded to call the captain if anything unusual occurred.

About 5:00 p.m. the captain was called to the bridge, the ship was encountering fog. The seas were calm but the fog was thick, visibility was but a few feet at times.

Captain Johnson listened to the fog signal soundings of the Rock of Ages Reef lighthouse in the distance. The sailors on the bridge searched the dense fog looking for other ships or rocky islands which dotted the area.

Rock of Ages Reef, only fifty-feet by 210-feet, is located about two miles off the southwestern tip of Isle Royale. Prior to construction of the lighthouse, two ships ran aground on the rocky prominence. In 1877 the 205-foot sidewheeler, *Cumberland*, in foggy conditions ran hard aground on the island. Salvage was attempted, but the ship could not be moved. A severe summer storm washed the ship off the rocks and she quickly sank.

The Rock of Ages Lighthouse. U.S. Coast Guard

The *Chisholm* was the second ship to run onto the reef. In 1898 the *Chisholm*, a 256-foot wood steamer, battled an October Lake Superior storm when it was virtually picked up by huge seas and thrown on the reef. The crew was able to escape in the lifeboat, but the ship was relentlessly battered by the waves and ultimately destroyed.

In 1907 Congress allocated funds to build a lighthouse on the desolate reef. The area was well known for ferocious storms and wicked winds. The lighthouse would need to be structurally sound to withstand the forces nature would throw at it.

The finished lighthouse would stand 130-feet above the mean water level and cast a beam nineteen miles from its Second Order Fresnel lens. The station was to be manned by a four man crew who lived within the lighthouse tower.

THE S. S. GEORGE M. COX IS ON THE ROCKS

John Soldenski, Keeper of the Rock of Ages Lighthouse, finished his supper, kissed his wife and started up the stairs. It was time to relieve Second Assistant, Joe Marshall. Soldenski, at only thirty-eight years of age, could feel a stiffness in his knees. The years of walking up lighthouse stairs at this and past stations was wearing on his joints.

He was in his second season as Keeper at the Rock of Ages Reef lighthouse, the fifth keeper to hold the duty since its first Keeper was appointed in 1908.

John climbed the stairs up the six decks to the gallery deck where he found his Second Assistant. They discussed the conditions, foggy with calm seas and the assistant, anxious for dinner, began to descend the stairs which wound along the lighthouse interior wall.

Keeper Soldenski looked over the log, pulled his coat collar tight around his neck and opened the curved metal doors to the gallery which encircled the tower.

He listened to the blare of the steam fog whistle as he looked out over the railing. The fog was low, from the water's surface extending up about twenty-five to thirty-five-feet. From his perch on the gallery deck, he looked out above the fog into clear sky, but below the water and the reef were shrouded in a dense layer of white.

On the bridge of the *Cox*, Captain Johnson realized that the *Cox* was operating at a speed in excess of that he had ordered. In fact, the ship was traveling through the fog at seventeen knots, a speed which was unsafe for the conditions.

Keeper Soldenski looked out into the fog and saw something moving. Above the layer of fog he saw the spars of a ship and they were too close to the reef!

The Keeper raced to the stairs, screaming to those below, "A ship! A ship is too close to the reef! Sound the siren!" The Second Assistant ran down one deck from the mess deck to the fog signal plant, threw a couple shovels of coal in the boiler firebox, turned the valve to produce the high, constant, shrill of the warning siren and raced back up the stairs.

Captain Johnson, who had taken over the navigation responsibilities, heard the fog signal of the lighthouse change from intermittent to a constant sounding. He assumed the ship to be two miles or more beyond the Rock of Ages light and ordered the ship to the north to better judge the location of the light.

Keeper Soldenski, on the gallery deck, watched the ship already much too close to the reef suddenly change course taking it directly towards the reef.

Onboard the *Cox* about 6:00 p.m., the thirty-two passengers sat down to dinner in the main salon as the ship cut its way through the thick fog. The men in their suits and the women wearing long dresses sat while the uniformed staff served the first course of the meal. A piano played softly in the background.

The ship smoothly cut through the calm waters without any rolling or pitching. The pleasant dinner conversation stopped when the ship suddenly jolted and rose at the bow. Screams replaced the piano as the passengers and crew were thrown to the floor by the sudden stop of the ship and they rolled aft on the incline of the decks. A large dinner buffet slid across the floor, narrowly missing several diners, crashing into the cabin wall in a shower of glass.

After the initial loud crash of the hull striking the rock, the passengers heard several other loud metallic crashes. The tremendous force of the ship impacting the rock at the speed they were traveling drove the ships bow high on one of the rock outcroppings near the lighthouse. The steel hull was ripped open allowing cold Lake Superior water to flood in.

The jarring of the ship striking the reef, the sudden stop and the angle of the ship with the bow high jolted the boilers and engine from their mountings and sent them crashing into the stern.

The ship came to rest, bow high, on Rock of Ages Reef listing to port. The weight of water rushing in and of the machinery shoved aft forced the stern down. The ship lie on the rocks, bow to the sky and the stern submerged below the surface.

The Cox *grounded on Rock of Ages Reef, off Isle Royale. From the H. C. Inches collection, Port Huron Museum*

Beatrice Coate, a housekeeper aboard the ship, was thrown backward against a cabin bulkhead and collapsed to the deck with severe pain in her neck and back. She laid there until passengers came to assist her. They called for Adeline Kieling, the ship's nurse, but she was busy in the ship's galley treating a cook who was scalded when a kettle of hot grease flew off the stove in the collision. He had burns on his face, arms and hands.

A deckhand, below in the engine room, was thrown into the machinery. He was found with a cut hand, bleeding profusely and a broken leg. Another of the crew had deep lacerations to his head and other injuries.

"Man the boats!" cried Keeper Soldenski. "There's a ship on the rocks!" He and his crew quickly lowered the lighthouse's small boat and the powered tender.

Captain Johnson climbed hand over hand along the railing, up the steep incline of the *Cox's* deck to survey the damage to his ship. Fearing the ship would slip backward into the depths of Lake Superior, he ordered the lifeboats lowered.

Because of the severe list to port, the lifeboats on the starboard side could not be lowered. The starboard lifeboats had to be released from their davits and slid across the deck and lowered off the port side.

The passengers, calm after the initial shock of the impact, gathered to board the lifeboats. Some, who had been fortunate enough to have been assigned forward cabins took the opportunity to go to their cabins for coats and personal items. However, most of the passengers climbed into the lifeboats dressed in dinner attire and the crew in work clothes.

The lifeboats floated in the fog near the ship until everyone was safely off the *Cox*. The passengers, frightened and shivering with cold, looked into the white of the fog. They could hear voices in the distance from the men of the Rock of Ages Lighthouse. The passengers cheered as the Keeper's power tender broke out of the fog.

The lines were thrown and secured to the tender, slowly the slack was pulled out and the tender pulled a parade of lifeboats to

The starboard side of the Cox. *From the H. C. Inches collection, Port Huron Museum*

the lighthouse. After several trips, the 120 passengers and crew had reached the safety of the lighthouse by 7:30 p.m.

The wireless operator on the *Cox* had sent an S.O.S. immediately after the ship had struck the reef. The freighter *S. S. Tremaine*, just miles away received the signal and changed its course to lend assistance.

The *Tremaine* anchored off the shallows near the Rock of Ages Reef. The three most injured were motored to the *Tremaine* to be transported to Port Arthur, Ontario for medical treatment. The ship did not have room to take on all of the survivors, but Mr. Cox, Nurse Kieling and the most severely injured were taken aboard the freighter.

The rest of the 115 survivors remained at the lighthouse awaiting the arrival of the Coast Guard vessels which were underway. After the harrowing experience of the crash and evacuation of the ship, the survivors were now crammed onto the eight floors of the lighthouse. Unfortunately, they all could not fit in the lighthouse at the same time. The survivors needed to take

The Cox high aground. From the H. C. Inches collection, Port Huron Museum

turns in the warmth of the lighthouse and outside in the cool Lake Superior spring night. They were kept warm by consuming large amounts of the Keepers wife's coffee and maintained this exchange routine throughout the night until the next morning when the Coast Guard was able to take them off the reef and transport them to Washington Harbor, on Isle Royale.

In the days that followed, the *S. S. Cox* slipped off the rock, sank below the waves and settled on the bottom. An investigation was held at Houghton, Michigan to determine the cause of the collision.

Mr. Cox gave his account of the wreck. "The crash sent the prow high in the air and the ship settled at an angle of about forty-five degrees. The keel was above the surface and the stern settling. Everybody was knocked about."

Captain Johnson and two other sailors on the bridge testified that First Officer Kronk changed the course the captain had ordered, steering the *Cox* on a collision course with the shallow rocky outcroppings near the Rock of Ages Lighthouse.

Other accusations were made against the First Officer. It was said that while the ship was under his command, he operated at an unsafe speed for the foggy conditions. Another serious accusation leveled at Kronk was that he deserted the ship in a lifeboat shortly after it struck near the Rock of Ages Reef, not waiting for women and children to board the lifeboat. A charge he vehemently denied.

In the end the cause of the collision was attributed to error on the part of First Officer Arthur Kronk. The ship was deemed a total loss without any possibility of recovery. The *Cox* eventually slid below the surface and remains on the bottom. The *Cox* is now one of the Great Lakes most popular wreck dives.

THE BURNING OF THE G. P. GRIFFITH

The mid 1800s was a period of growth in the United States. The cities of the east coast were growing and the vast stretches of land to the west were prime to be inhabited by industrious people who would take on the task of wrestling it away from the wild. Their reward was the opportunity of a better life and some of the best farmland available.

The prospect of inexpensive land and freedoms unheard of in their homelands drew millions of immigrants from Europe and Scandinavian countries. The Irish came to America looking for hope after the Potato Famine and economic depression. The Germans immigrated in large numbers to escape oppression and seek the riches America had to offer. Immigrants from Sweden crossed the Atlantic with nightmares of working someone else's land and dreams of working on their own farm. Over 1.5 million people immigrated to the United States in the decades of the 1840 and 1850s.

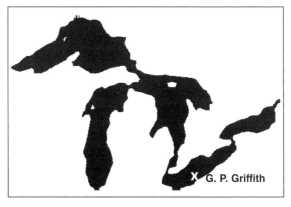

X G. P. Griffith

Historical Collections of the Great Lakes
Bowling Green State University

A drawing of the G. P. Griffith. From the Historical Collections of the Great Lakes Bowling Green State University

After a long and uncomfortable voyage across the Atlantic Ocean, the people landed, usually in New York City. In the strange land, the immigrants needed to find their way to the west, to the land being sold at next to nothing. From New York, the immigrants traveled on the Erie Canal or via railroad to Buffalo, New York, or other points on Lake Ontario or Lake Erie, to find passage west. Shipping lines were quick to see a very profitable opportunity. Passenger ships to carry the masses of immigrants on the lakes to such places like Chicago, Detroit, Cleveland and Toledo were put into service.

Among the ships involved in the lucrative immigrant trade was the 587-ton sidewheeler *G. P. Griffith*. The *Griffith* was built specifically to carry immigrants from eastern cities to ports on the western lakes. On the morning of June 16, 1850 in beautiful weather, over 300 passengers and crew departed Buffalo aboard the three-year-old *Griffith*, bound for Chicago and various ports in route. Onboard were a crew of twenty-five, 256 passengers in steerage and forty-five more affluent passengers in cabins. Most of those traveling in steerage were German, Irish, Scandinavian and a few English immigrants.

Captain C. C. Roby, Master and part owner of the *Griffith*, was joined on this trip by his mother, wife and young daughter. It was not common for his family to travel with him, but he knew the weather was going to be good and it would be an opportunity for him to spend some time with his family. His job took him away from them all too much.

The engine room was the domain of Chief Engineer, David Stebbins. Mr. Stebbins was not only Chief Engineer, but he also owned an interest in the ship. He was well aware of similar ships catching fire and burning to the waterline; so during construction of the *Griffith*, he incorporated measures to reduce the chance of fire. He insisted on water jackets and dead air space to dissipate the heat from the smoke stacks where they met the wood decks, a source of fire on previous ships. He also personally supervised the placement of cargo in the ships hold. Some ships became engulfed in flames because combustible cargo was stored too near the stacks and fireboxes.

The weather was calm and warm, and the spirits of the passengers were high. Many of the immigrants were eager to reunite with loved ones who had gone on before them. Most were leaving behind famine and oppression, seeking a new life in a new land. They dreamed of how they would transform the land in Michigan and Wisconsin, recently clear cut of the vast forests, or the prairies of Illinois and Ohio into their own homestead. Life was going to be grand. Their children would have opportunities not afforded them.

As night fell on June 17, 1850, the passengers and most of the crew bedded down for the night. Since the night was warm, many from steerage chose to sleep on the hurricane deck. Captain Roby and his family slept in his cabin as the First Mate, William Evens was on the bridge. Evens ordered Wheelsman Richard Mann to set a course for Cleveland running about two to three miles off shore.

About 3:00 in the morning the wheelsman noticed some sparks on the cabin roof near one of the smokestacks. He immediately notified Mr. Evens, who sent deckhands with buckets to extinguish the sparks. The crew always watched for errant sparks and quickly extinguished them before any damage was done.

Below in steerage, the sleeping immigrants were woken by the screams of a German man. "Feuer! Feuer!" He screamed as smoke began to fill the hold. Mothers and fathers woke sleeping children, grabbed their meager belongings and ran to escape. Panic soon spread through the hundreds in steerage, they began screaming and yelling in different languages, as they tried to escape up the narrow passageway to the open deck. Many families were separated. People fell and were trampled as the mass tried to leave the smoky confines.

First Mate Evens saw the sparks had not been extinguished, in fact they were now flames and were leaping from the cabin roof at midship. "To shore! Head for shore!" Evens screamed to Mann, who began porting the wheel. The telegraph called for all speed available. "We'll beach her," Evens told Mann, hoping they could travel the two to three miles quickly and allow the passengers an opportunity to escape the burning ship in shallow water.

The crew, armed with buckets and an abundant supply of water threw bucket after bucket on the flames but it was too little and too late.

Running at full speed towards shore, the flames were blown aft, igniting that part of the ship. Many of the passengers who were sleeping on the hurricane deck choked as smoke filled their lungs and ran from the flames until they had nowhere else to run. They jumped into Lake Erie in the black of night. Risking drowning but leaving a sure death by fire.

Captain Roby knew the lifeboats could not be lowered, they would capsize if lowered at the speed the ship was traveling and slowing or stopping was out of the question, it was imperative the ship make the beach to save the most lives.

Some passengers and crew caught near the flames were forced to jump over the rail. Those who could swim, swam clear of the ship, but found themselves too far from shore and eventually tired and drown. Passengers who could not swim away from the ship were sucked into the thirty one-foot diameter paddle wheels spinning at full speed. The paddles beat their bodies, killing them almost instantly. Some bloodied bodies were carried up on the paddles to the top of the arc only to be thrown ruthlessly back into the lake.

The *G. P. Griffith* was engulfed in flames from midship aft. Passengers on the bow screamed and prayed they would reach the safety of the beach where they could jump into the water and walk to shore, walk, because very few could swim.

Whole families huddled together, listening to the screams of passengers caught in their cabins as the fire reached them. A Swedish man ran towards the bow screaming in pain, his coat, hair and long beard in flames. He jumped over the rail and perished in the lake.

The night was filled with the cries of men, women and children, the screams of those whose clothes had ignited burning their bodies and the odor of burning wood and the stench of burnt flesh.

The ship, moving at full speed towards shore, suddenly stopped as it ground on the sandy bottom. Passengers and crew were thrown

An 1850 sketch of the passenger ship G. P. Griffith *burning on Lake Erie, 15 miles from Cleveland.* Great Lake Historical Society

to the deck by the sudden stop. They cheered and prayed aloud thanking God for delivering them to the beach.

When the ship was powering forward, the flames were swept astern. Now that the ship had stopped the wind coming onshore from the lake pushed the flames forward.

Frightened passengers, eager to get off the burning ship jumped off the ship in mass. Families hugged together and jumped, even Captain Roby threw his wife, daughter and mother into the safety of the water and jumped in after them.

In the dark, the panicked passengers had not noticed that the ship had not ground to a stop on the beach, rather it came to rest on a sand bar almost a half-of-a-mile from shore. They jumped into the lake expecting to walk to shore but found water eight to ten-feet deep.

Expecting to wade to shore they had not taken the precaution of throwing over items to float on. Without any form of flotation, the passengers had nothing to grab onto, nothing to float to shore on. The people made frantic movements to stay above the surface but quickly succumbed to the lake and drown an agonizing death. Some of those that could swim tried to save their loved ones but were grabbed by the drowning in a death grip and pulled under.

A custom of many of the immigrants was for the heads of the families to carry the families' life savings in a cloth around their waists. The gold, silver and other coinage, saved over the years to start a new life, quickly pulled the struggling men to the bottom.

Many women, fearful of thieves, had sewn coins into the hems of their garments and immediately sank under the excess weight. Clothing and heavy boots typically worn by the men filled with water, weighing them down. They fought to save themselves but soon joined their friends and loved ones at the bottom of Lake Erie.

The glow of the flames leaping from the *Griffith* lit the night sky. Residents in the area saw the orange glow and raced to the shore. They were met with horror. The bodies of passengers and crew illuminated by the burning ship could be seen floating on the surface and washed up on shore.

As day broke over the scene, the extent of the disaster could be fully realized. Bodies were everywhere, laying on the beach in a deadly repose and rising and falling on the gentle swells of the peaceful lake. Among them the lifeless bodies of the captain, his wife, daughter and mother. Clothing, steamer trunks, debris from the ship, personal belongings and papers were among the items that floated up on the beach while the remains of the *Griffith* lay smoldering offshore.

Entire families were pulled from the lake or washed up locked in an eternal embrace. Women clutching children to their breasts, infants with their faces frozen in terror and young men who just the day before dreamed of a better life for their families in the new world, were recovered from the lake.

Three hundred and twenty-six souls left Buffalo, New York, yet only forty lived through the night of flame and horror aboard the *G. P. Griffith* on the night of June 17, 1850. Two hundred and eighty six, mostly passengers nearing their dream of life in America, were drown or burned to death.

In 1850 the burning of the *Griffith* and the death of 286 of its passengers and crew, was the shipping disaster with the highest death toll on Lake Erie, to this day it still holds that dubious distinction.

THE DEMISE OF THE LITTLE
STEAMSHIP PILGRIM

The beginning of the 1907 season found Captain Cotton at the bridge of the steam passenger ship, *Pilgrim*. The vessel, 119-feet in length and 300-tons, was smaller than most passenger ships, but her size allowed her access to the smaller, shallow ports along Michigan's Lake Huron coast.

On April 29, 1907, the *Pilgrim* was downbound from Alpena calling at ports, delivering and taking on passengers and cargo. As she was nearing lower Lake Huron, she carried three passengers and a cargo which included shingles, barrel staves and barrels of apples, all bound for Port Huron. The crew, numbering twenty, consisted of the captain, mate, chief and second engineers, two firemen, a wheels-man, purser, steward, maid and ten deckhands.

The wind swept across Lake Huron, blowing cold that night. Remnants of winter's ice floated south as the *Pilgrim* left the

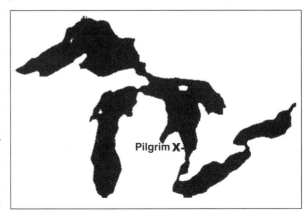

The Pilgrim was a favorite on the Lakes. From the H. C. Inches Collection of the Port Huron Museum

dock at Harbor Beach. The sky was ominously gray with a light rain falling, but twelve miles into the trip the sky opened and the rain became a cold downpour. The *Pilgrim* continued on its course.

About 10:30 p.m. while the *Pilgrim* was off Lexington, Chief Engineer "Win" Winterhalter found water accumulating in the bilge. "Win" took a quick look around the engine room and cargo hold, in the storm had a hatch cover or gangway opened, allowing rain in? He determined it wasn't from the storm.

Water in the bilge is common in a wood ship, but there was more than usual. He quickly notified Captain Cotton that the ship was taking on water and started the steam pumps. Winterhalter crawled in the dark, dank bilge looking for the source of the incoming water. Had an ice flow, abundant on the Lake this early in the spring, damaged the hull? Had the *Pilgrim* sprung a seam? Had a fitting come loose and begun to leak? A search of the ship to find the source of the leak turned up nothing.

The firemen, working in almost knee deep, cold spring Lake Huron water, were fearful the water would rise higher and put out the fire in the boiler's firebox. They called for Win to return. If the boiler fire was doused, the engine and the pumps would stop. Without steam, the vessel would be at the mercy of an angry lake.

The engineer shouted to the captain over the roar in the engine room, "The ship is filling and the pumps can't keep up with it!" Captain Cotton, realizing his ship was about to flounder, ordered the emergency steam whistle be blown to alert the Life Saving Service of their distress.

A surfman, patrolling the shore south of the Lakeview Life Saving station, had just turned the key in his patrol clock when he saw the lights of the *Pilgrim* and heard the distress whistle. Putting down the lantern and patrol clock, the surfman lit a Coston flare and frantically waved it to signal the lookout in the watch tower of a ship in need. Captain Plough, keeper of the station, was awakened and told an emergency whistle was heard. A ship was in distress.

Cold Lake Huron water continued to enter the ship. Captain Cotton, knowing his ship could not stay afloat much longer, ordered a course change. The wheelsman swung the wheel to starboard, turning the ship to the west, toward shore and toward shallow water.

The ship and passengers might fair better if they were in shallow water rather than in deep. Leaving a sinking ship in the yawl in rough seas mid-lake was always a dangerous endeavor. If the yawl should upset while being launched from a moving ship in rough seas or while it was being rowed to shore all aboard would surely perish in the cold lake.

If the *Pilgrim* could make it to the shallow water near the coast, lives could be saved, the cargo salvaged and the ship might be able to be repaired to sail again.

Winterhalter and the firemen, now working in near waist deep water, struggled to keep fire in the box for steam, steam for the pumps and steam to keep the engines turning and propelling the *Pilgrim* towards shore.

The men below knew if the ship were to go down, they probably would not be able to escape the engine room and get off the ship. Water would be pouring down in through all openings. The men would not be able to climb up the ladder from the engine room against the deluge pouring down. If the ship were to flounder, they would be carried to a cold violent death at the bottom of the lake.

Win and his men worked in freezing water, ironically, with beads of sweat rolling down their face. The firemen might have panicked and climbed to the main deck if it were not for Win encouraging them to stay and give it all they had.

Over the roar of the engine, the hissing of the escaping steam and the men yelling to one another, an unusual noise was heard. It started at the bow and moved aft. "We're breaking up!" screamed a young fireman. But a look of relief showed on their weary faces as they realized the noise they heard was the hull of the ship scraping the bottom as the *Pilgrim* reached the shallows.

The ship laid aground, bow towards shore. The waves from the east relentlessly assaulted the small vessel, forcing the ship to come abreast of the waves, lying bow to the north.

The ship was in the safety of shallow water, but now the waves crashed over the starboard side of the ship, rolling it violently. Water poured down into the engine room. Before Win left the engine room, water had risen to the level of the firebox extinguishing the fire.

The seas broke in the shoal water, crashing with a great roar upon the *Pilgrim*. The captain evaluated the situation with the First Mate. The ship's yawl was available, yet they knew it was not an option. The seas would throw the yawl into the rocks, casting all into the freezing lake. No one would be able to survive the pounding seas smashing their bodies into the rocks. Their only hope was to wait for the crew from the Lakeview Life Saving station to come to their aid. The surfboat was on the wagon and the team of horses was quickly hitched. Captain Plough and his crew raced from the lifesaving station along the shore road pulling the surfboat wagon and the beach rescue apparatus. They soon came upon the *Pilgrim*.

The Pilgrim *lies on the beach under the constant assault of the waves. From the H. C. Inches collection of the Port Huron Museum*

Captain Plough surveyed the situation. Should he use the breeches buoy to take the people off the *Pilgrim*? Shooting a line from shore to the vessel or can a surfboat rescue be made? The surf was breaking on the shore, but Captain Plough determined a surfboat rescue was the best option. The team pulled the wagon into the surf as far as the horses would go to float the boat off the wagon.

The surfmen in their white uniforms, dark oilcloth coats and cork jackets climbed into the surfboat and began pulling into the near shore breakers. Their rescue boat rode up the face of the waves, crashing through the white capped foam and coasting down the back side, only to plow into the next wave. The spray from the waves drenched the men with cold, lake water. Their hands froze to the oars. Icicles formed on their mustaches and noses. The thought of saving those on the *Pilgrim* never left their minds.

The *Pilgrim* had come close to shore and lay parallel to the beach. Waves continued to assault the length of the ship broadside. Anything loose on deck had long been washed away and the wood cabin work creaked with each wave's impact.

Captain Plough, standing at the stern of the surfboat holding the tiller with both arms, steered the surfboat into the lee of the ship. A surfman threw a heaving stick attached to a light line to the frightened deckhand awaiting their arrival. Blown back by the wind, the line was hauled in and thrown again. A deckhand, anxious to get off the ship, stretched to catch the line. Two other *Pilgrim* deckhands tied the heaving line to a heavy line. The heavy line was pulled over to the surfboat. First to be lowered to the surfboat were the three frightened passengers. They eagerly climbed down into the surfboat and several crewmen followed. The surfboat released the line and started towards shore with its cargo of cold, scared, but thankful people.

Captain Plough and his brawny men left their human cargo near shore to be retrieved by helpful onlookers and taken to the warmth of area homes. Without a thought of concern for themselves, the Life Savers jumped out of the boat to turn its bow to the lake to rescue more. That night the heroic men of the Lakeview Life Station made three trips back to the *Pilgrim*, rescuing all aboard.

Captain Cotton and "Win" Winterhalter, among the last to leave the ship, entertained the surfmen on the way in with their experiences of the night.

Throughout the day the *Pilgrim* lay in the shallows with the waves crashing down on her. The ship rolled violently port to starboard with the assault of the waves, grinding her hull on the rocky bottom. Captain Cotton said he hoped to have tugs pull his ship off the beach on the next day. But he feared an extended stay on the beach would cause more damage and possibly total destruction.

On the following day, the Thompson Brothers, owners of the *Pilgrim*, hired a local boat to take them to the wreck. They found the ship had sustained damage by the waves relentlessly beating her throughout the night. A large hole was broken in her starboard hull and the deck had a four inch tear about three-quarters of her length. The force of the waves had also shoved the cabin work several inches to port. The smokestack had been toppled and washed away. The rudder had been displaced and it looked as though her keel was broken.

The owners gave orders to remove the cargo and salvage anything of value. Salvagers were hired to strip the ship of her machinery for resale. The once proud *Pilgrim* was left grounded on the beach for nature to break her apart.

Word was sent to Harbor Beach to the friends and relatives of Engineer Winterhalter notifying them that he had escaped an angry Lake Huron. They responded with pleas for Win to retire, reminding him that this was his second wreck in just months. He had closed the previous season nearly losing his life on Lake Erie and this was a poor start to the 1907 season.

The nineteen-year-old steamer, *Pilgrim*, was always a welcome sight as it steamed into harbors along the lake where the larger ships no longer stopped. The small ship took on produce and goods from the small harbor towns and transported it, along with passengers, to the larger cities, a service which would be missed.

THE 1852 COLLISION OF THE ATLANTIC AND OGDENSBURGH

The early 1850s was a tragic time on Lake Erie. In 1851 the *Henry Clay* capsized killing an estimated twenty passengers and crew, while hundreds died in the 1850 burning of the *Griffith*. An estimated 250 more passengers and crew lost their lives in 1852 when the sidewheeler *Atlantic* and the propeller *Ogdensburgh* collided.

Excitement at the docks in Buffalo was contagious. Cabin passengers arrived from hotels and the railroad station in handsome carriages. The women, some carrying parasols, shielded themselves from the hot August sun. Their gentlemen, dressed in their finest, directed the porters who carried their steamer trunks to the gangway of the gleaming white, three-year-old steamship, *Atlantic*. Many of those boarding were returning from their honeymoon at Niagara Falls.

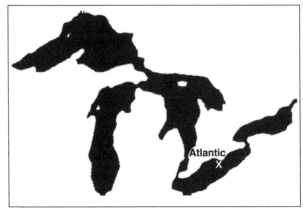

The steamer Atlantic. From the collection of the Port Dover Harbor Museum

Other passengers waiting to board the 265-foot-long ship were kept away while the affluent passengers boarded. Several hundred feet distant from the ship stood the immigrants, mostly from Norway and Ireland, en route for their new homes in Wisconsin and points west.

The immigrants stood in groups separated by nationality. The men discussed the torturous journey some endured, packed into the holds of ships as they crossed the Atlantic Ocean. A group of Irish men talked of the famine and pestilence which had ravaged their homeland. Some spoke of the hardships they suffered getting from New York and other Atlantic coast ports to Buffalo. Many others dreamed of the new life they would carve out for themselves in America. The women stared in jealous admiration at the fine clothing the wealthy cabin passenger women wore. The clothing would be discussed and dreamt about for many weeks.

Once the estimated 150 cabin passengers had boarded, the women supervised their domestic help in unpacking and arranging the cabins. The men found their way to the grand salon to have a drink and light up a cigar. Only then were the steerage passengers allowed to board. On the dock, the crewmen who had graciously assisted the cabin passengers for tips, now callously shouted orders to the 426 immigrants as they filed up the gangway. They reminded themselves they could endure the overcrowded and unsanitary conditions because it took them that much closer to their dream of freedom and prosperity. The *Atlantic* was carrying more passengers than she was certified for, but it was not uncommon for ships to do so. The ship owners put a lot of pressure on captains to maximize the profits on each trip.

The *Atlantic* built up steam and cleared the Port of Buffalo at approximately 5:30 p.m. on the afternoon of August 19, 1852. Captain Petty estimated they should arrive at Detroit around 10:00 the following morning. The orchestra entertained the cabin passengers in the main salon on the upper deck while steerage passengers walked the lower decks, listening to the methodic splash, splash, splash of the paddle wheels propelling the ship forward.

A 1852 steamer Atlantic *advertising poster. From the collection of the Port Dover Harbor Museum*

Among the passengers were Alfred and Ellen Birch, their daughter Phebe, Richard and Catharine Van Hovenbergh, Mrs. Birch's younger brother and sister. The party had left their homes in Albany and traveled by rail to Buffalo where they boarded the *Atlantic*. They had planned this summer trip for several months. They were impressed with the ship, especially their staterooms. Shortly after boarding, Phebe with her aunt and uncle, both close to her own age, was eager to explore the ship and pleaded with her father to go to the salon with them. "There is an orchestra!" she excitedly told them.

"Not until we review the safety instructions." Phebe's father said, as he turned over one of the footstools in their stateroom. "These stools are to be used in case of an emergency. There is a tin pan with trapped air in it to support a person in the water. It is the latest development in life preservers. So, if for some reason an emergency occurs, remember to use your stool."

The children, all in their teenage years, saw little importance in the knowledge, but the loss of the *Henry Clay*, which capsized on Lake Erie was weighing on Mr. Birch's mind. He had almost cancelled the trip, but his wife and the kids were looking forward to it and he didn't want to disappoint them.

Captain Petty set a course for the 257-foot *Atlantic*, which would take the ship on her regular route from Buffalo to Detroit along the north shore of Lake Erie. The captain then left the pilothouse to greet the affluent passengers aboard, leaving the ship in the charge of his first mate, Mr. Blogett.

The evening meal was served to the cabin passengers in the main salon. They reveled in the opulence of the salon. The gold leaf, accenting the carved woodwork, reflected the light from the oil lamps. The tables were richly set with fine china, complete with the ship's name and an etching of the ship at sea. After the meal the cabin passengers danced to the orchestra and strolled the decks enjoying the warm August night and the calm lake. As the evening wore on, many passengers retired to their cabins, exhausted from the excitement and festivities of the day.

Phebe and Catharine shared a berth and lay talking, too excited to sleep. The chatter and giggling was finally stopped by Mr. Birch and the teenage girls drifted off into slumber.

At midnight, James Carney, the second mate of the *Atlantic*, reported to the wheelhouse. He questioned the first mate about the weather, the sea conditions and the course they were following. The first mate then retired to his cabin.

Second mate, James Carney, peered out the wheelhouse window into the dark. The seas were calm and would pose no problem. There was a low layer of smoke along the surface, but it did not significantly reduce visibility.

About 2:00 a.m., Mr. Carney looked out of the wheelhouse and remarked to the wheelsman about sighting the Long Point light some two miles ahead. He continued to scan the horizon not seeing any other lights. About quarter after the hour of 3:00 Mr. Carney saw the lights of a ship about a mile distant.

First mate, Degrass McNell, was in the wheelhouse of the propeller steamer, *Ogdensburgh*. The *Ogdensburgh* had earlier departed Cleveland, Ohio bound for the Welland Canal at the east end of Lake Erie. First mate McNell saw the lights of a west bound ship. The ship was showing a red light aloft with two white lights below. Mr. NcNell estimated the ship to be about three miles off the *Ogdensburgh's* bow and thought they would pass about a half of a mile north of the other ship. No cause for concern. If anything, Mr. NcNell enjoyed seeing the other ship; it broke up the monotony of the night watch.

Absently staring out of the window at the red and white lights of the approaching steamer, Mr. McNell's eyes widened in disbelief, the ship had changed course, taking her across the *Ogdensburgh's* bow!

"Stop the engines." Mr. McNell shouted.

He watched the ship, becoming aware that a collision was very possible.

"Hard to starboard!" the first mate screamed to the wheelsman as he grasped the handle of the ships telegraph and rang the engine to reverse.

Mr. McNell instinctively reached to sound the ship's bell to alert the other ship of the *Ogdensburgh's* position but then remembered the bell was inoperable. He yelled… screamed out the window at the other ship trying to alert them of the impending peril.

Second mate, James Carney, aboard the *Atlantic*, maintaining their normal course across the lake ordered a slight correction to port. He could see a dim light of another ship. The ship was several miles distant, he determined, due to the fact that the light was so dim.

Suddenly, the bow of a ship appeared to the starboard of the *Atlantic*. There was nothing either ship could do, the *Ogdensburgh* crashed into the side of the *Atlantic*!

The two ships quickly separated since the *Ogdensburgh* had nearly stopped, but the *Atlantic* was running near full.

"Steer for shore!" the second mate screamed to the wheelsman, knowing they were four miles off. Mr. Carney then ran below to check the damage.

Running down below, Mr. Carney first ran to the steerage, which was forward and found it dry. The boiler room was next. There he found water gushing in from a rupture in the hull. The chief engineer was shouting instructions to the coal passers who were trying to stuff bedding and anything else into the gap to slow the incoming torrents of water. In the hold, Mr. Carney found the crew moving cargo to the port side of the ship, in an attempt to raise the gash in the starboard side above the waterline.

Due to the late hour, passengers and most of the crew were asleep. Some died in their berths as the *Ogdensburgh* smashed through their cabins. Many slept through the collision but were awakened by other passengers pounding on stateroom doors.

Mr. Kirby, a passenger from Detroit, was thrown out of his berth as a wall of his cabin collapsed on him. Pushing away boards and other debris which covered him, he stood up, bloodied, stunned and confused. Soon the reality of the situation struck him. He grabbed his cabin stool and hurried out the door. The ship was down at the bow, so he began to run aft towards the hurricane deck. Not seeing many others, he pounded on cabin doors in an effort to wake those still in slumber. Some passengers responded, but many did not.

The *Atlantic* had been dealt a fatal blow. The *Ogdensburgh* had smashed into the wooden hull of the *Atlantic* between the forward gangway and the wheelhouse, almost half way through her beam. The damage extended below the waterline.

An early illustration of the steamer Atlantic. *From the collection of the Port Dover Harbor Museum*

The collision had so damaged the ship that many stateroom doors were jammed shut. Jacob Nash, his wife and her friend were in a room with just such a problem. The wall of their cabin had been so distorted by the impact that their only door to freedom could not be opened. Mr. Nash quickly pulled the cabin stool to the door, broke out the glass light above the door and pulled himself through. His arms and legs were cut as he fell into the broken glass on the floor of the passageway. Jacob attempted to open the door, but it would not budge. He searched the nearby cabins for something to stand on, returning with a chair, he could hear the cries of the two women trapped in the cabin. He called to his wife to climb the stool and reach up, he was able to pull her through the light. Their friend sat on the berth, tears streaming down her cheeks, fully realizing her size would not allow her to escape the room through the light. Despite their efforts, and with help of others, the Nash's could not open the cabin door. Their friend perished that night, the cabin becoming her tomb.

The bow of the *Atlantic* sank low as water rushed into the ship. The steerage passengers, mostly immigrants, gathered there, screaming out of fear. Water rushed onto the forward deck as she made way towards shore. Many had jumped over the side in desperation, thinking the ship would sink quickly. Many others were washed off the deck as the bow sunk lower.

The cabin passengers on the aft hurricane deck were wrought in panic as well. Cries of anguish could be heard from those still trapped in the cabins. Someone screamed, "Fire!" sending the already terrified, screaming passengers scurrying about looking for safety. Some jumped into the lake even though the ship was still being propelled forward by the turning sidewheels.

Captain Petty and many of the crew had gathered at the hurricane deck, screaming orders at the terrified passengers. The captain began to lower one of the boats but in a panic allowed it to fall into the lake. The boat capsized and was rendered useless. The other two boats were lowered and crew quickly jumped in them. Horrified passengers watched as the crew rowed away from the stricken ship, their only hope for salvation disappearing into the night.

COLLISION BETWEEN THE STEAMER ATLANTIC AND PROPELLER OGDENSBURG ON LAKE ERIE, N.Y.

"Collision," from the front page of the Gleason's Magazine, *September 11, 1852. From the collection of the Port Dover Harbor Museum*

On the deck, the terrified passengers also watched the lights of the *Ogdensburgh* get smaller as the distance between the two ships grew. Men yelled until they could no longer make a sound, pleading for the crew and steamer to return and save them.

Mothers and fathers hugged their children. People alternately prayed and cried openly as the bow of the *Atlantic* slipped below the surface. The immigrants remaining on board were washed off the ship in mass, the lake becoming a sea of screaming heads bobbing on the surface. One by one the steerage passengers succumbed to the lake and the screams ceased.

The *Atlantic's* forward progress soon ceased as water reached the boiler room and doused the fires. The three year old ship sank, its last few moments on the surface filled with the sound of screaming passengers and the silence of the drown, floating on the surface.

Alfred Birch rolled out of his berth from the impact of the collision. He didn't know what had happened but he knew that a disaster was at hand. He woke his wife who almost immediately began to panic. They woke the children and with cabin stools Mr. Birch had found in other staterooms, walked the inclined deck up to the hurricane deck.

Alfred gave his family instruction, "Keep perfectly calm and hold onto the stool tightly. Trust in God to get us through this." He showed them how to hold the stool when in the water so as not to cause it to capsize.

"Stay apart from one another and remain tranquil in the water until a boat picks you up," he instructed.

Ellen Birch, the most terrified of the family, was the first to jump. Alfred wanted his wife in first to help the children when they reached the water. She fell through the air striking the water hard, yet she was able to hold onto the stool. She visibly calmed when she found the stool held her weight. Her brother, Richard, was next to jump followed by Catharine.

Catharine lost her stool upon impact with the water and started to panic. She reached out for her sister in the water, Catharine's panicked grasp ripping Mrs. Birch's hands from the stool. The two thrashed about in the water with of the rest of the party fearfully looking on.

Mr. Birch, witnessing the tragedy unfolding from the deck of the ship, jumped in to save his wife and sister-in-law. He hurriedly swam towards the two women hugging each other, their energy spent, slipping below the surface. They reached out to him as he approached, grasping him around the shoulders. He began to swim towards the floating stools, but the weight and thrashing of the frantic women was too much and all three of them sank below the surface locked in an eternal death grip while Phebe and Richard looked on in terror.

Onboard the *Ogdensburgh*, the crew ran throughout the ship to assess the damage.

Once it was established that the ship was taking on water but not in danger of immediately sinking the ship turned back towards the *Atlantic*. Ahead full was stuck on the telegraph as the *Ogdensburgh* steamed in a large circle to return to the sinking ship to render assistance.

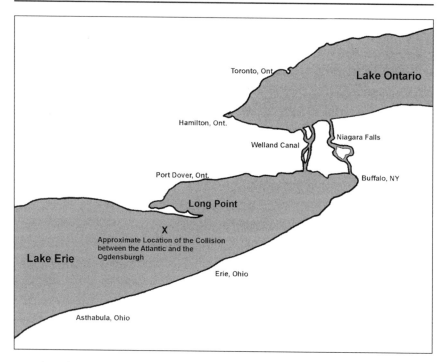

As the *Ogdensburgh* approached the *Atlantic* they found her bow submerged, with her stern remaining above the surface but sinking fast. There were no lights burning, no signals of distress, no emergency bells ringing. Only the sounds of screaming passengers on the decks and in the water filled the cool night air.

The *Ogdensburgh* slowly maneuvered next to the sinking *Atlantic*. Passengers jumped the distance to the relief ship. The *Ogdensburgh* lowered its boats to pick up those on the surface, still alive. Once all passengers were aboard, the ship backed away from the *Atlantic*. The *Ogdensburgh* made a circular passage about a mile distant from the *Atlantic*, her lifeboats in the center ignoring the dead and rendering assistance to those still moving.

The *Ogdensburgh* remained on the scene assisting the unfortunate souls of the *Atlantic*. They took about 200 victims off the ship and plucked another one hundred from almost certain death in the water. When the *Ogdensburgh* left the *Atlantic*, it was still afloat, its stern just above the surface. It continued to float until the next day when it was observed sinking by a schooner in the area. The ship took with it somewhere between 150 to 250 lives. The exact extent of the tragedy can not be determined, the passenger list went down with the ship and also an accurate count was probably not kept due to the ship being overbooked to maximize profits.

A maritime review was conducted and found that both ships were in error and shared the responsibility equally in the collision. The *Atlantic* had altered it course setting it on a collision course with the *Ogdensburgh*. The *Ogdensburgh*, despite the claims to the contrary, was found to be guilty of not displaying appropriate lighting, thus leading the mate on the *Atlantic* to believe the distance between the ships to be greater than it actually was.

The loss of the *Atlantic* affected many lives, those whose who died, those who mourned the dead and those who were permanently scarred by the tragedy they witnessed.

Phebe Birch and her Uncle Richard remained on Long Point for several days searching for the bodies of their loved ones who perished before their eyes.

THE PERE MARQUETTE NO. 18 IS SINKING

Chalmers Rosencrans stood at the bow of the car ferry, *Pere Marquette No. 18*, searching the wharf as the ship slowly entered the Ludington, Michigan harbor. He was looking for his wife and two-year-old son.

His job as the Assistant Engineer took him away from his family too often, but it was the nature of his vocation. They were only able to meet occasionally and for only brief times. The last time he saw his family was months earlier, but this layover would be special. They could spend a whole week together!

Chalmer's wife, Ethel, holding their baby, shook with excitement as her husband's ship steamed into port.

"Here comes Daddy's boat! Wave to Daddy!" she told the child.

It had been almost five months since they last saw one another, not

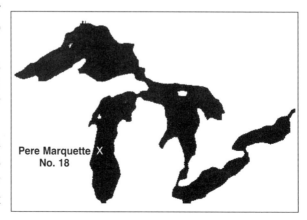

Pere Marquette
No. 18 X

The Pere Marquette Number 18. From the collection of the Michigan Maritime Museum, South Haven, Michigan

since early spring when he shipped out for the season. It was now the middle of September 1910.

She shielded her eyes against the sun, looking for Chalmers, wondering what he would think about the baby. Would he notice how he had grown, how much the boy had changed in the past months?

The home port for the *Pere Marquette No. 18* was Ludington, Michigan, but the ship had been chartered out of Chicago for the last two seasons. Since Chalmers was at sea so much, Ethel lived with her parents in Northport, some 120 miles to the north. She and the baby had taken the train down, arriving that day.

The couple had looked forward to this week. Chalmers had made plans on what they could do and Ethel was anxious to see the new merchandise at the shops. Muskegon was a thriving metropolis compared to Northport, she thought.

They dined out at a different restaurant each evening. Ethel shopped while Chalmers played with their son. They even had time to take in a motion picture. Ethel thought Chalmers would roll off his seat in laughter watching the Fatty Arbuckle and Harold Lloyd comedies.

The young family was so busy, the week practically flew by. All too quickly it was time for Chalmers to again leave on the *Pere Marquette No. 18* for a run across the lake to Milwaukee, Wisconsin.

As Chalmers prepared to board the big railroad car ferry, the husband and wife bid each other farewell under the cover of a porch at car ferry slip No. 1. Chalmers did not want to let go of his son or wife. He looked west, to the channel at the lake and knew it would be a rough trip. There was a stiff northwest wind building and the waves were crashing on the breakwater of the harbor. It was nothing worse than the ship had encountered before, but it makes for an uncomfortable trip down in the engine room.

The *Pere Marquette No. 18* was built to carry railroad cars across Lake Michigan on the Ludington to Milwaukee run. There the cars were coupled and their cargo distributed across the west. The ship, 338-feet in length, with a fifty-five-foot beam and capable of carrying 2,909 gross tons, was constructed with a steel hull so she could work year around, her steel hull capable of breaking winter ice.

The mate of the ship, Joe Brezinski, reported to the captain that twenty-nine cars, nine loaded with coal and the rest with general merchandise, had been loaded on the ship and were secured aboard. Supervising the loading of the cargo was one of his responsibilities. The sinking of the *Marquette & Bessemer No. 2* in Lake Erie the previous December was always on his mind. It was a common belief that the car ferry had capsized and sunk because of improper loading of the railway cars she carried.

Captain Peter Kilty, a well respected navigator on the lakes, was the skipper of the *Pere Marquette No. 18*. The ship had been launched in 1902 at Cleveland, Ohio, designed and built for the Pere Marquette Railway. She was the largest and best of the six ferries the company operated on the lakes.

Number 18, as she was often called, cleared the car ferry slip a few minutes before midnight and headed west out past the

The Pere Marquette *ferries loaded their cargo of railroad cars from the stern as can be seen in this photograph of the* Pere Marquette No. 19. *These ships carried the cars on four tracks across the ship. From the collection of the Muskegon County Museum*

breakwater. The captain blew a salute to the keepers at the Ludington North Pierhead lighthouse as the ship steamed west out into Lake Michigan.

This was her first trip across the lake with a load of rail cars in almost two seasons. The *Pere Marquette No. 18* had been chartered by the Chicago Navigation Company for 1909 and most of the 1910 season as an excursion steamer taking passengers out on lower Lake Michigan.

The ship had been retrofitted for the excursion market. Her rail deck was covered with wood planks and even slot

On the bridge of the Pere Marquette No. 18 *in 1910. (left to right) Wheelsman Simon Burke, Mate Walter Brown, Captain Peter Kilty and Mate Joseph Brezinski.* From the collection of the Michigan Maritime Museum, South Haven, Michigan

machines were placed on board.

Since she was changing operations back to transporting rail cars, the ship was docked in Ludington for a week for an extensive government inspection of her hull and machinery and refurbishing such as the removal of the planking and installation of new carpeting. The refitting wasn't completed at the time of sailing, so several of the workmen sailed with the ship to finish their work at sea.

On board were fifty-two crew, including the tradesmen and ten passengers. Due to the hour the ship departed many passengers retired to their cabins, but some sat and socialized in the main salon. However, the rolling and pitching of the ship soon sent all passengers to their cabins.

Captain Kilty set a course for Milwaukee, Wisconsin, located about ninety-five miles southwest of Ludington across Lake Michigan. The ship powered into the teeth of the wind, crashing into the waves, spray washing the forward deck.

About 4:00 a.m., First Mate, Joe Brezinski, told deckhand Herman Memrow, to follow him. They went below to the aft compartment to investigate a report of water coming in. They were amazed to find the aft compartment almost completely full of water. They wanted to check the deadlites to make sure they were closed but could not due to the water.

"Start the pumps!" the Mate screamed to Chief Engineer Leedham. Then turned to Memrow, "Go tell the captain what we found."

He hurried to the captain's cabin with the report from Mr. Brezinski. The captain responded to the urgent pounding. The young man told Captain Kilty that the ship was taking on water aft.

"What about the pumps?" the captain questioned.

The deckhand replied, "Mr. Brezinski started 'em!"

Running to the wheelhouse, the captain could feel the ship was low aft. A captain knows his ship.

"I've got a course change!" he shouted to wheelsman, Simon Burke. "Come about due west to Sheboygan."

With confidence in the seaworthiness of his ship, the captain knew they would make Sheboygan, Wisconsin, even with water in her aft compartment. She could probably make Milwaukee, but he preferred to err on the side of safety.

"Sczepanek!" the captain yelled to Steven Sczepanek, the ship's purser and wireless operator. "Send a message that we are taking on water and heading for Sheboygan. Request that *17* come to assist us." *Pere Marquette No. 17* was a sister ship to *18*. She could take *No. 18* in tow and assist her to Sheboygan.

Sczepanek tapped out the message which was picked up along both shores of the lake and by other ships so equipped. The initial message was sent, then nothing more as the captain and crew were busy assessing the conditions. Those who received the first message spent many anxious minutes before they again heard from the *18*.

Word of the *18* spread around Ludington quickly. At the homes of the men on board, tears and fear for their lives were abundant. On the waterfront, theories about what could have happened were plentiful.

"It must of lost a plate from 'er bottom," a well weathered sailor volunteered.

"Naw," butted in one of his drinking buddies, "I bet them cars busted the chains causing a bad list. She'll probably capsize. Them cars probably rolled all over the ship with the lake as rough as it is tonight."

"Maybe she wasn't loaded evenly. Ya know, too heavy on one side," someone interjected. But the thought was quickly discarded; they knew Joe Brezinski loaded the *18*, and if Joe did it, it was done right.

Out on the lake the big ship lumbered in the seas with its heavy load of twenty-nine railroad cars and the added weight of the water she had taken onboard. The stern gradually settled deeper.

After consulting with Mr. Brezinski and finding that the pumps were not keeping up with the torrents of water coming in, Captain Kilty realized that drastic measures needed to be taken. He told Mr. Brezinski to lighten the ship.

The first mate gathered most of the crew and several of the passengers as well, at the aft rail deck. He told them that they were going to roll the rail cars off the stern of the ship. By lightening the load, the stern would raise, hopefully enough to bring the cause of the incoming water above the surface and slow the ship's settling.

The crew, under the supervision of Mr. Brezinski, set to scuttle some of the cars. Loading a car ferry at a slip is a cautious and time consuming ordeal, but having to quickly push them overboard without the aid of a steam engine, on the rolling deck of a ship in the dark, was going to be a very precarious endeavor.

The cars filled the four rails across the ship. Chains securing the first car were released. As the *Pere Marquette* climbed a wave and her bow rose and the stern fell, the car was pushed by the men. With Herculean effort, the car slowly began to roll. The men cheered as the rear trucks of the car rolled off the stern of the ship. But, instead of dropping into the lake, the car came to a stop, its forward trucks still on the rail and its undercarriage resting on the deck.

Mr. Brezinski screamed over the wind to get the jacks. The crew set the pry bars, jacks and blocks to leverage the car off the ship. With men grasping the long steel shafts of the jacks and others pushing, the heavy rail car slowly fell off the end of the ship.

The crew ran toward the next car forward but were called back by Mr. Brezinski. "This one!" he shouted as he pointed to the last car on the portside. He knew the cars needed to be removed alternately from both sides or the ship would become unstable and could easily capsize.

Two Detroit men onboard the *Pere Marquette No. 18*, Thomas Kelley and his brother, came out of hiding when they heard all the commotion. They had stowed away on the big ship to get a free ride to Milwaukee.

"Come on!" yelled the first mate, waving them over to help. His concern was not with a couple of stowaways. It was with saving the ship and he could use all of the help they could get.

Below in the engine room, Chief Leedham and his assistant Chalmers Rosencrans, supervised the oilers and the army of coal passers frantically shoveling tons of coal into the firebox to provide the steam to keep the ship heading to Sheboygan and to keep the steam pumps working. The men worked in only their pants and undershirts; the heat in the boiler rooms was tremendous.

William Brown, the ship's second Mate, took a few men forward. He told them that Sczepanek, the ship's wireless operator, had tapped a message of their dilemma to *Number 17* and she was steaming towards them. They had to ready a hawser and a boat to take the line to *17*. The men dragged the heavy hawser along the deck preparing it to be played out when the line was taken to the tow vessel.

Sczepanek, remained at his wireless post and continually sent out a "C Q D" signal during the hours that the ship was settling. "C Q D" was the emergency code used prior to "S O S."

He also stayed in contact with the *Pere Marquette No. 17* relaying to them their position and updating them on the situation.

In Ludington the wireless operators of all ships monitored the transmissions of the sinking ship and relayed the information to the loved ones around town. Tears, panic and fear were the order of the day for those who had loved ones aboard the *Pere Marquette No. 18*.

Sitting in his cabin, unable to sleep due to the rolling and pitching of the ship, passenger Seymour Cochrane, sat reading when he heard a cabin boy in the passageway.

"Everybody get up!" he shouted as he pounded on cabin doors. "The ship is sinking!"

At the stern, work continued on lightening the ship. The cars were unchained and pushed, each one became hung up on its undercarriage. The men employed the jacks and succeeded, with much effort, in sending the railroad cars to the bottom. The mate and his men kept at their assignment until thirteen of the twenty-nine cars had been pushed off the *Pere Marquette No. 18*. Cars fourteen and fifteen dangled stubbornly off the stern of the ship. The crew not able to shove them off despite all of their efforts.

The stern of the ship had come up! The hours of hard work had paid off. The crew celebrated! There was even a smile on the face of the normally stern Mr. Brezinski as he reported the good news to Captain Kilty.

The crew rejoicing in the good fortune of their labors, went to the galley and consumed slabs of beefsteak between slices of bread and warmed themselves with the cook's hot coffee.

Unfortunately, the lightening of the vessel was only a temporary solution. The cause for joy was short lived as the *Pere Marquette No. 18* began to once again settle at the stern. Lake Michigan was still pouring into the ship.

"Where's *17?*" the captain called to Sczepanek. "She's steaming full towards us, captain. Just a few miles away. We should see her lights soon," he replied.

Captain Kilty privately prayed that the ship would make it to shoal water to save all those aboard, the cargo and his beloved ship.

Number 18 was now very low in the water at the stern and was making little headway towards the shallows of the Wisconsin coast. The crew was ordered to prepare the lifeboats and passed out life preservers to the passengers.

Patiently, members of the crew explained to the passengers what to do when they got in the water and what to expect if the ship sinks. "Get as far away from the ship as you can. When she goes down, she can suck you down with her." explained Mike Haythaler, who wished he was back on the family farm in Forestville, Michigan. He swore to himself that he was done sailing and was going home to work the land.

"Captain!" Roy Beckford, a porter on the *18* called as he thrust a life preserver towards the skipper.

"No! Give it to Burke," Captain Kilty yelled, pointing to the wheelsman struggling to hold the wheel.

Seymour Cochrane ran from the wireless room, where he had been assisting Sczepanek, towards the life boats. He saw Mrs. Marion Turner, the ship's cabinmaid, standing fully dressed as if she were preparing to go on a stroll in town. He shouted to her to follow him. She only stood there in a stately repose and said, "I don't mind it so much, but I can't stop thinking of mother." Seeing that she was not in a mind to run to the lifeboats, Seymour left her there. That was the last Seymour saw of Mrs. Turner.

At 7:35 a.m., just as the sun began to rise, the *Pere Marquette No. 18* began to rise at the bow as her stern slipped below the surface. The ship's buoyancy was no longer able to support the large vessel.

THE PERE MARQUETTE NUMBER 18 IS SINKING

Sinking Pere Marquette Carferry 18, Sept. 9, 1910,
Carferry 17 to the Rescue.

COPYRIGHTED 1910, BY F. W. ANDREWS & CO.

A popular postcard of the era showing the Pere Marquette No. 18 *sinking and many people in the water as the* No. 17 *steams to her rescue. From the collection of T. J. Gaffney*

On the *18* everyone knew that this was it, the great ship was going down. The boats were quickly lowered as the *Pere Marquette No. 17* steamed into view.

As the eighty men on the *Pere Marquette No. 17* looked on, the huge black bow of the *No. 18* rose high in the sky and then slipped stern first below the waves. They watched speechless and petrified as the horrible scene unfolded before them.

As she sunk, an terrible explosion filled the dawn air. "Her boilers blew," remarked the mate on *17* as they watched debris and bodies blown skyward.

Captain Kilty and wireless operator, Steven Sczepanek, remained at their posts until the concussion of the explosion blew their bodies airborne, landing in the rough sea. Captain Kilty's body was later recovered, severely cut and badly broken.

First and second mates, Joe Brezinski and William Brown, were killed as the ship turned skyward and the remaining railway cars broke their shackles and rolled and tumbled out of control on the sinking ship.

Below decks, the end came so fast that the men did not have time to escape. The engine room, boiler room and firebox became the tomb for Chief Engineer Leedham, second assistant engineer, Paul Renner, many firemen, oilers, coal passers. It also became the tomb of Chalmers Rosencrans, husband and father of a two year old son.

Roy Beckford was standing on the deck, tightening his life preserver as he felt the ship rising at the bow. Knowing the ship was heading for the bottom, Roy climbed the rail and jumped as far away from the ship as he could. He hit the water about the time the *Pere Marquette No. 18* exploded, sending men and parts of the ship in all directions. Trying to increase the distance between himself and the ship, Roy swam as fast as he could. He knew the sinking ship would create a whirlpool which would pull anything nearby down to the bottom with her.

Despite the urgency of his actions, Beckford was sucked below the surface by the sinking of the vessel. Timbers and other debris, including bodies of his crewmates, caught in the swirling vortex smashed into Roy, as he struggled against the force pulling him downward. The cork life preserver and Roy's strength enabled him to pull away. Roy broke the surface and inhaled frantically. Fortunately, he saw a lifeboat nearby and swam furiously for it.

The angry lake threw the remains of the ship around like they were toothpicks. Some of the lifeboats, loaded with human cargo, were struck by the heavy timbers of the ship and stove in and overturned or sank. The frightened passengers were thrown into the lake, many people who thought they were safe in a lifeboat were drown.

The boats from *No. 17* were lowered and hurriedly rowed towards the screams in the water. They dodged the debris thrown about by the waves and plucked survivors from the lake. One of *17's* lifeboats was crushed by a timber, casting the two life savers into the lake to perish in the turmoil.

Survivors were taken to the *Pere Marquette No. 17* where they were wrapped in blankets and warmed with restoratives. The dead were stowed away to be taken ashore to the morgue. The ship circled the last location of the *Pere Marquette No. 18* until they believed there were no more survivors and departed the area for Ludington.

Ethel Rosencrans sat on the bench at the Ludington railway station awaiting the train which would take her and her son back to Northport. She watched the boy peeping and giggling at a man across the way who was making funny faces at him.

She smiled slightly as she remembered the fun she and Chalmers had during the past week and how amazed Chalmers was at how much his son had grown. She was shaken back to reality when a man from the Pere Marquette railway office approached and asked, "Are you the wife of Chalmers Rosencrans, the assistant engineer on the *Pere Marquette No. 18?*"

THE MUSKEGON IS ON THE WALL

66The *Holland* is missing!" a man yelled as he ran into a waterfront tavern in Muskegon, Michigan.

The steamship, *Holland*, had departed Milwaukee on June 27, 1919 and had not arrived in Muskegon on the next day as scheduled. There was a heavy gale blowing and the worst was feared.

Relatives of the 125 passengers on board anxiously awaited word of their loved ones. They crowded the Crosby Transportation Company's offices on both sides of the lake for news. But, through the day and into the night, nothing was heard. Harbors and ports all along the southern Lake Michigan coast were contacted, the ship had not been seen.

Coast Guard stations in Wisconsin and Michigan were called out to search the waters of lower Lake Michigan for the ship or for a debris field, indicating the ship had come

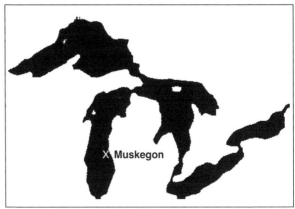

X Muskegon

171

The steamer Muskegon. From the collection of the Milwaukee Public Library

to a tragic end. All other ships on lower Lake Michigan were told to keep watch as well.

The *Holland* was built for the Goodrich Transit Company and launched in 1881 under the name *City of Milwaukee*. In 1906, when she was owned by the Graham & Morton Transportation Company, the vessel was given the name, "*Holland*." The missing ship was now owned by the Crosby Transportation Company.

The *Holland*, a sidewheeler with both port and starboard wheels, had a reputation on the lakes of being a troubled ship. In 1885, the four-year-old ship threw a cylinder rod which destroyed her engine. More recently, she was often delayed while operating on the Muskegon to Milwaukee run because of problems with the wheels and engines. The *Holland* was also easily blown off course in periods of high wind, an undersized rudder often the blame.

The Crosby Company officials were discussing hiring airplanes to search for the missing vessel, a search method not yet commonplace, when the fears of the relatives of those onboard the *Holland* were quelled. A wireless message came from Racine, Wisconsin that the ship had been found. A tug from the Great Lakes Navel Station, in Chicago had taken her in tow. The ship, its passengers and crew were all safe.

Once safely in port the story of the *Holland* was revealed. Shortly after leaving Milwaukee, one of the ships paddle wheels was damaged, which in turn damaged the engine, rendering the *Holland* helpless. The old ship, with no means of propulsion, drifted about the lake and with no wireless aboard, she could not reach anyone for assistance.

A freighter found the drifting ship off Racine, but while attempting to take her in tow, the freighter rammed the *Holland*, causing structural damage to her wooden upper works. The freighter backed off when a tug happened upon them thinking the tug was better equipped and had more experience in towing a vessel in distress. Unfortunately, while taking the tow line from the *Holland* in the rough seas, the tug also rammed the stricken ship further causing damage to her wooden superstructure.

The ship as she first appeared under the name City of Milwaukee.
From the collection of the Milwaukee Public Library

After all were safe, the Crosby officials sent the ship to drydock. After an inspection, she was found to be of sturdy construction and still seaworthy, even though the *Holland* was almost forty years old. With such a good report, the company authorized spending a considerable sum of money to refit the vessel. She received repairs to the damage caused by the rescue attempts and other necessary repairs. The old ship also received much needed new engines and wheels.

In an effort to free the old ship of her reputation as a "troubled ship," Crosby Transportation officials decided to rename the *Holland*. When she was put back into service the following August, her new name was the *"Muskegon"*.

On the afternoon of October 27, 1919, Mrs. Caroline Turck was excited but apprehensive as she stood at the Milwaukee waterfront. She was waiting to board the sidewheeler *Muskegon* for a trip across the lake, her first boat ride.

After boarding, a deckhand carried Mrs. Turck's cases to her stateroom on the lower deck. The accommodations were somewhat cramped, she thought, but adequate. After all, it was just going to be an overnight trip across the lake to Muskegon.

When the ship was first built and named *City of Milwaukee*, she was considered one of the finest passenger ships on Lake Michigan. She was also one of the fastest of the day, setting records for the Milwaukee to Grand Haven run.

With time to explore before it sailed, Mrs. Turck found the ship to be well kept and clean despite being thirty-eight years old. The ship's fresh paint and other improvements were noticed from the recent overhaul.

Mrs. Turck found the dinner, prior to departure delicious and the dining hall exquisite. The tables were set with linen, fine china, crystal and silver. Waiters and waitresses catered to the passengers' every whim.

Mrs. Turck shared the table with four other passengers. To her left, was an elderly woman, Mrs. Johnston. Mrs. Johnston proudly

The ship as the Holland. *Note the additional staterooms on her upper deck. The upper structure is not seen in the photograph of the* City of Milwaukee *and were removed before she was renamed* Muskegon. *From the collection of the Milwaukee Public Library*

announced that her son, Grant, was the Chief Engineer on the ship. She said she didn't want to be on the trip, but her son insisted she accompany him on his ship and stay with him at his home in Muskegon.

Also at the table was Mr. George Watson. Mr. Watson worked for the Anderson Sales Company, which sold milking machines throughout Wisconsin and Michigan. He said he was going to Michigan on a sales trip.

Blanche Cornell, a young girl barely in her teens, Mrs. Turck guessed, was also seated at the same dining table. She was a brave young lady traveling alone, returning home to Grand Rapids from visiting relatives in Wisconsin.

Mrs. Florence Rathbone completed the diners. Mrs. Rathbone, a widow from Milwaukee, talked with Blanche about Grand Rapids for she used to live there and was on her way there to visit friends.

At the next table were three women, the oldest Mrs. Turck had recognized from Milwaukee. It was Mrs. Frieda Beerman. She was in the company of her sister, Delia Beauleau and their cousin, Sina Samson. The two tables shared their excitement of the evening ahead and the pending cruise across the lake.

After dinner, Mr. Watson excused himself to the main salon for a cigar and Mrs. Johnston retired to her stateroom. Miss Cornell skipped off to explore the ship while Mrs. Turck joined Mrs. Beerman and her party to walk the deck in the cool autumn air.

The ladies watched cargo being carried into the ship and passengers boarding. They waved to some people on the wharf, but soon a cool breeze sent the ladies to their staterooms. They would go to sleep knowing that when they awoke, they would be in Muskegon.

Captain Miller, Master of the *Muskegon* for almost twenty years, was in the pilot house as the ship prepared for departure. The Mate, Albert Hoffman, reported all were aboard and the ship was ready to depart.

Captain Miller, always a cautious man, checked the barometer, its reading indicated fair sailing. Earlier the captain had checked the newspaper for the government weather report, as was his custom. It indicated moderate winds and a look around the harbor didn't show any storm flags raised. Fair weather was predicted by all indicators, so the Skipper gave the orders to depart.

Lines were cast off and pulled aboard by the deckhands, struggling with the weight of the wet manila rope. The *Muskegon's* steam whistle blew as she left the Milwaukee River and entered Lake Michigan just before 9:00 p.m. on the evening of October 27, 1919. The evening was cool and a light wind was blowing, a typical autumn evening.

Two sailors from the Goodrich Lines steamer, *Arizona*, were onboard the *Muskegon*. Their ship was in drydock for repairs, so they caught a ride on the steamer to Muskegon, where they both lived.

Shortly after leaving Milwaukee, the men had a feeling something was wrong. Harry Robinson, Chief Engineer on the *Arizona* and Clyde Boyle, his assistant, both felt as though something was not right.

"Clyde, I just don't like the looks of things. Let's take a look around the ship." Harry said to his assistant.

The two men left their cabin on the hurricane deck and walked the upper deck. "The ship was making all kinds of noises–creaking and cracking sounds," Harry later said. It so concerned them that they went below and stuck their heads in the crank room to seek the cause of the noises. Not finding anything to substantiate their fears, they returned to their cabin and retired for the night.

The beginning of the trip across Lake Michigan was uneventful. About an hour out, the captain checked the barometer. It read 29.3, an hour later it read 29.4.

"It sure is calm, Skipper," the wheelsman said to the captain.

"It's almost like a mirror," the Master replied, looking out over the unusual calmness of the lake. Another check of the barometer showed a drop to 29.3. By 1:00 a.m. it read 29.2. The dropping barometer reading indicated a storm, but the lake was calm... an eerie calm.

Without warning, a terrific gale roared down the lake from the northwest. The calm sea was whipped into heaving waves crashing onto the ship. The winds blew so hard it almost pushed the big ship off course. With the weather taking a turn for the worse, Captain Miller remained in the wheelhouse. He had a reputation of not trusting his ship to anyone when there was trouble at hand.

"Get McCue!" the captain yelled. He wanted his best wheelsman on the bridge in conditions like this. Ted McCue was an experienced and able seaman and Captain Miller could rely on him in an emergency.

The ship was buffeted by the northwesterly gale as she battled her way east on the lake. The wind whipped the sea into mountainous proportions which pounded on the ship.

Captain Miller stood in the wheelhouse, bracing himself against the pitching and rolling of the big ship in the storm tossed lake.

"We are going to have a bad gale, Ted," the Skipper said as Ted McCue entered the pilot house.

"It certainly is getting rough, captain. We could turn back to Milwaukee," McCue suggested.

The ship's master studied the wind and watched the waves breaking on the ship and washing the length of the deck. The old ship was holding her own, he thought.

"Running with the waves and wind is our only choice," Captain Miller reasoned. "We would flounder for sure if we tried to come about in these seas," the captain yelled over the storm.

The wind had veered from nor'west to nor'-nor'west, the captain observed.

"Test the rudder," Captain Miller told his wheelsman. Ted struggled to turn the wheel to port. The big ship slowly began to come about to port, despite the conditions.

"She's responding sir, but I think the wind is increasing," Ted said.

"In my thirty-five years of sailing I've never encountered such a sea," Captain Miller said to his trusted wheelsman.

The two men continued on, only speaking when necessary. Both thinking of the conditions, concern for the ship, the safety of the passengers and crew and of their loved ones on shore.

"We're about an hour out from Muskegon," the captain said to McCue.

"What do you think of running along the east shore to the city of Holland, then scooting farther inland back to Muskegon by bucking the waves?" the captain asked.

"I don't know, she' running a true course, despite the wind and waves, sir. And the rudder is doin' good," Ted responded, referring to the extension which was installed on the rudder during the ship's stay in drydock.

He searched the horizon for the familiar red light of the Muskegon pierhead light.

"There it is!" The captain exclaimed, as he spotted the light through the rain and spray. McCue was quietly thankful; his arms and shoulders ached from battling the wheel and he secretly worried about the old ship's seaworthiness.

"Only another thirty minutes," Captain Miller shouted to the wheelsman, yelling over the howling wind.

The waves tossed the ship around like a cork. Captain Miller gave the order to have the oil tanks on the port and starboard bow opened. Spreading oil on rough seas was a common practice of the

Light House and Pier.

The Muskegon south pier, in clear weather. Author's collection

A present day aerial view of Lake Michigan, the Muskegon Channel and Muskegon Lake in the background. The north and south piers can be seen jutting out into Lake Michigan. A breakwater was later built to calm the waters at the entrance. From the collection of the Muskegon County Museum

time. The oil coated the surface of the lake and tended to calm the sea near the vessel.

This time the oil had no effect on the waves, they continued to break over the bow of the ship.

Captain Miller yelled into the telephone for Chief Engineer Johnston to give full speed ahead and to be ready for the order to full astern. With the wind and waves beating across the ship's quarter, the speed was needed to safely steer the ship into the narrow channel.

"Yes sir," Chief Johnston replied.

Nearing the opening of the channel, an order was given to again release the oil at the bow to try to calm the waves and make for better steerage. Unfortunately, it still had no effect.

Robert Jaknowsky stood watch at the Muskegon Coast Guard station. He watched the waves crashing over the pier and noticed other waves finding their way into the channel and rolling all the way to Muskegon Lake. He marveled at the power of the waves as they passed him. The waves broke in the channel.

"White caps in the channel," he thought to himself. "That's something I never seen before. I hope we don't have to go out in this."

He knew that the channel was dangerous during a westerly storm. The natural current flowed from Muskegon Lake into Lake Michigan. Yet in a storm like this one, the waves traveled east, the length of the channel into the smaller lake, while the natural current moved west under the surface, creating a tremendous undertow.

A dim light on Lake Michigan caught his eye. It was a ship heading in for the Muskegon channel.

Captain Miller knew passing through the Muskegon piers in a storm was dangerous. He remembered the *Virginia* striking the

Goodrich Steamer Alabama.

In 1916 the steamer Alabama *rammed the pierhead while attempting to enter the Muskegon lake channel.* Author's Collection

south wall in similar conditions in 1911. He also recalled when in 1916 the Goodrich steamer, *Alabama*, drove her bow almost twenty-feet into the end of the pier. Captain Miller himself was all too familiar with the dangers of entering the Muskegon channel in a severe westerly storm.

Jaknowsky watched the ship nearing the pierheads, rolling and pitching violently in the big seas which broke in the shallow water.

The ship's two paddle wheels turned, propelling the ship toward the opening.

"Hug the north pier as we enter," The captain called to Ted, reasoning that the effect of the wind and waves breaking over the wall would push them towards the south pier.

Through the spray of the waves breaking on the breakwater, Jaknowsky saw the ship entering the channel. She was still rolling heavily in the seas but coming in straight.

Suddenly a great wave crashed over the north pier and rained down on the ship's port bow, carrying the ship's bow across the channel towards the south pier. Just as suddenly the ship's bow caught in the undertow and swung to port, away from the pier.

The men in the pilot house breathed a sigh of relief.

Another large wave crashed over the north pier. The big ship was then raised on the crest of the wave and pushed towards the south pier again. The huge wave did not subside, rather it lifted the *Muskegon* high and set her starboard side on the pier!

Her paddle wheel came to rest hung up on the south pier. The starboard side of the ship high on the wall and the port side lying low in the channel. The waves crashed into the ship, smashing it against the wall. Timbers could be heard cracking as the waves pounded the ship into the wall.

As Jaknowsky sounded the alarm, the night air was blasted by the shrill Coast Guard whistle.

The ship, her right side sitting high on the pier, sounded her emergency alarm as well. However, the water pouring into the severely damaged hull put out the fires and the ship's whistle quickly stopped. Worst of all, it also caused the dynamo to quit

S. S. Virginia.

The Virginia *at Muskegon, Michigan. The* Virginia, *while entering the Muskegon channel, had struck the south pier during a horrific storm in 1911. The pier was damaged to the point that large concrete blocks were needed to repair it.* Author's Collection

producing electricity, extinguishing the lights on the ship. All of the frightened passengers were now in a ship, rolling violently as the waves crashed into it. The *Muskegon* sat with a severe incline to port, making it almost impossible to walk on the deck, and the ship was pitch dark.

Harry Robinson, the chief engineer from the *Arizona*, did not sleep well and arose early in the morning. Partially dressed, he stood looking out the window at the storm that was lashing the lake and causing the *Muskegon* to pitch and roll drastically. He saw the red light of the pier and was happy the trip was nearly over. The ship only needed to nose into the seven tenths of a mile long channel which leads from Lake Michigan into Muskegon Lake. Once in the smaller lake, the seas would be calmer and the ship could safely dock.

There was a slight bump which startled the experienced lakeman. "Had the ship struck bottom? he wondered. Possibly the ship dipped down in the trough of a wave and hit the bottom, or maybe she had hit the sand bar near the channel entrance.

Blanche Cornell, the young girl traveling alone to her home in Grand Rapids, awoke with a scream as the water pitcher in her cabin was thrown to the floor and smashed into hundreds of pieces. The ship was at an odd angle, leaning severely to port and rocking. Knowing that something was wrong, she quickly removed her nightgown. But, before she could reach for her clothes, the lights went out. Feeling her way in the dark, she found the life preserver in her cabin and put it on. In a panic, she crawled from the room clothed only in her life preserver.

Passengers throughout the ship were awakened when the ship struck the pier. Some were thrown from their bed to the floor. Some

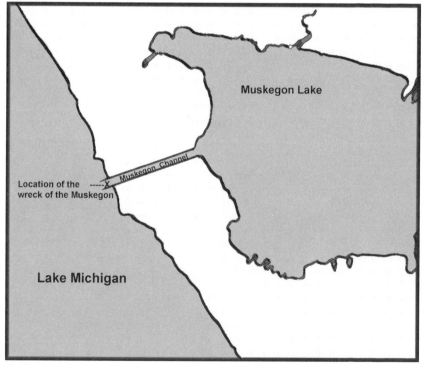

Lake Michigan is connected to Muskegon Lake through a narrow channel. Ships entering the channel in a north westerly storm face the challenge of negotiating the tight quarters with waves, wind and the undertow in the channel.

woke to the cabin boy pounding on the doors and others when debris from their shattered cabin walls rained down onto them. Some never woke, they were killed as they slept.

William Calahan, a coal passer, was bracing himself against the rolling of the ship as it entered the piers when suddenly the ship struck the pier.

"The first blow against the pier," he reported, "caved a hole a foot square through the side and water came rushing in." The water rushing over the hot boilers created steam, adding to the confusion among the crew in trying to escape.

"Get out!" Chief Engineer, Grant Johnston, screamed to the oilers and coal passers, as he climbed up from the engine room. He knew his mother could not save herself and ran through the halls towards his mother's cabin.

"Jump off the starboard side to the pier!" he instructed passengers, climbing the incline of the floor, bouncing from one wall of the passageway to the other with each wave that pounded down on the ship.

Standing at his mother's cabin, he could hear her inside pounding on the door and screaming for help. He tried the door, but it wouldn't open. When the ship was slammed down on the pier, floor timbers were broken and many cabin doors were jammed shut. Realizing the problem, Johnston yelled to his mother that he would return, but he had to find an axe.

Each wave that smashed into the *Muskegon* ripped away large pieces of the wood upper structure. The wreckage was pushed by waves down the channel into Muskegon Lake.

Chief Engineer, Grant Johnston, an axe in hand, was trying to get back to his mother's cabin when the lights went out. The waves crashing into the ship had destroyed much of the vessel, rendering it's passageways virtually impassable. Johnston tried, but was unable to reach his mother's cabin in the dark.

Harry Ries, Assistant to the Engineer, knew that Mrs. Johnston would be incapable of saving herself and went to her rescue. He struggled to crawl up against the incline of the rolling deck. The darkness, debris and frightened passengers hampered his progress.

Waves breaking on the ship washed the decks with streams of rushing water carrying shards of lumber and passengers and crew fighting to save themselves.

Harry, on hands and knees, was working his way towards the port passageway where Mrs. Johnston's stateroom was when a wave smashed into the ship and washed Harry into the channel.

Harry tried to swim towards the south pier, but the undertow sucked him below the surface and carried him out into Lake Michigan. Harry's body was found the following day on a beach north of town.

Mrs. Beerman, her sister Delia and cousin Sina were awakened by the cabin boy pounding on their door and telling them to hurry and dress. They did not have time to dress before the ship was jolted and the lights went out. They found their way to the ship's deck next to the pier where others had gathered. The younger women hugged Mrs. Beerman and were crying when two men grabbed Delia and lifted her over the rail and lowered her to the pier. Sina was next to be lowered from the doomed vessel. The ship was quickly sliding off the pier as she broke up in the waves. Mrs. Beerman waited until the deck was almost at the level of the pier and jumped to safety.

Sleeping soundly despite the raging storm, George Watson was awakened when the ship struck the pier. Whistles began blowing and he could hear screams coming from all points of the ship. He quickly put on his union suit and pulled on his trousers. As he reached for his overcoat, the lights went out.

Mrs. Caroline Turck, asleep in her stateroom on the lower deck, was also awakened when the ship struck hard on the pier. The drastic incline of her cabin floor alerted her that there was a problem, a major problem. She grabbed for the life preserver, pulled it on over her nightgown and opened the door. She was met by screams and unsteady passengers crawling in the damaged passageways, the ship was rolling as the waves pounded it against the pier. Once the lights were extinguished, Caroline crawled on her hands and knees through the halls to the stairwell. Some passengers pushed and shoved their way up the stairs, yet others assisted those, like Mrs. Turck, who were too panicked and incapable of negotiating the severe angle of the stairway.

On the deck, Caroline found she wasn't able to climb the railing, but a man came from behind and lifted her over the railing and lowered her down into the waiting arms of a large man on the pier.

Caroline looked around confused, not knowing which way to go.

"This way!" someone yelled over the crash of the waves.

Caroline followed the lady who was screaming to the passengers on the pier. The ladies trudged along towards the safety of the Coast Guard station, with waves crashing over the pier, covering it with streams of water almost a foot deep. The torrents knocked Caroline and others to the pier, threatening to wash them into the lake like the remains of the ship.

At 4:30 in the morning it should be a quiet, reflective time, but this morning was far from quiet. A multitude of sounds filled the morning: gale force winds howling, waves crashing on the pier,

The pilothouse of the ill fated Muskegon *adrift in the waves. Second Officer, Fred Steffens, was the last man to leave the ship. He was rescued by the Coast Guard, he was hanging onto the pilothouse after it had been washed off the ship.* From the collection of the Muskegon County Museum

people screaming in fear and the sound of the steamer *Muskegon* being ripped apart as the huge waves smashed her against the stone filled timber caisson.

It wasn't until Mrs. Turck was safely in the Coast Guard station that she became aware that she was dressed only in her nightgown. The heavy life preserver weighed her down while running towards the station, so she had removed it.

She and several other survivors were given blankets to cover themselves and hot coffee for warmth. Looking across the room, she saw the young girl from dinner the night before. The girl stood, wrapped in a blanket, shivering. Mrs. Turck waved her over, the motherly instinct in her coming to bare.

"Caroline! Yoo-hoo Caroline!" came a call from across the room. Caroline was relieved to see Mrs. Beerman, her sister and cousin had been rescued.

"Have you seen Mr. Watson or Mrs. Rathbone?" Freida Beerman inquired of Caroline.

The ship's debris filled the beaches. Police and Deputies were called out to stop the looting of the belongings of the passengers.
From the collection of the Muskegon County Museum

This photograph shows the twisted remains of one of the Muskegon's *paddlewheels. From the collection of the Muskegon County Museum*

"No, Blanche is the first person from the ship that I knew," Caroline replied, her arm wrapped around Blanche's shoulder, rubbing to warm and comfort her.

The ladies talked of the horror of escaping the ship and of seeing people being washed down the channel, some screaming for help and others floating by in a deadly repose.

Young Blanche told her tale of leaving the ship clothed only in a life preserver. While she was running on the pier, a man had stopped her and given her his overcoat.

"I was so scared I didn't even know I was naked," she said, embarrassed.

Sina Samson, Mrs. Beerman's cousin, said they were just beginning to dress when the lights went out. They left the ship in quite a state of dress as well.

Delia spoke, "I took off my night clothes after the cabin boy woke us, but barely had time to put on my skirt before the lights went out. I left the ship with only a skirt and life preserver to cover me."

The ladies laughed at what they must have looked like sloshing up the pier half naked. Their merriment ceased when they remembered the passengers who weren't as fortunate.

"Ladies, you're safe!" came a man's voice above all the other noise in the building.

"Mr. Watson!" Blanche exclaimed. "You've been rescued as well!"

George Watson told of his escape from the ship as it was being ripped apart.

"My stateroom was on the starboard side, just north of the wheel which was hooked on the pier," Mr. Watson said. "I had previously noted the position of hallways and doors. When the lights failed, I remembered my position and left my stateroom. In creeping along the steep angle of the cabin, I met a woman crying in the darkness for a life preserver. I endeavored to quiet her and together we found the life preserver and made our way out to the housing over the wheel. A rope dangled from the side of the boat down to the pier. The woman slid down first and I followed."

The ladies listened intently and then told of their frightful run along the pier and the horrible screams of those trapped in the rooms as the ship was torn apart by the waves.

"That trip down the pier, with the gale raging around us and the waves breaking at our feet was a journey not to be forgotten," declared Mr. Watson. "You could not see a step ahead. The waves would chortle down through the stones of the pier and we could not tell whether we were headed to safety or the black waters of the lake."

"Have you seen Mrs. Johnston or Mrs. Rathbone?" Mr. Watson asked.

A lady next to the group told them that Mrs. Johnston had been trapped in her room and couldn't get out.

"We tried to help her, but the door wouldn't open. It was hard to leave hearing her screaming and weeping, but there was nothing we could do," the lady said, slowly shaking her head as tears ran down her cheeks.

The autumn storm continued to rage throughout the remainder of the morning and the *Muskegon* continued to beat against the wall until all of its wooden upper structure had been reduced to splinters and her debris clogged the channel. The hull sunk to the bottom with only the ship's walking beam and stack breaking the surface of the channel.

The bodies of those who did not survive the wreck of the *Muskegon* were found floating near the beach, entangled in the wreckage or were washed into Muskegon Lake and surfaced in the following days. In all, twenty-nine passengers and crew lost their lives. Most of their bodies were taken to the morgue where relatives of the missing began the torturous task of trying to identify their loved ones.

For days, crates of general merchandise, part of the eighty-tons of cargo the ship carried, washed up on the beach, along with steamer trunks and suitcases filled with the personal belong-

Debris from the Muskegon *clogged the Muskegon channel. The photograph shows remains of the ship at the Muskegon Life Saving station. The lifeboat is from the destroyed ship. From the collection of the Muskegon County Museum*

ings of passengers. Muskegon police, Coast Guardsmen and Sheriff's deputies were called on to guard the shore from the hordes of greedy looters who tried to turn the tragedy into personal gain.

Even while the gale raged, looters were seen pulling in pails of lard and candy as the tins were washed away from the ship as it was beaten on the pier.

The walking beam and stacks are all that remain of the steamship Muskegon *after it struck the south pier at Muskegon and was beaten to kindling by the mountainous waves against the pier. From the collection of the Michigan Maritime Museum, South Haven, Michigan*

A woman was found on the beach carrying seventy-two pairs of silk hosiery that she had recovered from a cargo crate which had washed ashore.

The police even found people walking off with life preservers from the ship and armfuls of wood, mere kindling which the upper structure of the ship had been reduced to.

When survivors and the relatives of the dead reclaimed their trunks, there were endless reports of missing articles, jewelry and money.

Rollie Joslin, a serviceman stationed at Camp Jackson, South Carolina was anxious to hear he had received a telegram. "Who's it from? Who's it from?" his comrades inquired. He was afraid to open it, telegrams usually meant bad news.

It read, "Private Joslin, we are sorry to inform you that your sister, Florence Rathbone, was killed in the wreck of the steamship *Muskegon*."

GLOSSARY

Aft - Towards the rear end of a ship.

Ballast Tanks - Tanks on the port and starboard sides of a ship to take on sea water to counter act the listing of a ship.

Beach Apparatus - A cart pulled to the location of a shipwreck by the Life Saving Service. The cart contained lines, breeches buoy, Lyle gun and various projectiles. The apparatus was used to shoot a line to a ship grounded near shore and retrieve those aboard.

Beam - The biggest width of a ship.

Becalmed - A ship in a calm, windless sea.

Bilge - Lowest part of the interior of a ship's hull.

Boilers - A metal container where water is heated to create steam to power the steam engines.

Bollard - A post or cast metal device on a dock or wharf. The mooring lines of a ship are secured to it to hold the ship to the dock or wharf.

Bow - The front end of a ship.

Breeches Buoy - A device to remove people from a ship it danger. A line is run from the ship to the shore. Hung from the line is a ring bouy with a canvas pair of pants (breeches) sewn into the ring. The sailor steps into the breeches and is pulled along the line to safety.

Bridge - The pilot house or location on the ship where the ship is steered.

Capsize - When a ship turns over; rolls over with the hull or the port or starboard sides up.

Car Ferry - A ship designed to transport automobiles or railroad cars across a lake or river.

Checking Speed - To reduce speed.

Chief Engineer - The crew member who is in charge of the engine and machinery of the ship.

Coal Passer - A crew member whose duty is to shovel coal into the firebox.

Companionway, Passageway - A passage, corridor, or hallway on a ship.

Coston Flare - A night signal carried by the Life Saving Service while on shore patrol. The flares were used to notify the station of a ship in peril and to inform the sailors on the ship that their situation had been seen.

Davits - The brackets which hold lifeboats on the ship and are used to raise or lower the lifeboats.

Deadlights - Portholes

Deck Cargo - Cargo transported on the deck of a ship rather than in the hold below deck.

Deck Passengers - Passengers who did not book a stateroom or cabin onboard a ship and must remain on the open deck throughout the trip.

Distress signal - A signal used to alert others of a disaster at sea and call for assistance.

Excursion Ships - Ships which transport passengers on short trips not requiring overnight accommodations.

Ferry - A ship designed to transport people across a river or small lake. The trip lasts from minutes to a few hours.

Firebox - The chamber in which a fire is built to heat the boiler on a steam powered ship.

First Mate - Second in command of the ship behind the captain.

Fog Signal - A steam or compressed air powered whistle sounded in times of reduced visibility to notify other ship

Fore - The forward or front of the ship.

Foredeck - A deck towards the bow of a ship.

Flounder - To sink.

Freshening - The wind increasing; The wind is freshening.

Full Ahead - A ship moving at top speed in a forward direction.

Gale Force Wind - A strong wind from 32 to 63 miles per hour.

Gangway - A passageway in a side of a ship where passengers and cargo enter and depart the vessel.

Harbor of Refuge - A harbor, natural or man made, designed for ships to seek refuge in times of severe weather.

Hawser - A large rope used to tow or secure a ship.

Hold - An area on a ship below the deck where cargo is stowed.

Hull - The body of the vessel.

Hurricane Deck - Usually the upper deck of a ship where passengers may stroll. Also called a Promenade deck.

Keel - A large wood beam running fore and aft at the lowest point of the ship. It forms the backbone of the ship.

Knot - Speed of a ship which equals one nautical mile per hour.

Lee - Protection; the side of a ship protected from the wind.

Lifeboat Station - The location of a lifeboat on a ship.

Life Jackets, Wood Preservers, Flotation Vests, Cork Jackets - a personal floatation device used to support an individual at the surface of the water.

Lightened - Intentionally reducing the weight of the ship.

Lines - Ropes used on a ship.

List - When a ship leans to port or starboard, left or right, due to unevenly stored cargo or from taking on water.

Mid ship - In the middle of the ship from the bow to the stern.

Oilcloth /Oilskin - A cloth treated with oil to make it water repellant.

Paddlewheel - Rotating wheels at the sides of a ship which propel the ship forward.

Passenger Ship - A ship designed to transport passengers on journeys extending more than just a few hours.

Pike Poles - A wooden staff with a metal tip.

Pilot House - The Bridge of a ship; where the ship is controlled, steered, and navigated.

Pitch - The forward and aft rocking of a ship.

Port - The left side of a boat when looking towards the front.

Promenade Deck - Usually the upper deck of a ship where passengers may stroll. Also called a Hurricane deck.

Radar - A device which sends out a strong beam of radio waves. When it strikes an object it reflects back. The radar can then determine the distance away, direction of movement and speed of the object.

Reef - A rocky or sandy feature at or near the surface of the water.

Roll - The sideward, port to starboard, movement of a ship.

Salon - A large usually elegant room on a ship where passengers gather.

Schooner - A sailing craft having two masts, one fore, the other aft.

ShippingLane - Areas of a lake which ships must be traveling in a specific direction; up bound or down bound lanes.

Shoal Water - Shallow water.

Side-wheeler - A ship propelled through the water by two large paddle wheels on both sides of the ship.

Slow Astern - A ship operating at slow speed in a backward direction.

Soo Locks - Situated between Lakes Superior and Huron the locks raise ships 22 feet to the higher level of Lake Superior, or lower downbound ships to the Lake Huron level.

Spar - A rounded wood piece of the rigging of a sailing vessel used to support part of the sail.

Starboard - The right side of a boat when looking towards the front.

Stateroom - A cabin used by passengers while on a ship.

Stern - The aft or rear of a boat.

Stove In - A puncher in the hull of a ship caused by striking a rock or some other object.

Telegraph - A mechanical devise used to transmit instructions to and from the bridge of a ship to the engine room.

Tender - A small boat which carries passengers and supplies between a ship or lighthouse and shore.

Ways - As in a ship slide down the ways; a track a ship on land would slide down into the water.

Wharf - A structure built along a waterway where ships can tie up and discharge or take on cargo or passengers.

Wheelsman - The person who steers the ship.

Wireless - In today's terms a wireless is a radio.

Yawl - A small boat on a ship.

BIBLIOGRAPHY

The Collision of the *City of Cleveland lll*
Historical Collection of the Great Lakes, Bowling Green State University
The Bay City Times, June 26, 1950
The Benton Harbor News Palladium, June 26, 27, 28, 29, 1950
The Harbor Beach Times, June 30, 1950
The Huron County Tribune, June 26, 1950
The Huron County Tribune, July 5, 1950
Swayze, David D., "Shipwreck!", Harbor House Publishers, Inc., Boyne City, Michigan, 1992

When Ships Collide; the Story of the *Lady Elgin*
Grand Traverse Herald Weekly, September 14, 1860
http://www.lakemagazine.com/poetry/lady_elgin.html
Historical Collection of the Great Lakes, Bowling Green State University
History of the Great Lakes, http://www.mfhn.com/glsdb/archivestemp/ldyelgin.html
Marine disaster, http://www.linkstothepast.com
"The wreck of the *Lady Elgin*", Brendon Baillod, http://www.baillod.com/elgin//milwaukee/marinrdis.html
Swayze, David D., "Shipwreck!", Harbor House Publishers, Inc., Boyne City, Michigan, 1992
"Wreck of the Steamer *Lady Elgin*", Brendon Baillod, http://my.expecpc.com/~drewitz/elginh

The Passenger Ship *Hamonic* Burns In The River
The Port Huron Times Herald, July 17, 18, 1945
Historical Collection of the Great Lakes, Bowling Green State University
Swayze, David D., "Shipwreck!", Harbor House Publishers, Inc., Boyne City, Michigan, 1992

The Rise and Fall of the Famous *Tashmoo*
Detroit Times, December 8, 1927
Historical Collection of the Great Lakes, Bowling Green State University
The Detroit Free Press, May 8, 1901
The Detroit Free Press, June 19, 1936
The Detroit Marine Historian, http://www.mhsd.org/publications/dmh/samdmh.1.htm
The Detroit News, June 19, 1936
Rearview Mirror, "The *Tashmoo* and her date with doom", http://.detnews.com/history/tashmoo/tashmoo.htm
Race between two centuries, http://.detnews.com/history/boatrace/boatrace.htm
Swayze, David D., "Shipwreck!", Harbor House Publishers, Inc., Boyne City, Michigan, 1992

The Collision of the *Pewabic* and the *Meteor*
Historical Collection of the Great Lakes, Bowling Green State University
Thunder Bay National Marine Sanctuary and Underwater Preserv, Shipwreck Salvage,

GREAT LAKES PASSENGER SHIP DISASTERS

http://thunderbay.noaa.gov/history/salvage.html

"The *Pewabic*," James Donahue, http://www.oweb.com/upnorth/shipwreck/ship9.html

Great Lakes Dive Center,
http://www.greatlakesdivecenter.com/divesites/localdivesites/pewabic.shtml

"The *Pewabic* and the *Meteor*, 1865," http://my.execpc.com/~drewitz/pewabic.html

Swayze, David D., "Shipwreck!", Harbor House Publishers, Inc., Boyne City, Michigan, 1992

The St. Clair Republican, August 9, 1860

The Burning of "Queen of the Lakes", the *Noronic*

Historical Collection of the Great Lakes, Bowling Green State University

Swayze, David D., "Shipwreck!", Harbor House Publishers, Inc., Boyne City, Michigan, 1992

The Detroit News, September 17, 18, 19, 1949

The Detroit Times, September 17, 19, 1949

The Detroit Sunday Times, September 18, 1949

The Port Huron Times Herald, September 17, 18, 19, 1949

The Tragic Tale of the *S. S. Eastland*

Bell System Memorial, http://www.bellsysyemmemorial.com/eastland.html

Chicago Historical Information, http://www.chipublic.org/004chicago'disasters/eastland_photos.html, http://www.chipublib.org/004chicago/disasters/eastland_photos.html

Eastland Disaster Historical Society, http://eastlanddisaster.org.html

Hilton, George, W. Eastland Legacy of the Titanic, Stanford University Press, Stanford, California, 1995

Historical Collection of the Great Lakes, Bowling Green State University

Swayze, David D., "Shipwreck!", Harbor House Publishers, Inc., Boyne City, Michigan, 1992

The Chicago Sunday Tribune, July 25, 1915

The Daily News, "Lake Steamer capsizes in Chicago River," http://www.inficad.com/~ksup/pm_oct15.html

"The *Eastland*," http://www.rmstitanichistory.com/eastland.html

"The *Eastland* Disaster," http://chicago.about.com/library/blank/bleastland01.html

"The *Eastland* Disaster of 1915," http://www.novagate.net/~bonevelle/eastland/

The Huron County Independent, July 30, 1915

The Ferry *Omar D. Conger* Made Its Mark On Port Huron

Historical Collection of the Great Lakes, Bowling Green State University

Swayze, David D., "Shipwreck!", Harbor House Publishers, Inc., Boyne City, Michigan, 1992

The Port Huron Times Herald, March 27, 29, 1922

The Port Huron Museum

The *Alpena* Sailed Into the Storm

"*Alpena* Goes Missing!" http://www.macatawa.org/~crich/alpena.html

Bay City Evening Press, October 20, 21, 1880

Detroit Free Press, October 19, 20, 1880

Grand Traverse Herald Weekly, October 21, 1880

BIBLIOGRAPHY

Historical Collection of the Great Lakes, Bowling Green State University
Swayze, David D., "Shipwreck!", Harbor House Publishers, Inc., Boyne City, Michigan, 1992
The Grand Rapids Daily Times, October 19, 20, 1880
The Port Huron Weekly Times, October 21, 1880

The *S. S. George M. Cox* Is On the Rocks!
Chicago Sunday Tribune, May 28, 1933
Historical Collection of the Great Lakes, Bowling Green State University
http://www.superiortrips.com/cox_history.html
http://www.superiortrips.com/cumberland_history.html
http://www.terrypepper.com/lights/superior/rockofages.html
Swayze, David D., "Shipwreck!", Harbor House Publishers, Inc., Boyne City, Michigan, 1992
The Bay City Sunday Tribune, May 28, 1933
The Evening News, May 29, 31, June 1, 1933
The Daily Mining Gazette, May 27, 30, 31, June 11933
The Daily Mining Journal, May 29, 30, June, 1, 2, 1933
The Sunday Mining Gazette, May 28, 1933

The Burning of the *G. P. Griffith*
Boyer, Dwight, "Disaster off Willoughbeach," http://www.willowick-ohio.com_Willowick/history/disaster/disaster.html
"Burning of the *G. P. Griffith*," Inland Seas, Volume 12, number 3, 1956
Detroit Daily Free Press, June 18, 20, 1850
Hawkins, Lawrence J., "The Most Dreadful Calamity,"
http://www.willowickohio.com_Willowick/history/Calamity/calamity.htm
Historical Collection of the Great Lakes, Bowling Green State University.
Swayze, David D., "Shipwreck!", Harbor House Publishers, Inc., Boyne City, Michigan, 1992

The Demise of the Little Steamship *Pilgrim*
Swayze, David D., "Shipwreck!" Harbor House Publishers, Inc., Boyne City, Michigan, 1992
The Harbor Beach Times, May 2, 1907
The Port Huron Daily Times, April 30, 1907
The Port Huron Weekly Times, May 3, 1907

The 1852 Collision of the *Atlantic* and *Ogdensburgh*
Historical Collection of the Great Lakes, Bowling Green State University
The Great Lake Historical Society, "The Loss of the Steamer *Atlantic*," by Gerry Barker, Pg 211-214, 1964
The Detroit Daily Free Press, August 20,23, 25,26, 27, 30, 31, 1852
The Grand River Times, September 1, 2, 8, 1852
"The *Atlantic*," http://www.rmstitanichistory.com/atlantic/antlantic.html
"The *Atlantic* Story," http://www.kwic.com/~pagodavista/atlantic.html
Swayze, David D., "Shipwreck!", Harbor House Publishers, Inc., Boyne City, Michigan, 1992

GREAT LAKES PASSENGER SHIP DISASTERS

Hawkins, Lawrence J., "The Most Dreadful Calamity",
http://www.willowickohio.com_Willowick/history/Calamity/calamity.htm

The *Pere Marquette No. 18* Is Sinking!

Caesar, Pete "Who sunk the *Pere Marquette 18?*" Green Bay, Wisconsin, Great Lakes Marine Research, 1992

Historical Collection of the Great Lakes, Bowling Green State University

The Daily Tribune, South Haven, Michigan, September 10, 1910.

The Evening Record, Traverse City, Michigan September 9, 10, 1910.

The Grand Rapids Herald, Grand Rapids, Michigan, September 11, 1910.

The Grand Traverse Herald, Traverse City, Michigan,   September 13, 1910.

Swayze, David D., "Shipwreck!", Harbor House Publishers, Inc., Boyne City, Michigan, 1992

The *Muskegon*

Historical Collection of the Great Lakes, Bowling Green State University

The Grand Haven Daily Tribune, Grand Haven, Michigan, June 28, 1919.

The Grand Haven Daily Tribune, Grand Haven, Michigan, October 28, 29, 30, 31, 1919.

The Grand Haven Daily Tribune, Grand Haven, Michigan, November 1, 3, 4, 5, 6, 8, 1919.

The Muskegon Chronicle, Muskegon, Michigan, June 28, 1919.

The Muskegon Chronicle, Muskegon, Michigan, October 28, 29, 30, 31, 1919

The Muskegon Chronicle, Muskegon, Michigan, November 1, 1919

Swayze, David D., "Shipwreck!", Harbor House Publishers, Inc., Boyne City, Michigan, 1992

ACKNOWLEDGMENTS

No historical endeavor can be accomplished without the assistance and aid of many. I want to thank all of those who contributed:

Bad Axe Public Library, Bad Axe, Michigan

Bayliss Public Library, Susan James, Sault St. Marie, Michigan

Benton Harbor Public Library, Jill Rauh, Reference Librarian, Benton Harbor, Michigan

Bowling Green State University, Historical Collections of the Great Lakes, Bowling Green State University, Robert Graham, Archivist

City of Harbor Beach, Michigan Tom Youatt, Marge Montgomery, Holly Brown, Leslie Woycehoski, Mary Woycehoski and Ron Wruble

Dossin Great Lakes Museum, John Polacsek, Curator of Marine History, Detroit, Michigan

Eastland Disaster Society, Ted Wachholz, President and Director, Chicago, Illinois

Harbor Beach Public Library, Vicky Mazure, Director, Harbor Beach, Michigan

Historical Museum of Bay County, Ron Bloomfield, Curator of Collections and Research, Bay City, Michigan

Library of Michigan, Lansing, Michigan and Carol Fink of the Rare Books department

Michigan Maritime Museum, Ronniee Harrell, Researcher and Sheri Lemon, Research Assistant, South Haven, Michigan

Muskegon County Museum, Noah Phelps, Archivists, Muskegon, Michigan

Point aux Barques Lighthouse Society, Captain Ron and Judy Burkhard, Port Hope, Michigan

Port Huron Museum. Special thanks to T. J. Gaffney, Curator of Collections for all of his assistance in the project. Port Huron, Michigan

St. Clair Public Library, Port Huron, Michigan

Terry Pepper, "Seeing the Light", www.terrypepper.com/lights

The Great Lakes Historical Society, Peggy Becktol, Vermillion, Ohio

The Grice House Museum, Harbor Beach, Michigan

The Port Dover Harbor Museum, Ian Bell, Port Dover, Ontario

The Sarnia Observer, Sarnia, Ontario

Traverse City Public Library, Traverse City, Michigan

Wisconsin Maritime Historical Society, Catherine Sanders, Milwaukee, Wisconsin

ABOUT THE AUTHOR

Geography has played an important part in shaping Wayne "Skip" Kadar's love of the Great Lakes. Throughout his life he has lived in the downriver area of Detroit, Marquette, Harbor Beach and at the family cottage in Manistique, Michigan. Growing and living in these rich historic maritime areas has instilled in him a love of the Great Lakes and their maritime past.

Photo by Karen Kadar

This love has taken him in many directions. He is a certified S.C.U.B.A. diver and avid boater, having owned most all types of boats from personal water craft to sailboats to a small cruiser. He is involved in lighthouse restoration, serving as the Vice President of the Harbor Beach Lighthouse Preservation Society and a consultant in lighthouse restoration.

Mr. Kadar enjoys studying and researching Great Lakes maritime history and has made presentations on maritime history on a local and state level.

An educator for thirty years, Mr. Kadar has retired after 15 years as a high school principal.

Skip lives in Harbor Beach, Michigan with his wife Karen, their dog and two cats. During the summer Skip can usually be found at the Harbor Beach Marina, on the family boat "Pirate's Lady" or at the lighthouse.

Also by Wayne Louis Kadar:
- *Great Lakes Freighter, Tanker & Tugboat Disasters*
- *Strange & Unusual Shipwrecks On The Great Lakes*

Avery Color Studios, Inc. has a full line of Great Lakes oriented books, puzzles, cookbooks, shipwreck and lighthouse maps, lighthouse posters and Fresnel lens model.

For a free full-color catalog, call **1-800-722-9925**

Avery Color Studios, Inc. products are available at gift shops and bookstores throughout the Great Lakes region.

After Christianity

Italian Academy Lectures

Italian Academy Lectures

∼

UMBERTO ECO
Serendipities: Language and Lunacy

CARLO GINZBURG
*No Island Is an Island: Four Glances at English Literature
in a World Perspective*

After Christianity

~

Gianni Vattimo

translated by Luca D'Isanto

Columbia University Press   New York

Columbia University Press
Publishers Since 1893
New York   Chichester, West Sussex

Library of Congress Cataloging-in-Publication Data
Vattimo, Gianni, 1936–
After Christianity / by Gianni Vattimo ; translated by Luca D'Isanto.
p. cm. — (Italian Academy lectures)
Includes index.
ISBN 0–231–10628–9 (cloth : alk. paper)
1. Christianity. I. Title. II. Series.
BR121.3 .V38 2002
230—dc21
2001047502

∞
Columbia University Press books are printed on permanent
and durable acid-free paper.
Designed by Chang Jae Lee
Printed in the United States of America
c 10 9 8 7 6 5 4 3 2 1
p 10 9 8 7 6 5 4 3 2 1

Chapter 5, "The West or Christianity," was first published in Italian
as "L'Occident o la Cristianità," in the book *Cristianesimo ed Europa*
(Citta Nuova, 1993).

~

Contents

After Christianity

⁓

Believing That One Believes

THE ITALIAN TITLE of a recent book of mine, translated into English as *Belief*,[1] was *Credere di credere* (believing that one believes). It was a difficult title to translate, though it contained the meaning I wanted to convey in the text. The expression "believing that one believes" sounds paradoxical in Italian, too: to believe means having faith, conviction, or certainty in something, but also to opine—that is, to think with a certain degree of uncertainty. To clarify the title, then, I would say that the first *believing* has the latter meaning, while the second use of the term has the sense of having faith, conviction, and certainty. It is rather difficult to put the two meanings of the verb together: if I merely opine, if I think, I hold with some probability that I have certainty and faith. This sounds unclear as well as suspicious.

However, this expression's meaning, unclear as it may be, seems to correspond to an experience that is widespread and comprehensible, and of which many of us are aware. As I say in my book, it came to mind one day while I was speaking on the telephone—indeed, on a public telephone set in an open space, in the midst of traffic and of chatting people—with an old professor of philosophy who was also a fervent believer. I had not seen him for a long time, and he asked me whether I still believed in God. I answered, "Well, I believe that I believe." This is still my attitude today. Upon reflecting on that spontaneous response I came to understand, or I believe to have understood, that this unclear meaning of faith is entirely bound up with my experience as a scholar of philosophy, and perhaps as an intellectual belonging to this specific epoch, too. I say this without any presumption. On the contrary, I recognize that what I hold to be "exemplary" is such only in the sense in which people generally call "an example" something corresponding to a number of similar objects, a car of a certain type, or a statistical sample (which has nothing exceptional about it either).

Why, then, do I think I have understood that for those like me who have any familiarity with contemporary philosophy, but above all with postmodern life, religious belief can only have this meaning characterized by a deep uncertainty of opinion?

My itinerary toward the Christian faith, too, makes me a statistical sample, of which quite a few people who have had training similar to mine also are part. After World War II, when I was about ten years old, I used to go to the parish church, where I developed my basic attitudes toward the world and others, including my social, political, and religious interests. Indeed, it was to live up to this blend of interests that I decided to study philosophy at the university: I wanted to contribute to the formation of a new Christian humanism, which would be free from liberal individualism and from collective and deterministic Marxism. Those were the years when we—the Catholic youth—studied the works of Jacques Maritain, a distinguished neo-Thomistic and antifascist French thinker, who had written a book entitled *Integral Humanism*. I inherited from Maritain a diffidence toward certain dogmas of modernity. For this reason, after finishing my doctoral thesis on Aristotle, I became engrossed in the study of Nietzsche and Heidegger, who to me appeared to be the most radical critics of modernity. Now, it is precisely through these authors, who were not merely antimodern but also anti-Christian (especially Nietzsche), that I paradoxically was led back to the Christian faith, or to something that bears a striking resemblance to it.

Here I shall stop dwelling on my autobiography. Instead, I would like to explain my paradox of having recovered Christianity—in the form of believing that I believe— through Nietzsche and Heidegger. Nietzsche's announcement that "God is dead" is not an atheistic thesis like "God does not exist." Nietzsche could not state a thesis like the nonexistence of God because the claim to its absolute truth would have to be upheld as a metaphysical principle, that is, as the true "structure" of reality, having the same function as the traditional God of metaphysics. Wherever there is an absolute, even if it is the sheer affirmation of the nonexistence of God, metaphysics is always present in the form of the supreme principle, namely the God whose superfluousness Nietzsche believes to have discovered. In sum, for Nietzsche "God is dead" means nothing else than the fact that there is no ultimate foundation. An analogous meaning, albeit unacknowledged, is found in Heidegger's polemics against metaphysics—the whole European philosophical tradition from Parmenides on—which believes itself capable of grasping the ultimate foundation of reality in the form of an objective structure like an essence or a mathematical truth, which is given outside of time.

Just as Nietzsche cannot state that God does not exist (otherwise he would have to say that he knows the true structure of the real), Heidegger cannot dismiss metaphysics by stating that reality has a different structure, which is not objective but rather mobile. He would still be affirming another structure. Indeed, Heidegger dismisses the meta-physical—objective, stable, and structural—conception of Being only in the name of an experience of freedom: if we exist (with our projects, hopes, aims, and fears) as finite beings who are not just appearance but rather beings who have a past and a future, then we cannot conceive of Being in accord with the objectivistic terms of metaphysics.

Actually, Heidegger's denial of metaphysics articulates the attitude of a large part not only of philosophical thought but also of artistic, literary, and religious thought at the beginning of the twentieth century, when humanistic culture began to feel the need to rebel against the total organization of society ("*die totale Verwaltung*" in Adorno), which had increasingly imposed itself through the ration-alization of labor and the triumph of technology.

For much of twentieth-century philosophy it is no longer possible to think of Being as foundation, not simply because of the risk that objectivism might lead to a totali-tarian society—to Auschwitz or to the Gulag—but above all because European culture has become aware that there are other cultures that cannot be merely classified as "prim-itive," that is, as lagging behind the West in the way of "progress." The 1800s were the century in which the his-torical sciences, including cultural anthropology, arose: there was a ripe awareness that there was not just a single course of history (culminating in Western civilization) but different cultures and different histories. This awareness would be decisively advanced through the wars of libera-tion of the colonial nations. Algeria's revolt against France as well as the petroleum war of the early 1970s were the last episodes within the theoretical, practical, and political rupture of Eurocentrism, i.e., of the idea of a unique human civilization of which Europe was conceived to be the leader as well as the apex.

How are all these themes—Nietzsche, Heidegger, the end of colonialism, and the Christian faith—related? It may be possible to say that the epoch in which we live today, which is rightly called postmodern, is the epoch in which reality can no longer be conceived of as a structure solidly tied to a sole foundation that philosophy would have the task of knowing, or perhaps that religion would have the task of adoring. The pluralistic world in which we live cannot be interpreted by an ideology that wants to unify it at all costs in the name of a sole truth, which some academic disciplines would have the task and capacity of knowing. This ideology would stumble against, among other things, any ideals of democracy. It would affirm, as we have recently heard many Catholic politicians say, at least in Italy, that a law wanted by the majority but without truth (i.e., in contrast with the teachings of the Catholic Church) has no legitimacy. Hence, one must infer, it is a law that does not deserve to be obeyed.

Here one might proceed in different ways. For example, one might ask how we can rationally argue once we forgo the claim of grasping an ultimate foundation that would be valid for all, above and beyond any cultural differences. To this one might answer: the universal validity of an assertion can be construed by building consensus in dialogue, though without claiming any right in the name of an absolute truth. Dialogical consensus may be reached by acknowledging that we share a heritage of cultural, historical, and technological-scientific acquisitions.

Instead, here I intend to show how postmodern pluralism has enabled (for me, though I mean it in a more general sense) the recovery of the Christian faith. If God is dead, if philosophy has recognized that it cannot with certainty grasp the ultimate foundation, then philosophical atheism is no longer necessary. Only an absolute philosophy can feel the necessity of refuting religious experience. Yet, perhaps there is something more important in Nietzsche's announcement of the death of God. Nietzsche writes that God is dead because those who believe in him have killed him. In other words, the faithful, who have learned not to lie because it was God's command, have discovered in the end that God himself is a superfluous lie. However, in light of our postmodern experience, this means: since God can no longer be upheld as an ultimate foundation, as the absolute metaphysical structure of the real, it is possible, once again, to believe in God. True, it is not the God of metaphysics or of medieval scholasticism. But that is not the God of the Bible, of the Book that was dissolved and dismissed by modern rationalist and absolutist metaphysics.

Furthermore, if there is no longer a philosophy (like Hegelian or Marxist historicism or like the various kinds of scientific positivism) claiming to be capable of demonstrating the nonexistence of God, we are free, again, to hear the words of Scripture. Moreover, in the postmodern end of the absolute philosophies, we become aware that once we discover that the vision of Being as eternal structure of objectivist metaphysics is untenable, we are left with the biblical notion of creation, namely with the contingency and historicity of our existing. To translate all this in secular and philosophical terms: it is above all because of the experience of postmodern pluralism that we can think of Being only as event, and of truth not as the reflection of reality's eternal structure but rather as a historical message that must be heard and to which we are called to respond. This conception of truth is not only valid for theology and philosophy. It is the same truth that, more or less explicitly, is upheld by a large part of the sciences, at least by those that have become aware of the historicity of their paradigms.

As is well known, this term has been characterized by its usage in Thomas Kuhn's *The Structure of Scientific Revolutions* in 1963, whose meaning concerns us here. It is only based on certain presuppositions—methods, theorems, axioms, etc., which in turn are not verifiable or demonstrable or else one would go on *ad infinitum*—that the sciences verify or falsify hypotheses. The rise and fall of scientific paradigms are complex historical events, which cannot be explained according to the logic of the proof and of confutation. What occurs in our everyday language also occurs within science: we experience things in the world only on the basis of forms that we have inherited, together with the other forms of our existence. For a long time, philosophers and linguists have dismissed the idea that first we see things and then attribute them their names. On the contrary, we encounter the world already possessing forms, words, grammatical structures through which we give it order, otherwise to us the world would appear to be an indistinct mess.

Here we don't need to develop further this mode of conceiving knowledge. I only intend to say that if we suppose, as I believe we should, that the postmodern conception of truth (understood as historical message, rise and fall of paradigms, interpretations of things in light of inherited historical languages) makes sense, it becomes possible to take the Bible seriously. Indeed, it becomes essential to take the Bible seriously, insofar as it is the principal book that has marked deeply the "paradigm" of Western culture. "Thank God, I am an atheist," says an Italian (not too) paradoxical expression. It is only as the heir of a Judeo-Christian tradition that conceives of the real in terms of creation and the history of salvation that postmodern thought has freed itself from the objectivistic metaphysics of scientism so that it can live up to its experience of cultural pluralism, namely of the historicity and contingency of existing.

Why, then, and in what sense, can one "believe that one believes"? The God I have recovered after liquidating metaphysics and the illusion that one could demonstrate that the real has a certain structure and a determinate foundation is not the God of metaphysical certainties, of the *preambula fidei*. The natural theology expressed by scholastic metaphysics was grounded on the idea that a healthy, natural reason was capable of demonstrating the existence of a supreme Being—cause and *telos* of the world—so that one might then move on to hear revelation. Instead, the God recovered in the postmetaphysical and postmodern epoch is the God of the Book. This is not only in the subjective sense of the genitive—meaning God as the author of biblical revelation—but also in the objective sense of the genitive: the God who is given to us in the Book and who does not "exist" as an objective reality outside of salvation's announcement, is always handed over in historically changing forms offered, in the sacred Scriptures and in the living tradition of the Church, to the continuing reinterpretation of the community of believers. It is not possible to "believe" in this God in the strong sense of the word, as if God's reality were more demonstrable than the reality of sensate things or of the objects of physics and mathematics. "*Fides ex auditu*," a motto that stems from the New Testament, also means that one believes in the God of revelation because one has "heard" about him. Hence it has all the uncertainty associated with all the things we take to be true because they are told by someone we trust, though it is a trust that has its precondition in the feeling of friendship, love, and respect. And we also know that "blind" love does not see things in their objective "truth."

Yet if paradigms—the horizons through which we experience the world—are historical, existential, and transmitted, and therefore are not objects of demonstration or proof, this kind of believing is a primary and fundamental mode of encountering truth. In this sense, every authority comes from God: all verification and falsification of statements about the world is made possible by a foregrounding, albeit determining, faith that has the look of a conjecture, a risky wager, and ultimately a loving acceptance, devotion, and pietas.

This concept of postmodern faith has nothing to do

with the acceptance of strictly defined dogmas or with disciplines imposed by a single authority. The Church is certainly an important vehicle for revelation, but it is above all the community of believers who, in charity, hear and interpret freely the meaning of the Christian message, mutually helping and correcting one another. It is an idea of Church, found in many Romantic thinkers such as Novalis and Schleiermacher, that is wrongly treated as a utopia to be dismissed with the other theses of eighteenth- and nineteenth-century German idealism. Perhaps it is only by taking seriously this utopia that Christianity will be able to realize in the postmodern world its vocation as a universal religion.

I

~

The God Who Is Dead

IN ONE OF the long fragments on nihilism from the 1800s (which was first published in *The Will to Power*), Nietzsche asks whether nihilism is compatible with some form of faith in the divine and conceives of the possibility of a pantheistic religiosity, since "after all only the moral God is denied"[1]). After all, there are other, well-known passages in Nietzsche's more mature work where he speaks of the creation of new gods. Let me remark that when announcing the death of God, Nietzsche anticipates that the latter's shadow will continue to be cast upon our world for a long time. As with the emperor's message in Kafka's story, time is necessary so that the message will reach the most remote provinces of the empire, or the most secret corners of our consciousness. On the basis of these fragments, it is possible to draw not only the idea of the religious, Christian character of Nietzsche's inspiration (on which there is an abundant literature, for example Karl Jaspers's study) but also the impression that the announcement of the death of God does not definitely close off Nietzsche's engagement with religion.

My aim here is not to explore the meaning of the possible "return" of religion in Nietzsche's philosophy, which constitutes a problem (after all, still largely unresolved) for the Nietzsche-*Forschung*. Instead, I want to ask more generally whether and to what extent the end of all possible religious experience constitutes the implication of what Nietzsche calls the death of God (or the overcoming of the moral God), which in contemporary thought is described as the end of metaphysics.

I begin by explaining why I interpret the Nietzschean death of God as the end of metaphysics, which, as is well known, is Martin Heidegger's idea. Here too I have no intention of providing a thematic or historical reconstruction of Heidegger's thought. I argue instead that the Nietzschean announcement of the death of God and the Heideggerian announcement (let me stress the character of *announcement*: neither a theory nor a thesis) of the end of metaphysics can provide the general framework for characterizing late-modern experience. This is how I will discuss these thinkers (on the basis of historical analysis I have undertaken elsewhere).[2]

We are all aware of the meaning of Nietzsche's announcement of the death of God. The belief in God was a powerful instrument of rationalization and discipline, which enabled man to leave the primitive state of the *bellum omnium contra omnes*, favoring the constitution of the "scientific" world view and paving the way for technology, with its reassuring effects that facilitate existence. For this reason, today's "civilized" man no longer needs to believe in God. Now, those who were always commanded in the name of God not to lie have recognized that this belief is useless and obsolete. This is why Nietzsche argues that believers have killed God. However, this statement must be read beyond its literal meaning, in light of the general phenomenon of the lightening of existence brought about by the rationalization that was initially related to belief in

God. This phenomenon has made useless and obsolete the radical hypothesis concerning the existence of a supreme Being as the ground and ultimate *telos* of the world.

Let me stress that the Nietzschean doctrine has only the character of an announcement: Nietzsche is not putting forward an atheistic metaphysics, which would imply the claim to describe reality correctly as something from which God is excluded. This claim, like the claim advanced by the faith in the truth discussed in *The Gay Science*, would still entail a form of faith in the moral God as the founder and guarantor of the objective world order. Only if we keep this in mind can we recognize the analogy, or close continuity, between the Nietzschean doctrine of the death of God and the end of metaphysics of which Heidegger speaks. It is not a matter of discovering a philosophical truth superior to that of past metaphysical philosophies. Like the death of God, the end of metaphysics is an event that cannot be ascertained objectively, one to which thought is called to respond. It is an event that transforms the existence of the person who receives the announcement—or which is entirely constituted by this transformation.

In Heidegger's thought, the event of "the end of metaphysics" has basically the same meaning of the death of God: the moral God, in Nietzsche's view, is "*ueberwunden*," overcome, or put aside. Indeed, what Heidegger calls metaphysics is the belief in an objective world order, which must be recognized so that thought might conform with it its descriptions of reality and its moral choices. This belief in the objective world order evaporates when it is revealed to be untenable. Briefly, and provocatively, let me observe that this happens in the twentieth-century existentialism that is represented, more radically and more consistently, by Heidegger's *Being and Time* (1927). Existentialism "corresponds" to the completion of metaphysics in the world of the incipient "total organization" of society, made possible by modern science, which has brought the premises of Greek metaphysics to their logical conclusion. Metaphysics endured only as long as it was a belief in the ideal world order—in a kingdom of essences that lay beyond empirical reality—which made knowledge and the critique of reality's limits possible. Now metaphysics has come to deny itself, through a chain of events associated with the development of the modern sciences, where the truth of the Platonic ideas has become more and more identifiable with the objectivity of the statements of physics. Metaphysics has unmasked itself as an untenable and inefficacious belief insofar as the ideal order, to which it always in principle related itself, has become the *de facto* order of the rationalized world of modern technological society. This order makes it *de facto* impossible to think of existence as project, opening, unpredictability, or ultimately as freedom. If true being lies in the objectivity of the objects ascertained by the sciences and codified by the laws of physics, then human existence cannot be conceived of as being and thereby becomes theoretically unthinkable. Heidegger's effort to move beyond metaphysics (which he describes as "the forgetting of being") into beings reflects the theoretical impossibility of thinking about human existence with the concepts inherited from tradition, as well as the practical—ethical and political—rebellion against what Adorno called the world of the total organization.

However, the self-dissolution of metaphysics cannot be described in these terms only. It is not confined to the view of being as objectivity, which has become untenable for theoretical and ethical-political reasons. After *Being and Time*, during the years that he himself described as the "turning" point of his thought, Heidegger increasingly insisted on the nihilistic outcomes of modern techno-science. However, in addition to the total organization of society, what refutes metaphysics, thereby making the belief in an objective, stable, and instituted order of being untenable, is the inexorable proliferation of world "pictures." The specialization of scientific languages, the proliferation of cultures (which are no longer hierarchically brought together under the Eurocentric myth of progress), the fragmentation of the life spheres, and the Babel-like pluralism of late-modern society have made the thought of a unified world order impossible to conceive. Now, all the metanarratives—to use Lyotard's well-taken expression—that claimed to mirror the objective structure of being have been discredited. Thus, the end of metaphysics is not merely the discovery, by a philosopher or by a school of thought, that Being is not the objectivity to which science has reduced it. It is above all associated with a series of events that have transformed our existence, of which postmetaphysical philosophy gives an interpretation rather than an objective description (an interpretation is not neutral but engaged knowledge, because it is not placed at an ideal point that would claim to be external to the process).

In other words, it is precisely the Babelic world of late modernity that "verifies" the Nietzschean announcement of the death of God and the Heideggerian announcement of the end of metaphysics—which are identical in meaning—by legitimizing them. In a certain sense, which cannot be systematized, this is the world where "the moral God" as metaphysical ground is dead and buried. But the moral God is only what Pascal referred to as the God of the philosophers. There are many indications, therefore, that the death of the moral God has paved the way for the renewal of religious life.

This seems clear, at least for me, in the realm of theory. The decline of metaphysics as a systematic philosophy, which conferred a consistent, unified, and rigorously grounded representation of the stable structures of Being, has made the philosophical denial of God's existence impossible. This was, after all, already one of the principles Kant had set for himself in the *Critique of Pure Reason*. To defend the possibility of religious experience, Kant had to show that reason couldn't speak objectively of God and of the *noumenal* world. Thus, he grounded religious experience on practical reason only, against efforts to deny it on the basis of metaphysical arguments. Today, it seems that the main philosophical outcome of the death of the metaphysical God and of the almost general discrediting of philosophical foundationalism is the renewed possibility of religious experience. This possibility returns to philosophy in the guise of the liberation of metaphor.

It seems, then, that Nietzsche may have been right in forecasting the invention of new gods. Narratives proliferate without any stable center or hierarchy in the Babel-like pluralism of late-modern society. No master narrative or normative metanarrative is any longer capable of legitimizing or delegitimizing them. The social hierarchy among languages, of which the young Nietzsche spoke in the long fragment "Truth and Lies in an Extra-moral Sense," has been overturned. In that fragment, Nietzsche asserted the metaphorical character of language: everybody associates freely a mental image with an object and a sound. Nietzsche illustrates how the obligation to "lie by following an instituted rule," that is, by adopting the master's metaphors as the only proper language, arose only through the institution of society and of a cast of masters. Consequently, the other languages were degraded to the realm of the poetic, namely to the status of purely metaphorical languages. But the pluralism without center of our postmetaphysical epoch has undermined the theoretical possibility of distinguishing between metaphorical and proper language. Wherever it survives, this distinction is revealed to be a pure effect of social power's unequal distribution. This was, for example, the sense of Michel Foucault's inquiry. To be sure, the liberation of metaphor from subordination to the proper sense has taken place in theory only. In practice, our pluralistic societies are still far from having achieved the perfect equality of the life forms (different cultures, groups, minorities of different kinds) embodied in the different metaphorical systems. The demise of hierarchical principles and norms is, at least, sufficiently clear in the theoretical discourse of philosophy, literary criticism, and several genres of writing. We have at our disposal not only the explicit theory of the end of metanarratives advanced by Lyotard but also the theories of redescription such as Rorty's, who believes it is necessary for human culture to generate infinite redescriptions so that "the conversation might continue." A symptom of metaphor's liberation is visible in recent Italian philosophy and also in a lot of Continental philosophy in the flexible use, without any explicit justification, of mythological and religious terms. This began (following in Heidegger's footsteps) with philosophy's dialogue with poetry but went on as an autonomous phenomenon. Nowadays, it is more and more frequent for philosophers to speak of angels and redemption without providing an explicit justification for the use of these terms, or to refer to classical or preclassical mythologies extracted from the commentary of poetic, theological, or mythological texts. The distinction between philosophical and poetic—or creative—writing has been apparently erased.

The end of metaphysics and the death of the moral God have liquidated the philosophical basis of atheism. Contemporary philosophers seem to be mostly religious or irreligious as if out of inertia, rather than for strong theoretical reasons. In modernity, the theoretical reasons for being religious or not were associated with positivist or historicist metaphysics. God was denied either because his existence was not verifiable by scientific experiment or because he was a stage ineluctably overcome in the progressive enlightenment of reason. But the end of metaphysics has now discredited these metanarratives.

The revival of religion in late-industrial society corresponds, though without any direct causal link of dependence, to the liberation of metaphor and to the dismissal of the philosophical reasons of atheism. To be sure, many explanations have been advanced to explain this revival, which have to do in the end with the historical circumstances that have ushered in the end of metaphysics—for example, the demise of colonialism, which has *de facto* liberated "other" cultures, thereby making Eurocentric historicism itself impossible. The end of Western colonialism has also meant the possibility of developing a multiethnic society in most of the industrialized nations. Even though it has been less peaceful than the textual liberation of philosophy or of literary criticism, multiethnic pluralism can be treated as a phenomenon of the liberation of metaphor. The other cultures have made their voices heard in Western societies but have also brought with them their own theologies and religious beliefs. Perhaps the phenomenon of the rebirth of local religious traditions in Western societies is a mimetic and defensive reaction to this very pluralism. It is possible that the demise of proper language and of the hierarchy of world pictures has provoked a phenomenon of rejection, thus creating a need to return to some forms of belonging that are at the same time as reassuring and as dreadful as all forms of fatherhood. We may add to these phenomena, on the one hand, the popularity acquired by the Roman pope because of his contribution to the collapse of communist dictatorships; on the other hand, the seriousness of problems posed by developments in the life sciences, which cannot be resolved by the pure means of modern reason and thus may have driven people to seek deeper and "essential" truths.

I am sure that all of us could add to the list of reasons for the rebirth of religion and the forms that it is taking in our world. Now it is already possible to see, even in the brief outline drawn here, the configuration of a paradoxical situation: the return of religion, in all its theoretical, social, and historical aspects (like the fall of Eurocentrism and the political liberation of other cultures), seems to depend on the dissolution of metaphysics, that is, on the dismissal of all doctrines, which claimed absolute and definitive values as the true description of Being's structures. Whereas the liberation of metaphor has allowed philosophers to speak of God, angels, and salvation once again, it is only the pluralism of late-modern societies that has conferred visibility to religion. In turn, though, the renewal of religion configures itself necessarily as the claim to an ultimate truth, which is indeed an object of faith rather than rational demonstration but which in the end tends to exclude the very pluralism of world pictures that has made it possible.

Once we acknowledge this paradox, we should ask whether the death of the moral-metaphysical God must necessarily lead us to the rebirth of the religious fundamentalism and of the ethnic-religious or religious-communitarian fundamentalism that are spreading around us. The same question, albeit slightly modified, can be raised at the philosophical level, too. It would seem paradoxical that the effect of the overcoming of metaphysics (which was theorized by Heidegger but also is central to a large part of twentieth-century philosophy) is the pure and simple legitimation of relativism and its shadow, fundamentalism, and communitarianism, its democratic version. Judging from the many signs, this is precisely what is happening—for example, Rorty's relativism and the communitarianism of philosophers like MacIntyre and Charles Taylor.

To return to the theme of religion, which is my topic here, it seems clear that the return of religion in the discourse of philosophy and in our shared experience has acquired visibility through the liberation of metaphor from subordination to the proper sense. But the condition of such liberation is entirely bound up with the end of metaphysics. I am thinking of Christian philosophers in contemporary Italian and French thought, who declare themselves to be "postmetaphysical" insofar as they treat the end of metaphysics as a process that has undermined philosophical atheism, paving the way for a Pascalian wager or decision of faith. The theses that I and other Italian post-Heideggerian philosophers have called "weak thought" have become very popular in a certain part of Italian Catholic thought because they have been interpreted, though with a degree of partiality, as a pure and simple confession of reason's weakness. True, the demise of the metanarratives is a recognition of weakness in this sense; just as "weak" is Nietzsche's recognition that one cannot avoid speaking metaphorically, that is, in a nonobjective and nondescriptive manner, without mirroring a state of affairs. However, this is just a small part of the whole picture. To extract it from the whole is to reduce the end of metaphysics and the death of the moral God to a pure and simple legitimization of relativism and fundamentalism, whether communitarian or not.

Once we acknowledge that, at the end of metaphysics, we have no ground for unmasking the truth hidden in our myths and ideologies because we have discovered that the belief in an ultimate truth is a myth and that the very idea of the unmasking of ideologies is itself an ideology, shall we just return to placing our faith in myths and ideologies? My impression is that this is precisely what is happening in many aspects of contemporary culture, even though it is not explicitly acknowledged. When, for instance, postmetaphysical philosophy limits itself to the defense of pluralism for its own sake or to the legitimization of proliferating narratives without hierarchy or center, it ends up preaching a pure and simple return to myth and ideology without setting up any critical principle, apart from the important principle of tolerance. Are not tolerance and pluralism themselves ultimately myths and ideologies, which cannot claim the status of normative metadiscourses? For anyone who acknowledges the impossibility of judging the

Babel-like pluralism of world pictures from an external point of view—a view from nowhere—the appeal to tolerance is insufficient. This, I believe, is the force of the communitarian objection to liberal relativism.

It seems, then, that only when we reflect on the difficulties emerging from the end of metaphysics and the death of God, philosophy meets religion, and not just as a possibility disclosed in "negative" fashion, that is, by recognizing philosophy's defeat and weakness. The radical overcoming of metaphysics cannot be reduced to the pure and simple legitimization of myth, ideology, and the Pascalian leap of faith. Let me turn now to discussing Heidegger's interpretation of the overcoming of metaphysics, since he is the philosopher who has theorized it more radically. The effort to think of Being—for the reasons mentioned at the outset—not as an objective structure projected by the mind to conform itself to in all its practical choices led Heidegger to practice philosophy as the recollection of the history of Being. The expression "history of Being" or "destiny of Being" (a word play on the German terms *Geschichte* and *Geschick*) is central to the later Heidegger. This is because, for Heidegger, only the thought that conceives of Being as event or as occurrence rather than objective structure is a nonmetaphysical and nonobjectifying way of recollecting Being. In other words, the objects of our experience are given only within a horizon; this horizon, like the light that makes things appear, is not in turn objectively visible. If we are capable of speaking of Being, we must conceive of Being as horizon and as light, rather than the general structure of objects. Since it is not an object, Being does not possess the stability assigned to it by the metaphysical tradition. Hence, the event of Being lies in the double sense of the genitive: the horizon is the opening belonging to Being, but it is also that to which Being itself belongs. Being is not given as a stable and eternal structure. Rather, Being gives itself, again and again, in its occurrence.

Heidegger believes that to think of Being as event means recollecting Being's history: for him, *Denken* is *an-denken* (thinking is remembrance). This is not because, from the perspective of objective correspondence, it is necessary to know historical being in its totality—as Hegel ultimately argued. Rather, the point is "to take a leap in the liberating abyss of tradition."[3] It is a liberating leap because it shakes the claim of the order of beings to be held as the eternal and objective order of Being. The leap does not give us more truthful or more complete knowledge of what Being objectively is; it only tells us that Being is neither objective nor stable. Being manifests itself as an event with respect to which we are always engaged as interpreters somehow "on the way" (Being and man).

What I have proposed to call weak thought emphasizes this aspect of Heidegger's recollection: the leap in the abyss of tradition is also the weakening of Being, insofar as it shakes all claims to peremptoriness advanced by metaphysics's ontological structures. On the other hand, in the leap Being does not manifest itself abstractly as event—as if Being were "always" event, in accordance with a concept of historicity as the eternal finitude of existence or as the eternal fall into time. The *Ereignis* is an event that happens to us, here, today. Thus, the weakening generated when, in the leap, Being reveals itself as event is also, inseparably, a weakening understood as the sense and historical common thread of the tradition, onto which we leap. The recollective retracing of the history of Being is a philosophy of history, too, which is directed by the idea of weakening: i.e., consummation of strong structures on the theoretical level (from the metaphysical metanarrative to local rationality; from the belief in the objectivity of knowledge to the awareness of the hermeneutic character of truth) and on the level of individual and social existence (from the subject centered on the evidence of self-consciousness to psycho-

analysis's subject; from the despotic State to the constitu-
tional State; and so on).

So far I have outlined two salient aspects of the death
of God. I have shown how the end of metaphysics (the
belief in an order of being as stable, necessary, and objectively knowable foundation) is accompanied in contemporary thought and social practice by the death of the moral
God, namely the God of philosophers. The end of metaphysics, however, is also and above all the rebirth of the
sacred in its many forms. For Heidegger, the end of metaphysics means moving from a conception of Being as structure to one of Being as event characterized by a tendency
toward weakening.

The conclusions I want to draw from these two long
premises are the following: first, the revival of religion in
the postmetaphysical age is not exclusively the outcome of
a misunderstanding. Rather, it can appear in its theoretical
legitimacy if we recognize the deep family resemblance—
at present I can refer to it only in this manner—between
the Western religious tradition and the idea of Being as
event with the destiny of weakening. Second, the recognition of this family resemblance offers philosophy the basis for a critical reflection on the forms that the sacred has
taken in our time. Therefore, whenever it betrays its constitutive, antimetaphysical inspiration, the revival of religion must be subjected to philosophical criticism.

The recognition of the "family resemblance" is not realized "logically" as a conceptual necessity. As is often the
case with most philosophical points of departure, it is
somehow impure. However, it will be rationally legitimated on the basis of meanings, links, persuasiveness generated in the course of its development. If we ask why this
vision of the history of Being as the destiny of weakening
should be persuasive (as I, at least, believe), the following
answer comes to mind: it is because we are the heirs of a
tradition that has absorbed "Christian" values like broth-

erhood, charity, and nonviolence. This vision has its foundation in the idea of redemption (which already appears in the Old Testament) and in the idea of incarnation, the *kenosis* of God, as Saint Paul calls it. I am aware that these "humanitarian" values belonging to our tradition are the same ones that Nietzsche believed were the causes, and expressions, of nihilism and decadence. But Nietzsche, and above all Heidegger, also taught us that nihilism (and the democratic humanitarianism of our tradition) is the way in which metaphysics has come to closure and in which Being reveals itself, gives itself, as event. Postmetaphysical philosophy, which conceives of the history of Being as a destiny of weakening, cannot be separated from the tradition to which it belongs. Furthermore, to recognize this belonging is not to ascertain a phenomenon objectively.

As I mentioned above, this somehow reopens the philosophical debate on the end of metaphysics, and provides the basis for a critical evaluation of the forms in which the rebirth of the sacred appears in our time. The term around which these two aspects of my argument can be further developed is *secularization*. Having recognized its family resemblance with the biblical message of the history of salvation and with God's incarnation, philosophy can call the weakening that it discovers as the characteristic feature of the history of Being secularization in its broadest sense, which comprises all the forms of dissolution of the sacred characteristic of the modern process of civilization. If it is the mode in which the weakening of Being realizes itself as the *kenosis* of God, which is the kernel of the history of salvation, secularization shall no longer be conceived of as abandonment of religion but as the paradoxical realization of Being's religious vocation. From the perspective of secularization—of the vocation for weakening—postmetaphysical philosophy will understand and criticize the multifaceted phenomena of religion's return in our culture, thus inescapably putting itself in question.

2

~

The Teachings of Joachim of Fiore

THE RECOGNITION THAT the history or weakening of Being is akin to the secularization of the sacred in the Western tradition discloses a broad area of reflection for philosophy, and for the self-interpretation of religious experience. My purpose in this chapter is not to reconsider, from the perspective of philosophy, philosophy's relationship to religion so that we might clarify the meaning of their family resemblance (as I have called it, leaving the meaning undefined), which is an important aspect of my reflection. Nor is it to discuss whether the recognition that secularized philosophy is akin to Christian revelation implies that the former has a duty to return purely and simply to the Bible, and eventually to the Church. This would amount to understanding secularization as an abandonment that needs to be revoked and put aside so that authenticity—the proper meaning of religious language—might be recovered. Instead, my intention is to trace the implications of the idea of secularization as a constitutive aspect of the history of Being, and therefore of the history of salvation, for our way of living the return of religion.

Nietzsche is right: the faithful have killed God. The death of God, of the moral-metaphysical God, is an effect of religiosity. In its most immediate and literal meaning, we might understand this statement in relation to the—not paradoxical—fact we have just seen: the dissolution of metaphysics generates an openness to religious experience in the philosophical thought, culture, and collective mentality of our society. It is possible that the renewed religious sensibility has killed metaphysics. But the charge that the faithful have killed God has an even more radical and perhaps scandalous significance; secularization, the departure from the sacred characteristics of Western modernity, is an occurrence within the history of Western religiosity. It is not alien and hostile toward Western religiosity but rather characterizes it very deeply. If modern civilization secularizes itself, this is the positive mode in which it responds to the announcement of the religious tradition. My argument here is that the radical meaning of this occurrence is that the religious experience that has incorporated itself into Western culture—the land of the sunset, as Heidegger calls it, though we might call it the land of the sunset of the sacred—constitutes the long "murder" of God, understood as a task that exemplifies the meaning of religion.

Joachim of Fiore offers us a model for living postmodern religious experience on the basis of the specific content of his teaching on the age of spirit and of his general theological tendency to understand salvation history as the story of the transformation in which the Scripture's meaning is spiritualized. From his perspective, biblical revelation does not consist in the communication of a message that would have to be understood as faithfully and definitely as possible to be applied to existence. The promised salvation is above all an increasingly "fuller" and more perfect—rather than more literal or objective—understanding of the message. Salvation history is not just about those who receive the announcement. Rather, it is above all the history of an announcement whose reception is its constitutive, rather than accidental, moment. Perhaps this is the essence of the Judeo-Christian message, which makes it a unique case in the history of religions and a reasonable candidate to be a universal religion—above and beyond imperialist or Eurocentric claims. The defense of universality cannot be reduced to the claim to speak the sole truth in contrast with the errors of false and mischievous gods. On the contrary, such a defense must present itself as a capacity for "assimilation," understood not as a practical political adjustment (like the Roman Imperial Pantheon) but as the meaning of the doctrine of incarnation. Let me observe that many Catholic thinkers, such as Luigi Pareyson, who declare themselves to be strictly orthodox and who situate themselves in the perspective of postmetaphysical philosophy, do not suggest that the incarnation of God in Jesus Christ undermines—and delegitimates—the myths of other religions; in many senses, they rather suggest that it implicitly validates them. Since the Christian God was incarnate in Jesus, we may also understand God through the other forms of natural being appearing in many non-Christian religious mythologies. Natural and historical symbols (up to the ciphers of which Jaspers speaks) can really symbolize God only because God has become a human being in Jesus, disclosing that he is akin to finitude and nature and—I would say—inaugurating the dissolution of divine transcendence.

However, the Christian tradition has understood only retrospectively the central dogma of incarnation's capacity for assimilation, by showing the ultimate truth of Christ as the definitive fulfillment that closes the epoch of mythical and symbolic revelations. One might argue, then, that it is no longer possible to believe in myths. Indeed, myths are recognized to be true but are immediately "sublated" and overcome, following a scheme that is repeatedly used in Hegel's philosophy of history. It is not by chance that He-

28

THE TEACHINGS OF JOACHIM OF FIORE

gel declares himself to be an authentic Christian author, and that he has been reproached for the anamnestic character of his thought. It is Joachim of Fiore, the medieval prophet of the so-called "third age" of salvation history, or the age of spirit, who emphasizes the openness to the future implicit in the dogma of incarnation. His theology of history has precedents in early Christian thought, too; for example, in Gregory of Nazianzus, who may well be his most important precursor. In the subsequent history of Christian thought, there is a broad crowd of conscious and unconscious followers of Joachim.

Joachim marks a decisive shift in the medieval exegesis of sacred Scripture insofar as he modifies and brings to completion the various theories of the multiple senses of Scripture. (The theory of the four senses of Scripture, which is the most famous, is found in Dante as well: literal, moral, allegorical, and anagogical; *litera gesta docet, quod credas allegoria, moralis quid agas, quo tendas anagogia.*) The theory of the four senses is known also as the doctrine of the spiritual intelligence of Scripture. Without denying these various aspects, Joachim places them in a more comprehensive or fundamental scheme, which can be rightly called "historical." The spiritual intelligence of Scripture is above all the capacity to grasp the events narrated in the Bible as "figures" of other historical events, rather than as parables aimed at the edification of the faithful. This means not only that the facts narrated in the Old Testament are read as figural symbols of New Testament events, as prophetic exegesis had already taught, though mainly for apologetic reasons (Jesus realized the prophecies, thereby legitimating them, and in turn was legitimated by them) or for the sake of edification. Joachim argues that his method enables one to prophesy in the proper sense by foretelling future events of salvation history on the basis of the figural exegesis of past events within the same history. I am not appealing to this prophetic aspect of Joachimite theology, which betrays a literalism that contradicts the very idea of the age of spirit and risks lapsing to the level of Nostradamus. If by now we are, at least in principle, in the age of spiritual interpretation rather than the age of literal interpretation of sacred Scripture, it seems clearly a contradiction to demand that biblical narratives be read as narratives of events that are "objectively" true or as prophecies of events that are "really" destined to take place in world history. Eugenio Trias might be right in arguing that spirit can only unfold in a symbolic form, which leaves behind a concealed remnant and which by definition cannot be reduced to the literalism required by Joachim's specific and realistic prophecies.[1] An event can never become the pure symbol of another discrete historical event. Spiritual interpretation cannot be reduced to a chronological displacement of the past to the future, or vice versa.

What I find interesting in Joachim's teachings is the idea that salvation history is still in progress; in fact, we can speak of prophecies of the future only because salvation history remains unfulfilled. But for the same reason, prophecy cannot claim, without contradicting itself, to be realistically literal. For Joachim, the conviction that we live in the age of spirit in which the Bible can no longer be interpreted literally provides the only legitimation—apart from Jesus—of the prophetic interpretation of Scripture. This phenomenon, however, excludes literalism.

The three ages that make up Joachim's scheme of history are relatively known. They are modeled on the three persons of the Trinity:

> Three are the stages of the world indicated by the sacred texts. The first is the stage in which we have lived under the law; the second is that in which we live under grace; the third is one in which we shall live in a more perfect state of grace. . . . The first passed in slavery; the second is characterized

by filial slavery; the third will unfold in the name
of freedom. The first is marked by awe, the second
by faith, the third by charity. . . . The first period
regards the slaves; the second regards the sons; the
third regards the friends. . . . The first stage is as-
cribed to the Father, who is the author of all things;
the second to the Son, who has been esteemed
worthy to share our mud; the third to the Holy
Spirit, of which the apostle says, "Where the spirit
of the Lord is, there is freedom."

Moreover: "As the letter of the Old Testament appears
to belong to the Father for its symbolism, and the letter of
the New Testament to the Son, so the spiritual intelligence
generated by both belongs to the Holy Spirit."[2]

For Joachim, we are clearly not yet in the third stage,
that is, the age of spirit; but he prophesies it as imminent
on the basis of figural correspondences with the events narrated in the Bible. The birth of Benedectine monasticism
plays a determining role in these correspondences (which
are too complex to be discussed here). Indeed, the third
stage supposedly begins with the "time of Saint Benedict";
the order of the monks (after the order of the married and
that of the preachers, corresponding respectively to the
first and the second stage or age) "to which the great final
period has been assigned belongs to the Holy Spirit" (*Expositio* f. 5 b–c). The monastic character of the third period
is grounded on another aspect of the threefold division,
according to which the first period is "distinguished by calamity, the second by action, and the third by contemplation" (*Concordia* 5:112 b–c).

The third age, therefore, is merely announced. Joachim's prophecy remains only a prophecy, namely a reading
of the "signs of the times" that occur within the historical
process. Yet he is able to read these signs because he is
already, at least in part, living in the age whose imminence

he glimpses. This is not an unusual mode of reasoning in the history of religion: it is because salvation has already taken place that we are called to save ourselves. This, however, shows that salvation history is still in progress. If this scheme holds for all the religious announcements of salvation, its Christian form has the more radical implication because it concerns the content of the message and the mode in which the announcement is received by the faithful. The configuration of the history of creation and redemption as the articulation of the three ages "belonging" to the three persons of the Trinity introduces historical rhythm into the divine life, which constitutes the "content" of revelation.

So far, the meaning of Joachim's teachings for our discussion seems to lie in the "discovery" that historicity is constitutive of revelation. This historicity, in my view, corresponds to the "event" character of Being discovered by postmetaphysical philosophy. It is useless to stress, once again, that for philosophy this "discovery" has the same character of Joachim's prophecy of the third age. The end of metaphysics is an event that announces itself and demands to be recognized, promoted, and realized, or at least to be explicitly clarified as the guideline for our choices. The signs of the approaching third age, which today we call the end of metaphysics, are obviously not the same ones observed by Joachim. However, Joachim's text can still be our guide because of the general meaning of the age of spirit, which stresses not the letter but the spirit of revelation; no longer servants but friends; no longer awe or faith but charity; and perhaps also not action but contemplation. We could dare to think of the long process of secularization that separates us from the historical epoch of the abbot from Calabria as the realization of the conditions that are bringing us closer to the advent of the third age. We also cannot honestly say this age has been fulfilled. Perhaps, given its "spiritual" character, the third age cannot be really conceived of as an actual fulfillment; however, this clearly raises significant dogmatic problems. The spirit breathes wherever it wants; its kingdom is one of freedom; and therefore one cannot establish definitive limits to it without reducing the spirit to the letter. However, this does not seem to challenge the kernel of Joachim's teaching, namely the idea that salvation takes place at a specific time—which is an intrinsically historical matter—and the idea that this history is still in progress, like the divine life that unfolds in the three persons of the Trinity.

The *Wirkung*, the reception of Joachim of Fiore's doctrines, constitutes this kernel throughout the history of European thought. De Lubac tells this history in a book[3] whose importance is undeniable, although he is too constantly preoccupied with demonstrating the thesis, from the perspective of orthodox Catholicism, that the most radical aspects of Joachim's thought are untenable. To counter De Lubac's thesis, one could refer to the reading of Joachim proposed by Ernesto Buonaiuti, the great inspiration of Catholic modernism condemned by Pope Pius X at the beginning of the twentieth century. Many European thinkers, philosophers, and poets have been fascinated by Joachim's spiritual heritage, particularly by his idea of the essentially historical character of salvation, insofar as it is still in progress and involves the history of the world; therefore, it does not concern only the individual decision to assume the heritage of faith, taken once and for all. Among the "spiritual" posterity of Joachim, analysts like De Lubac, Novalis, Schleiermacher, and Schelling, are the thinkers who seem more in accord with the argument I am developing in this chapter. I am thinking not only of Schelling's *Philosophy of Mythology* (which I cannot discuss in depth) but also of his *Aeltestes Systemprogramm des Deutschen Idealismus*, initially attributed to Hegel but actually created by Hegel, Schelling, and Hölderlin when they collaborated in Tuebingen. The program announces with a prophetic tone (let us acknowledge) the advent of the kingdom of freedom that will be realized only on the basis of a "sensible religion," understood as the "monotheism of the heart, the polytheism of the imagination and of art," and the "mythology of reason." A more detailed analysis of this fragment could show the close proximity of this prophetic tone to Joachim. The program certainly takes up and emphasizes the idea of the spiritual interpretation of Scripture, as it speaks of "overturning all superstition, and persecution of the clergy" and predicts that the "blind awe of the people toward the wise and its priests" shall be no more. Although Joachim did not go that far, it is clear that after the demise of the age of the letter of Scripture and the realization of the kingdom of freedom and charity, the interpretation of sacred texts will no longer be the exclusive heritage of a priestly authority. Perhaps the aesthetic feature of the kingdom of freedom, appearing in the program, is closer to Joachim's third stage insofar as it is an age of contemplation. Schelling writes: "Poetry will reach a superior dignity, it will become in the end what it was in the beginning—the teacher of humanity." These points are even more explicitly made in Novalis's essay "Christendom or Europe," which was wrongly received, because of his radical Catholicism, as a "reactionary" text. The choice for Catholicism against Protestantism echoes Joachim's tone to the extent that it is a choice against the strict literalism of the Bible. Luther introduced philology in the matter of faith through the principle of *sola Scriptura*, "whose wearing influence has been irresistible since then."[4] "Nothing destroyed religious feeling like the letter"; when, after Luther, "the absolute popularity of the Bible was asserted . . . the inadequate content, the rough, abstract sketch of religion in these books was all the more noticeably oppressive, and made it infinitely difficult for the Holy Spirit to bring about true vivification, penetration, and revelation" (Ibid.). Novalis believes that Romantic and Idealist Germany are the precursors of a new religion, where "an infinite amount of intellectual spirit is being developed" (147), the announcement of "a great time of reconciliation, a savior who like a true genius will be at home among men, who can only be believed in and is not seen, and who is visible to the faithful in countless forms, consumed as bread and wine, embraced like a beloved woman, breathed as air, heard like word and song, and with heavenly delight, amid the pangs of love, taken up in the form of death into the innermost part of the body whose turbulence ceases at last" (148).

We are—perhaps luckily—no longer used to this visionary style. Rather, we tend to be suspicious of it because of its impact on German culture, the same culture that in the twentieth century has given birth to many political monsters. But the spirit breathes where it wants, and the Romantic dream of a new religion remains, albeit partially, our dream. Such a religion, as Novalis tells us at the end of the essay, must be founded on the ruins of the papacy and of sectarian Protestantism "and again form as a visible church without regard to national borders, one which will take up in its bosom all those souls who thirst for the supernatural, and gladly become the mediator between the old world and the new" (Ibid. 148). Joachim's heritage is even more visible and explicit in Schleiermacher's *Speeches on Religion*, in such theses as that the Bible should not be interpreted literally, because each religious spirit should be able to write one of its own. The *Speeches* belongs to the same epoch as Novalis's essay, to the same cultural milieu, that of the *Atheneum*, the journal of the Schlegel brothers.

Is it possible that Joachim's presence within the modern European tradition—of which I have given just a few examples—might be close to the events characteristic of modernity that I have treated under the general title of secularization? I am trying to clarify and verify (I am not sure whether in this context one may speak of a proper proof, or of falsification) the hypothesis that the secularization of modern thought and society embraces the meaning of the end of metaphysics and the "discovery" of Being as event and destiny of weakening. Today, these are the signs of the age of spirit that could be compared to the central role played by Benedictine monasticism in Joachim's scheme.

If we briefly come back to Novalis's conclusion in the essay mentioned above, we see that there is a political or cosmopolitical modulation. Novalis's hope for a new Church is fostered by the analysis of a series of historical events: the fall of the papacy brought about by the French Revolution (Novalis wrote the essay in 1799, when Rome had been occupied by the troops of Napoleon since 1798, sending Pius VI into exile to Valencia); and the crisis of the Protestant confessions, which were closed in their own sectarianism. Above all, Novalis had the impression that "the other continents are awaiting Europe's reconciliation and resurrection so that they might follow and become citizens of the Kingdom of heaven" (Ibid. 151).

Perhaps we no longer face the crisis of the papacy or of the Protestant confessions. However, the ecumenical question seems as urgent as ever, not only as a theoretical problem of the Christian West's relationship with other religions and with the societies reflected in them. What upsets, but at the same time makes concretely promising, the present world epoch is precisely religious and cultural pluralism. It would not be too daring to say that today the ecumenical feeling expressed in Novalis's essay is driven by more concrete motives. It has shifted from the order of the dream and of individual poetic intuition to the everyday order of international politics. The determining factors that have brought about this transformation are largely socioeconomic; they depend on the outcome of unification and rationalization that technology has brought about in the lived world—the *ecumene*. The meaning of secularization illustrated here refers clearly to Max Weber's description of modernity as the epoch of the capitalist rationalization of the world, grounded on a specific "application" of the Protestant ethic, and more generally of Judeo-Christian monotheism. To understand modernity as secularization, namely as the inner and "logical" development of the Judeo-Christian revelation, and to grasp the dissolution of metaphysics as the manifestation of Being as event, as its philosophical outcome, means to read the signs of the times, in the spirit of Joachim of Fiore and of his spiritual disciples such as Novalis, Schelling, and Schleiermacher.

If, in light of Joachim's teachings, we interpret the death of the God who is killed by the faithful as the secularization upon which modernity has construed itself, then it acquires a meaning that takes up and completes, albeit transforms deeply, the way in which much of contemporary Christian theology speaks of secularization and of the death of God as events linked to the renewal of religion. In general, when it does not stigmatize secularization as an abandonment of the sacred or as a widespread sinful condition, theology recovers secularization only as the manifestation of the radical difference of God and earthly reality. This is the atmosphere of Karl Barth's theology, though it is not always explicitly made in the doctrines: he understands the secularization of modern man as the paradoxical affirmation that God radically transcends any worldly realization. The secularized world is correlative to the wholly other. The same idea appears in Dietrich Bonhoeffer—in "religionless Christianity"—who dismisses the concept of God as a stopgap, namely the idea that God's truth might be proved by emphasizing the inexorable insufficiency of man. To be sure, Bonhoeffer is closer than Barth to the "positive" concept of secularization, at least insofar as he explicitly dismisses a view of secularization as a paradox that reveals God's transcendence. (This would be the metaphysical God, the stopgap and the supplement of human and worldly reality, which remains totally closed in the horizon of finitude and sin.) However, neither Bonhoeffer nor—I suspect—other theologians of the death of God such as Cox, Altizer, Hamilton, and Van Buren has articulated an explicit theory of secularization and of the death of God as the positive affirmation of divinity based on the idea of incarnation. The presence of Nietzsche's idea of the death of God in contemporary theology appears in doctrines that assume consciously the attitude of paradox. To be sure, I do not exclude the possibility that there might be exceptions (which would require a more detailed analysis). Contemporary thought emphasizes the disappearance of the sacred from the world precisely by affirming transcendence as the total "alterity" of the biblical God.

In a certain sense, the God who at the end of the secularization process is recovered as wholly other is the God of the Old Testament (let me say this without any anti-Semitic implication), and not the God incarnate in Jesus Christ, of the New Testament revelation, and even less the God understood as spirit in the third age prophesied by Joachim of Fiore. The reference to Joachim clearly shows the radical difference between the position I am illustrating here and the one more common in contemporary culture, which understands the recovery of religion only as openness to the wholly other. I am thinking of the widespread influence of Emmanuel Lévinas and of Derrida's deconstruction. In Joachim's terms, these positions go back to a theology of the first age, ignoring incarnation and consequently conceiving secularization as the fall in which God's transcendence as the wholly other can be revealed through a dialectical reversal. God's divinity would then consist in his radical alterity (for Derrida, the openness to the divine seems to have this meaning only: to say "*Viens*" to someone of whom we know absolutely nothing). The preference for Joachim against the theologies of the wholly other is not justified merely by the decision to remain faithful to the Christian tradition, as the historical tradition to which we belong. This tradition—which addresses, appeals, commits, and binds us—comprises the Jewish heritage as well. It is only in the hardening of dogmatic systems and church disciplines that the two souls of our tradition—Judaism and Christianity—are separated from and juxtaposed to each other. The philosophical reasons, too, that lead us to recover religion—summed up as the manifestation of Being as the destiny of weakening at the end of metaphysics—oblige us to be suspicious of an excessive emphasis on the transcendence of God, as mystery, radical alterity, and paradox. Only the "leap" of faith, understood as the acceptance of absurdity, could correspond to that concept of God. In other words, God as the wholly other of which much of contemporary religious philosophy speaks is not the incarnate Christian God. It is the same old God of metaphysics, conceived of as the ultimate inaccessible ground of religion (to the point of appearing absurd) and warranted by his eminent objectivity, stability, and definitiveness—all traits belonging to the Platonic *ontos on*. If we were to follow contemporary theologies inspired by Barth and Bonhoeffer, conceiving of secularization as the locus where God is revealed in his radical transcendence, we would have to understand this process not so much as a leap or as an overturning, but as the fulfillment of the history of salvation, which is directed from the outset by the death of God as the dissolution of the sacred—the event Saint Paul calls *kenosis*. My interpretation of secularization is clearly inspired not only by Joachim of Fiore and Heidegger's ontology but also by René Girard's religious anthropology. In my view, Girard has persuasively demonstrated—for example, in *Violence and the Sacred*—that if a "divine" truth is given in Christianity, it is an unmasking of the violence that has given birth to the sacred of natural religion, that is, the sacred that is characteristic of the metaphysical God. God as the wholly other, toward which much contemporary philosophy inclines, retains too many features of the "violent" God of natural religions. Transcendence, understood as inaccessibility to reason, paradox, and mystery, belongs to the "capricious God" of stupid and ferocious brutes who—according to Vico—worshipped and feared him in the *ingens sylva* because of thunder and other natural catastrophes to which they were continually exposed. By contrast, the God of Joachim's age of spirit is not revealed in the mirror and enigma of these kinds of experiences. To be sure, Christ legitimated, through the event of incarnation, the many natural ciphers of the divine. However, for us these ciphers are valid only because they are the modes in which God descends from the heavens of transcendence, where primitive mentality had placed him, thus fulfilling the transition announced by the gospels, after which we shall be no longer called servants or (for Joachim) children, but friends.

3

~

God the Ornament

WHAT ARE THE consequences of the fact that philosophy has recovered its provenance from the Judeo-Christian tradition, interpreted in light of the ontology of the event rather than of a metaphysical conception of Being? In the two preceding chapters, I have tried to establish, or at least to suggest, that on the basis of these two premises it is possible to construe an image of postmodern religious experience. I do not renounce using the word *postmodern*, because I am convinced that the history of salvation announced by the Bible realizes itself in world historical events—in this I remain faithful to Joachim's teaching. But these events cannot merely signify the trial man has to undergo to gain eternal life or a condition of exile from which he must escape. My argument is that the history of salvation takes place through the events of modernity, and possibly of its crisis—since postmodern theories speak of the end of modernity and of the concept of history as unilinear progress. However, this end transforms into a paradoxical thesis the very idea of a postmodern religious experience, which goes back to Joachim of Fiore and to his theological "progressivism."

Contemporary thought seems to find no place for this progressive conception of history. Karl Löwith, who illustrates the modern philosophy of history (up to Comte, Hegel, and Marx) as the secularizing interpretation of the Judeo-Christian idea of salvation, observes that this interpretation went into its deepest crisis with Nietzsche and his announcement of the eternal return. The reasons for this crisis, according to Löwith, are the same ones leveled by Kierkegaard at Hegel in the middle of the nineteenth century. Other reasons are associated with the explosion of the inner contradiction of historicism illustrated by Nietzsche in "The Uses and Abuses of History." We might also add that the widespread dismissal of historicism has to do more with the reasons given by Karl Popper, namely with the suspicion that faith in history as progress toward a condition of perfection might lead inescapably toward the political outcome of totalitarianism. This suspicion resounds in the negative character usually attributed to the word *millenarianism*, which is perhaps wrongly attached to the name of Joachim of Fiore. If salvation, paradise, and eternal perfection are conceived of as outcomes of the historical process realizable in this world, it is almost fated that a politics inspired by these beliefs would plan to establish by any means the perfect order, thus generating repressive regimes. If this were the case, then Hitler and communism would be placed along the trajectory of Joachim of Fiore's spiritual posterity, as in De Lubac's work mentioned above.

The idea of the divine as wholly other, which has inspired many religious philosophies in the second half of the twentieth century, has become very popular at a time of disillusionment with the revolutionary millenarianisms that have stained with bloodshed our most recent history. Postmodern theories are also the effects of this disillusionment: the catastrophic outcome of millenarian revolutions has undermined the "metanarratives" (Lyotard's term) that inspired them. But the end of the metanarratives that grounded modernity is not only the consequence of this catastrophe. These metanarratives have become unacceptable also because Eurocentrism has been undermined, like the historicism (i.e., positivism, idealism, Marxism) that inspired revolutionary millenarianism, in political practice. It would seem, then, that Joachim's metanarrative has becomes untenable as well. Thus, the only way of encountering religion at the end of historicist modernity would be that of Karl Barth and Emmanuel Lévinas, who speak of the divine as the "wholly other." I have already shown that, for philosophical reasons, this position is untenable, because it falls back on the metaphysics of Being as stable and eternal structure, given once and for all, which is inaccessible to rational discourse and therefore even more strictly "objective." Indeed, God could be conceived of as the wholly other, who in absolute transcendence overwhelms thought, only in these metaphysical terms. From the perspective of our Judeo-Christian heritage, the theologies of the wholly other do not seem to take too seriously the dogma of incarnation, even when they declare themselves to be Christian. By contrast, Joachim's theology of history is based on this dogma.

As I have argued elsewhere, if we interpret the end of modernity outside of objectivistic metaphysics, we may construe postmodern religious experience in light of Joachim's teachings. The way out of modernity cannot be found by retrieving the concept of Being as stable and eternal—suprahistorical structure—but rather by thinking, more radically, of Being as event. Being gives itself as an announcement or "sending," as Heidegger says, that comes from the tradition of which postmodern thought is the heir. There are good reasons to think that such a sending belongs to the history of salvation developed by Joachim of Fiore, insofar as it retains all the features of what Joachim called the beginning of the age of spirit.

Why call it "the age of spirit"? Joachim was led to do so by the demand for a reformation in the Church of his time, which he wanted to be less involved in earthly quarrels. To pave the way for salvation, the Church would have to constitute "one sheepfold under only one shepherd," by converting all nations and above all the Jews to Christianity. For Joachim, the reformation of the Church hinged on a new spiritual interpretation of Scripture. It was "spiritual" in the sense that it was oriented toward the inner conversion of the human being and toward contemplation, and less involved in power struggles. Joachim, then, reread the Bible in light of the demand for moral and religious renewal in the Church of his time.

However, we have rediscovered Joachim's teaching by starting from the thesis of the end of metaphysics, that is, the idea that Being announces itself as event and destiny of weakening. Philosophy, or at least a good part of it, has not autonomously "discovered" the end of metaphysics. If the observations I have made in the preceding chapters are true—i.e., that philosophy, today, conceives of Being as event and as destiny of weakening—there is every indication that the message of the Judeo-Christian heritage is still alive in philosophy. What happens to philosophy with the end of metaphysics also belongs to the history of salvation construed by Joachim as the moment of the "third age." I have repeatedly said that I do not intend to follow Joachim of Fiore in his too literal, insufficiently "spiritual" effort to forecast future events on the basis of complex symbolic deciphering of scriptural texts. What seems still valid in his teaching, from the perspective of a postmetaphysical philosophy, is the idea that the history of salvation occurs today as the spiritualization of Christianity. What follows is an attempt, on the one hand, to clarify the relationship between spiritualization and weakening, and on the other hand, to show that in contemporary culture there are visible signs of a transformation that can be interpreted in this light.

These two steps cannot be taken in strict sequence. I have already alluded to the secularization characteristic of the modern world, in order to suggest that the weakening of Being of which postmetaphysical thought speaks is a spiritualization of the meaning of Scripture. If we look at the fundamental text for a description of modernity as secularization, namely Max Weber's *The Protestant Ethic and the Spirit of Capitalism*, we see that capitalism's relationship to Christian ethics is one of interpretive application rather than abandonment or polemical opposition. According to Weber, modern capitalism can be understood only as the outcome of the ethical principles of Protestantism. This is the sense in which I employ the term *secularization*: it is an interpretive application of the biblical message that situates it beyond the strictly sacramental, sacral, or ecclesiastical realm. Whoever argues that this gesture betrays the biblical message obviously defends the literal interpretation of Christian doctrine, which, therefore, can be legitimately opposed by the idea of secularization as "spiritual" interpretation. Weber's model may well be extended to the whole relationship of modernity with the Bible, which, after all, has explicitly been the most eminent textbook for all Western interpretations of the world, from the perspective of politics to that of family life, up to the natural sciences (as, for example, in the case of Galileo's dispute over heliocentrism or in the debates about evolution). In the wake of the emancipatory struggles of modern reason, the Bible has played a less central role. However, the opposition between modern "enlightened" reason and religious faith seems to be nowadays a matter of the past, because awareness of "the dialectic of the Enlightenment" has radically limited the claim to dismiss religious belief on the basis of purely rational explanations of the world.

Christianity's encounters with other religions, which have freed themselves from the stigma of barbarism and primitivism that colonial missionaries had attributed to them, have radically reduced the claims of the Christian churches (most of all the Catholic Church) to be the repository of the sole true religion. In this atmosphere, which is dominant in our society, it is no longer possible to separate secular history from sacred history. Modernity seems to occur within the history of salvation—not only because capitalism stems from the Protestant ethic (and even before then, from the scientific vision of the world made possible by biblical monotheism) but for other constitutive reasons as well. It would be difficult to conceive of the democratic evolution of modern political forms apart from the Christian concept of the brotherhood of men as children of the One God: the rejection of war, inscribed in the charter of the United Nations, is at least in principle an effect of the deep influence of Christian or religious ideas. The distinction between the public and the private sphere of existence, too, has to do with religious experience, namely with the relationship between religion and mundane life.

The difficulties that have obstructed the recognition of the proximity or identity of secular history with sacred history may be easily traced back to the persistent prevalence of the "literal" interpretation of Scripture. A lay spirit might immediately reply to this argument that the Christian churches, above all the Catholic Church, have contested the accomplishments of modernity mentioned above, starting with the heliocentric hypothesis, up to the Democratic and Republican Constitutions. However, the well-known example of Galileo's condemnation shows that the Church's attitude was inspired by the literal—and therefore authoritarian—interpretation of the biblical text. When the Church nowadays condemns secularization in both individual and social life as abandonment and betrayal, it still appeals to the literal interpretation of Scripture. In certain cases, this is so obvious as to appear in all its absurdity: consider the interdiction of women's ordination, which is justified only by the fact that Jesus chose men as his apostles. Examples like this, which for good reasons are central to debates in many Catholic circles, show that literalism is based on specific links with a historically determined culture falsely assumed to be "nature." What did lead Jesus to choose men as apostles, and still leads to the interdiction of women's ordination in the Catholic Church, is women's social condition of inferiority. At the time of Christ this inferiority was widespread and taken for granted. Today it is just a vestige of the past that is assumed by the Catholic Church to be an eternal norm of nature consecrated by the actual choices of Jesus.

My argument is that our epoch must be treated as the age of the spiritual interpretation of the biblical message. The active presence of the Christian heritage is recognizable only if the literal, and authoritarian, interpretation of the Bible is abandoned. Let me insist on the example of women's ordination, because it is emblematic of our situation: there is no doubt that it is more Christian, for women, to desire to accede than to forgo the priesthood. This inclusion should be interpreted as the positive phenomenon of the extension of the priestly vocation. But the Catholic Church does not conceive of the priesthood in this way, because it is incapable of freeing itself from the letter, that is, from the history of the first apostles' appointment. Analogously, if literalism no longer holds sway in the reading of Scripture, we will be able to recognize the genuine history of salvation in many aspects of the modern world and of our actuality, which instead appear to a rigorously "orthodox" mentality to be abandonment of and breaking from religion. From this perspective, we should examine the spread of marginal, heterodox, and syncretistic religions in various parts of the late Western world. The official churches generally tend to condemn these religious phenomena as aberrant or even as fraud, whereas perhaps they should be treated with more tolerance and more openness. In other words, once examined from the perspective of a more flexible interpretation of the Bible, most of the nonreligiousness in lay society and in marginal or spurious religiosity appears to have different aspects and values.

One might ask whether there are any limits to the acceptance of secularization. Is there any distinction between legitimate and aberrant interpretations of the Christian message? The criterion indicated by the Christian tradition, beginning with Saint Augustine, is "*ama et fac quod vis.*" Charity is the only limit to the spiritualization of the biblical message; the same principle characterizes Joachim's third epoch of the history of salvation. It is not at all a generic or vague principle. Consider, again, the moral preaching of the Catholic Church: a sexual ethics that defines love as not confined to traditional family structures and not governed by the principle of reproduction does not clash with the commandment of charity. The ecclesiastical teaching, however, continues to oppose to charity a discipline that is entirely grounded on specific biblical texts (for example, the destruction of Sodom and Gomorrah) and on a philosophically outdated metaphysics of "nature," which amounts more or less to the Aristotelian doctrine of the "natural places."

The spiritual reading of the biblical text, and more generally of the Christian dogma, is needed to recognize the pervasive religious essence of many aspects of secularized society and to enable the ecumenical dialogue of the Christian churches among themselves and with other religions. The recognition at the closure of colonialism that other cultures have equal rights, which was accomplished theoretically through the dissolution of Eurocentric metanarratives, demands that Christians abandon their missionary attitude, that is, their claim to bring the sole truth to the pagan world. The recognition of other religions' truth, which begins to happen for many Christian theologians (for example, I have in mind uncomfortable figures such as Hans Küng) requires an intense attempt at a spiritual reading of the Bible and of much dogma of the ecclesiastical tradition, to the point of disclosing the kernel of revelation, charity. The price to be paid for all this is a weakening of all claims to the literal validity of biblical texts and to the peremptoriness of the churches' dogmatic teaching.

However, here we are not concerned with a new reading of sacred history, namely with the destiny of Christianity and of the Christian churches. From our perspective, sacred and secular history are, at least in principle, no longer distinguishable. This is the first meaning of the family resemblance we have recognized between postmetaphysical philosophy and the Western religious tradition. The spiritualization I am illustrating (employing freely Joachim's term) is not exclusively linked to the problem of reading the biblical texts. It occurs in all the spheres of life as the postmodern outcome of modernization. Just as the spiritualization of the biblical text's meaning imposed itself upon the churches through the problem of meeting other religions, so the spiritualization of the sense of reality itself is brought about by the general effects of cultural, political, and social pluralism characteristic of our postmodern world. One of the most famous works of Paul Ricoeur is entitled *The Conflict of Interpretations*. This title, above and beyond Ricoeur's intention, can be useful for disclosing the essence of the postmodern world. The most radical version of hermeneutic philosophy, to which Ricoeur refers in this book, can be summed up with Nietzsche's statement: "There are no facts, only interpretations." Since we are aware—after Nietzsche and Heidegger—that every relation to the world is "mediated" (the epistemologists would say "theory laden") by cultural schemes, that is, by historical paradigms that are the true *a priori* of all knowledge, we can no longer deceive ourselves (or worse, let ourselves be deceived) into thinking that what we say and what is said to us is an objective description of a reality that is given out there. The idea of a destiny of weakening somehow inscribed in the history of Being claims to interpret this specific situation: a reality understood not as the stable presence of things clearly defined in themselves that the mind can mirror objectively but as the play of interpretation is in many senses a diminished reality. If, as many contemporary philosophical positions argue, we understand truth not as the correspondence of the mind with the thing (the faithful description of a state of affairs) but instead as plausibility and persuasiveness that is linked to a set of premises (or to a community of competent speakers), we meet a phenomenon of weakening again. Furthermore, we could take the central role that the notion of consensus has assumed in contemporary philosophy, the very definition of truth, as an indication that charity has replaced the traditional conception of what truth means (see for example Davidson's use of the term *charity*).[1] This mode of characterizing postmodernity sees spiritualization as the meaning of the weakening of Being's strong structures due to the triumph of technology in our world. Technology, which in the beginning was just an engine technology, developed first a mechanical ability that lightened reality, thereby making manual labor less burdensome; today, computer technologies increasingly reduce reality to the play of interpretation. It would be too much to attempt to show that the first meaning of spiritualization—the more appropriately theological meaning realized in the spiritual reading of the Bible and of Christian dogma—is bound up with this more general process of reduction of the sense of reality. This link is slightly visible in the question of ecumenism, the relationship with other religions, which has to do with a more flexible reading of the sacred text that imposes itself on the churches precisely in the world of the communi-

cation technologies characterized by the conflict of interpretation.

When facing the task of reducing the weight of the
biblical letter and dogma to understand the truth of other
religions, Christian thought discovers that charity is the
only thing that really matters. Indeed, charity is the only
limit and criterion of the spiritual interpretation of Scripture. Analogously, if in the epoch of the end of metaphysics
philosophical thought understands the history of Being as
a destiny of weakening (i.e., in which reality is "reduced"
to the conflict or play of interpretation), it takes this destiny
as the only guiding thread to which it can refer to judge
the plausibility of interpretation and to decide moral options. After Nietzsche, Freud, Marx, and Heidegger, there
is no ultimate and indubitable metaphysical foundation in
which we might put our trust; nor is the voice of Kantian
reason, which would speak in all men in the same manner,
given. Cultural anthropology has made us sensitive to the
irreducible pluralism of cultures. To interpret the world
and evaluate alternative ethics, we can only refer to the
appeal that comes from the history in which we are always
already involved. To be sure, it is an appeal that does not
speak univocally but rather involves us as interpreters.
True, the decision to interpret our provenance as moving
toward weakening is already a way of explicitly assuming
the Judeo-Christian heritage that we carry within us. This
is also an interpretation, not a fact. Even the assumption
of the heritage is an interpretation. Then what? We are
ready to abandon this interpretation only if someone will
propose a better one. But we will not abandon it on the
basis of the "realistic" argument that it is "only" an interpretation.

I cannot draw in detail the ethical consequences of
reading the history of Being as weakening. These are not
limited to grounding the choice for tolerance. Rather, they
foster an active commitment to diminish violence in all its

forms, which therefore appears synonymous with what religious language calls "charity," thus testifying not only to an analogy but also to a real family resemblance between postmetaphysical philosophy and the Christian tradition (from which it originates).

However, the acknowledgement of a family resemblance in the end clashes with questions of ultimacy, that is, eschatology. The history of salvation of which we have spoken with regard to Joachim is the history *of salvation*. Let me make a few remarks on the mysterious meaning of this chapter's title, "God the Ornament." It is an expression that came to my mind while reading the Book of Revelation (as is well known, this text is central to Joachim, since he dedicated to it one of his most important works) years ago. What struck me in those pages was the overabundance of forms, lights, and colors, as if the revelation (according to the etymology of *apokalypsis*) of salvation at the end of time was not so much a destructive catastrophe as a transfer of things on the plane of phantasmagoria, a dissolution of the real into "secondary" qualities bound with the perception of the senses. We should not forget that the word *spirit* (*pneuma*) means etymologically breath, wind, blowing, something volatile, fleeting, of which thought lost the memory when it began conceiving of spirit as the evident and indubitable foundation of self-consciousness, up to Hegel's "absolute spirit." I cannot avoid recalling here another idea that comes often to mind when I think about *What Computers Still Cannot Do* (which is the title of a famous book by Hubert Dreyfus). It seems to me, whether rightly or wrongly, that what computers cannot do is precisely perceive secondary qualities, or at least the most secondary among them: a certain perfume, an atmosphere, the threatening air that in certain circumstances warns us that we have to be on the alert, even though there is nothing "concrete" that might be grasped by a computer or a robot.

The weakening of Being toward which, in my hypothesis, the history of our civilization is directed can be described as a history of salvation insofar as it prepares for the transfer of reality on the plane of secondary qualities, of the spiritual, and of the ornamental; we might even add, the virtual. We might then draw closer to the spiritual—not literal—meaning of *kenosis* of the divine *Verbum*. The Logos did not humiliate himself just so that we might understand his teaching, and then go back to the heavens to prepare for us an eternal life that can be reached only in another world. Despite his authentic faithfulness to the Church of his epoch, Joachim does not say much about the transition from the third epoch to salvation occurring in another world. True, even if he does not deny the immortality of the soul, eternal life appears to him only as the epoch of spirit. This epoch does not consist in the mere preparation for something else. World history is not exclusively a time of trial that will end with the destruction of the natural order and the transition to the supranatural realm.

Although philosophy does not have any means of deciding the question of immortality, it is at least clear that, after the end of metaphysics, philosophy cannot support (provide the support Thomas Aquinas found in Aristotle) arguments about nature and supranature. The philosopher, like any other religious man, can only hope that life will not end with the death of the body. It is not an unreasonable hope to the extent that there are no "metaphysically" certain limits of nature (which, for some, preclude the survival of the individual soul). Whether salvation is realized in this world or beyond death, the salvation addressed by the Judeo-Christian revelation, understood spiritually in light of Joachim's teaching and of the end of metaphysics, appears as the lightening and weakening of the "heavy" structures in which Being has manifested itself throughout human civilization. Hence, we retrieve here the dream of Idealism, which is not exclusively Hegel's but also Marx's:

the world becomes truly the dwelling of man (where man can feel at home, *bei sich*) only if man becomes, in multiple senses, spirit: spirit as pneuma, breath, the lightest breath that moves the air around us. (I am thinking of Heidegger's passage on the *Gering*, the marginal.[2]) This spiritualization is not too different from the total disclosure of self-consciousness in Hegel's absolute spirit, or from Marx's unalienated humanity. The idea of spiritualization I have illustrated here emphasizes the aesthetic aspect of these two versions of salvation (Hegel's and Marx's), though not so much, or not only, in the sense of the realization of harmony (which echoes Dewey's idea of fulfillment). The aesthetic here is the term, which reveals a condition in which reality dissolves its strict contours. It is the plane in which reality is no longer distinguishable from fantasy—what we also call the "poetic." Let me remark that Heidegger, in his commentary on Hölderlin, gives a lot of weight to the verses that say: *Voll verdienst, doch—dichterisch wohnet der Mensch auf dieser Erde* (full of merit, yet poetically, man inhabits this earth).

Our civilization, which we have reached through mechanical and computer technology, political democracy, social pluralism, and the availability of goods necessary to ensure survival, offers us the chance to realize the kingdom of spirit, understood as lightening and poeticization of the real. I am saying that it *offers* the chance. I am fully aware that poeticization is at the present moment absolutely imaginary. Even when Joachim spoke of the beginning of the epoch of spirit, he predicted that the struggle to realize it in this world would be hard. Spiritualization, which is today within the realm of technological possibility and of the evolution of ideas, demands to be pursued with a difficult kind of action. The appearance of easiness and moral disengagement, which this thesis might stimulate, has to do with the fact that the salvation—or emancipation—it prefigures has a densely aesthetic and poetic connotation.

This, however, is the only connotation that can fill the otherwise empty *figure* of the end of human history, no matter how it is conceptualized: whether as the *telos* of emancipation, which bestows meaning upon the life of each of us within the unsurpassable earthly limits of birth and death, or as a condition realizable in the eternal life after death. Even in the latter case—as Joachim and (my) philosophy teach—salvation must begin in the here and now, otherwise the story of its development would no longer make sense. Then, the play would be entrusted to a divinity that transcends any capacity for relation that we might possess—of which, therefore, it would be preferable not to speak at all.

If there is salvation somewhere, it has the features of lightening rather than justice. Might this be one of the meanings of the divine mercy and forgiveness running through the Bible? The passage of the gospel in which Jesus promises the apostles that in eternal life they will sit upon the twelve thrones and judge the twelve tribes of Israel should probably not be taken in legal but rather in aesthetic terms. Eternal life is nothing but the "perfect" enjoyment of meanings and spiritual forms generated by the history of humanity, which now constitute the "kingdom" of immortality. To draw closer to that life here and now would mean to realize the conditions in which a more perfect aesthetic enjoyment of meaning can be increasingly given. The establishment of "righteous" historical orders has only this aim.

It would not be scandalous to put Herbert Marcuse's name (in addition to Nietzsche's and Heidegger's, to which I have already referred) next to that of Joachim of Fiore. The idea of weakening that I have described as the guiding thread of a nonmetaphysical ontology that recognizes its family resemblance with the religious tradition of the West calls attention to the fact that today the human being has at his disposal the technological, conceptual, and political possibilities to begin to realize the kingdom of sense. The simultaneity in which the world of generalized communication makes available, at least in principle, "all" that human culture has produced or produces, as in a sort of imaginary museum, orients us toward weakening. If we do not welcome the appeal of aesthetic emancipation offered to us by the new condition of existence, it is because we are still oppressed by the letter—the literalism of the sacred texts (the fetish of fundamentalism of all sorts) and the world's materiality, the unsatisfied needs and injustices in the distribution of goods that are indispensable to life. Although we can only catch a glimpse of this possibility, the epoch of spirit announces itself to us with a specific strength, which is bound up with the postmodern condition. To hear this announcement, if only in theory, is already a way of preparing for its realization.

4

History of Salvation, History of Interpretation

A COMMA DISJOINS the two parts of the title. It is clearly a patch: for lack of a better term, it is an approximate solution. There could have been a colon or a dash; however, it would have not been possible to replace the comma with a *sive*, a "that is." Somehow—and I do not think that it is just a deconstructive chattering—this is the real topic of the following remarks.

The comma is not a neutral joint, as a simple conjunction might have been, bringing near the two terms so as to announce, more simply, an analysis of their relation. The preference for a comma here—or a colon, or a dash—underscores that it is not a question of analyzing two themes, which are anyway defined in their own terms, in order to establish the relations or differences between them. The theme arises properly out of the recognition that it is possible for us today, if not obligatory, to move from one term to the other. One does so by following a type of relation that cannot be easily recognized as a simple identity—*seu*, *sive*, that is—or as a difference between two autonomous thought-contents, which would disclose their proximity or distance. What I mean to suggest with this title is the need to thematize the point of departure where we find ourselves—no matter how problematic that "we" may be—that is to say, the pre-understanding in which we are placed, and of which we become aware when we problematize our pre-understanding. Our point of departure is that the relation between these two terms is closer, and yet more vague or opaque, than would have been suggested by a relationship of identity or by a simple parataxis.[1]

I do not mean to say that the history of salvation is the history of interpretation, or that there are significant relations between the two terms (notions, events) that would be worthy of inquiry with the right kind of research. Rather, I mean to echo a "crossing," the rustle of a slippage from one term to the other, a slippage of which we are all aware. Our pre-understanding of this slippage constitutes our common, historical belonging to the world (epoch, history, culture) of the religions of the Book. If we replaced the comma with an *is*, we would have to make an effort to hear it as a transitive verb: the history of salvation lets be the history of interpretation, or the history of salvation occurs, gives itself, as the history of interpretation.

It seems to me that it is justified to insist on what might appear a marginal question of punctuation. In fact, a more appropriate tone for this discourse is not that of a "scientific" investigation (or only apparently scientific, as it can be in disciplines like philosophy), but that of a meditation seeking to grasp a relationship, which seems to impose itself with a certain undeniability and which is nevertheless a fleeting relationship.

Interpretation—primarily of sacred texts—has always dealt with the issue of salvation in the Judeo-Christian tradition. (Note that there is already a meaningful difference between a discourse on interpretation and salvation, and a discourse on the history of the one or the other. I shall not dwell on this, as it may become clearer later on; yet this

difference resonates and echoes in the title as well as in its
immediate illustrations.) From its beginning, modern hermeneutics has reflected on salvation, as in Schleiermacher,
whose work in its most immediate sense has to do with
preaching and with pastoral explication of sacred texts to
the faithful (*subtilitas intelligendi*, *subtilitas explicandi*, in the
hermeneutical terminology of the time). Salvation requires
understanding the Word of God in Scripture and its cor-
rect application to our condition and situation (*subtilitas
applicandi*). Furthermore, it is necessary to interpret Scripture without contradicting reason, making use of our fac-
ulties to respect thoroughly the Word of God and avoiding
the attribution of aberrant meanings to Scripture (even
Spinoza, after all, is motivated by this essentially pious purpose; however, during the Enlightenment, it was on this
terrain that criticism arose).

In another sense, however, salvation and interpretation
are joint in the Christian tradition, linking Jesus to the
prophets, as heard in New Testament expressions like: "You
heard it was said . . . , but I say. . . ." Here interpretation
is no longer only a tool (of the faithful) for understanding
what God reveals and expects; the event of salvation (Jesus'
coming) is itself, deep down, a hermeneutical occurrence.
But it can be called hermeneutical only to a point: it is true
that Jesus is the living interpretation of the meaning of the
law and the prophets (here another meaning of the Logos
that becomes flesh: the incarnation of the Logos, of meaning, of the Jewish Scriptures), but somehow, he is also its
fulfillment. Thus Jesus seems to be announced as the definitive deciphering of sense—as if after him there were no
longer any space or necessity for interpretation. Yet (it
would suffice to reflect on the interpretations of the so-
called consequent eschatology) although salvation is essentially "fulfilled" in the incarnation, death, and resurrection
of Jesus, it awaits a further fulfillment. Thus the Paraclete,
the Spirit of Truth bestowed upon the faithful at Pentecost,

has been assigned the task of assisting them in this further hermeneutical project. We should not forget that the Spirit (the one who gives life to the text, the true sense of the "letter"), namely the more exquisitely hermeneutical person of the Trinity, is also the one through whom the Son becomes human in the bosom of Mary. The Trinity is a hermeneutical structure *par excellence*, for the Son is the Logos of the Father and the Spirit is their relation, the hypostatizing of their love-understanding. If we follow through these elementary subjects of the Christian teaching in a spirit of loyalty to the catechism, the relationship between interpretation and salvation becomes more complex: it introduces overwhelmingly the feature of history into the main picture. It is more and more difficult to attribute the pure sense of a subjective genitive to "the history of interpretation," according to which interpretation has a history but is basically something that takes place in the immediate relation between reader and sacred text, the latter being posited once and for all with its definitive sense, which the believer must only decipher and apply.

If interpretation continues after the resurrection of Jesus (indeed by virtue of the resurrection, as its continuation and authentication), this means that interpretation and salvation, too, have a history that is not only an accidental occurrence crossing above or near their supposedly stable kernels. Rather, this history affects them deeply, in a sense that can only be explained by emphasizing the "objective" genitive in the two expressions. Salvation takes shape, takes place, gives itself, and constitutes itself through its history, and thus the history of interpretation, too—through a series of connections that can be only with difficulty frozen into a scheme. It is true that the announcement of salvation is given once and for all—in Jesus and the prophets—but it is equally true that, having given itself, it needs interpretations that receive it, actualize it, and enrich it. The history of salvation that continues in the age of the Spirit, after the descent of the Paraclete at Pentecost, is not simply driven by the biological fact of the presence of ever new human generations that must be evangelized. Rather, it is history, just as the Old Testament narrative up to the Messiah's coming was history. This history has a meaning and a direction, and the interpretation of Scripture that takes place in it is its constitutive dimension. It is not only a tale of errors, or conversely of close or literal understanding of meaning given once and for all in Scripture (which would be as inessential in itself as the errors). The history of salvation continues as the history of interpretation in the strong sense in which Jesus himself was the living, incarnate interpretation of Scripture.

But, even assuming that we have given an accurate—albeit cursory—representation of this event, is it not in the end only the business of theologians, of historians of religions? In other words, the interpretation of which we speak in the title, whose history stands in a deep and complex relationship with the history of salvation, seems to be finally only the interpretation of Scriptures. Would it not be better to add this qualification in the title in order to avoid inappropriate generalizations, or confusion and equivocation?

The fact is that it seems difficult to bring the issue to closure within such restricted and precise (disciplinary) boundaries. Is ours a "religion of the Book," which we will leave eventually behind through the irresistible process of secularization? Or, more important, do we belong to a culture or civilization of the Book that still affects us deeply, even when we think, or might think, that we no longer have anything in common with the religion of the Book? Does this culture or civilization of the Book not have any relation—at the same time both vague and deep—with the religion of the Book, so much so that it becomes difficult to confine our "history of interpretation" to the history of the interpretation of Scripture?

Of course, one can rightfully argue that the relationship of modern European civilization with sacred Scripture is only a particular instance of the civilization of the Book, which has deeper and more distant origins. In this civilization of the Book, or of writing (in lower case), interpretation is a general phenomenon that is not based and does not depend on the interpretive model of Scripture. This can be granted. Indeed, the Greeks used Hesiod and Homer as the foundational texts in their education, and conceived of their culture as interpretation of these texts—at least to some extent.

Thus the formation of modern Europe has revolved around not only the interpretation of sacred Scripture but also around the interpretation of the Justinian Code and the reading and rereading of the canon of classic literary texts—a textual *corpus* that is not directly related to the sacred Scripture (although this could be debated, too). But the idea of the productive act of interpretation could not have originated in the interpretation of legal codes or in the interpretation of literary and poetic classics, even though it is obvious—as Gadamer illustrates in *Truth and Method*—that the notion of application makes juridical hermeneutics more sensitive to this idea. By contrast, consider the classicist tradition that runs through the whole history of European art and literature, wherein one can read of an ever-returning negation of the productiveness of interpretation on behalf of a literal loyalty to models (a loyalty that is always conceptualized rigidly even when one becomes nostalgically aware of its impossibility, as in Romanticism).

What I want to suggest is that the idea of the productiveness of interpretation could only originate as an "effect" of the Judeo-Christian (or specifically Christian) concept of the history of revelation and salvation. By the productiveness of interpretation, I mean that interpretation is not only an attempt to grasp the original meaning of the text (for example, the authorial intention) and to reproduce it as literally as possible but also to add something essential to the text (to understand it better than its author, the adage resonating in eighteenth-century hermeneutics). This effect is itself an occurrence of interpretation and salvation—and here we find again one of those vertiginous circles, albeit not vicious ones, that unfold when we speak of hermeneutics: in other words, the fact that the European culture of late modernity "discovered" the productiveness of interpretation or—which is the same—the nonepiphenomenality, instrumentality, or secondariness of the commentary. I take this fact, to the extent that it has taken place, as an effect of the interpretation that this culture has given of the Christian message. It is an inseparable effect, or undoubtedly *the* effect, of the Christian event.

But has such a hermeneutical event—an effect of interpretation as well as a way of construing interpretation—really taken place? As I pointed out at the outset, even the argument that such an event has taken place cannot be submitted as an objective or literal description of a state of affairs, but only as an interpretation of the situation in which we are always already thrown.

I take this hermeneutical event to coincide with the phenomenon that in Heideggerian language is called the end of metaphysics in the world of techno-science. Briefly, let me remark that Heidegger calls modern techno-science the end of metaphysics, because science "consumes" definitively the idea that Being is what is indubitably given as simple presence. The ascertained and indubitable presence of the "thing" becomes explicitly an effect of representation in experimental science and in the universal (at least tendentially, in principle) technological manipulation of the world that it has made possible. In other words, the certainty of the object is a pure effect of the process of verification carried out by the subject. When one reaches this stage by consistently developing the premises already implicit in classical metaphysics, it becomes impossible to identify Being with simple presence.

Although Heidegger did not go very far beyond this simple negation, that is, beyond the recognition of the unfolding of the radical difference between Being and beings, it is easy to see how and why precisely this ontology provides support (in his own work and in that of those who appeal to him) for the broad direction of thought called hermeneutics, which has become a sort of *koine*, a commonplace of contemporary culture. However, one can assign a nonderivative, noninstrumental, or accidental sense to interpretation only through the denial of the identification of Being-true with what is completely and indubitably present.

But is Heidegger's ontology—and the hermeneutics that depends on it—at all connected with the history of Christian revelation? Is this, after all, only a question of hermeneutics unfolding within European culture initially and primarily in relation to the problem of reading and interpreting the sacred Scripture, as can be easily seen by tracing the history of interpretation theory? This fact conceals a larger issue that can be articulated in the following terms: if an ontology of Heidegger's type, which does not want to contradict its own conclusions, "denies" the identity of Being with the objectively present, it cannot announce itself as the description of an "objective structure," that is, present, given, of Being. Rather, it must argue necessarily on the basis of an "interpretation," as a response to a message, a reading of texts, a sending that comes from tradition. (As is well known, terms like *sending* and *tradition* are central to the philosophy of the so-called second Heidegger). Now, it can be argued, even diverging from the Heideggerian texts on this topic—which are very obscure, if not reticent and inconclusive (at least, so it seems to me)—that the sending to which postmetaphysical philos-

ophy, ontology, or hermeneutics corresponds is the tradition of Western Christian civilization.

The thesis thus enunciated seems both too rigid and
too generic. Instead, it should be taken mainly as a project of inquiry, which is still largely unfinished (even in
Heidegger himself). Only if the interpretive and non-
metaphysically descriptive status of ontological hermeneutics is radically acknowledged—a recognition not explicitly
made by Heidegger or by his first and most authoritative
hermeneutical interpreters, such as Gadamer—can it be
both possible and necessary to clarify the link between
postmetaphysical ontology and the Western tradition, that
is, the fact that ontological hermeneutics is nothing but the
theory of Christian modernity.

The basic continuity of Western civilization with the
message of the Judeo-Christian Scriptures is generally acknowledged. Here, however, the issue is radicalizing the
implications of this recognition. First of all—and this can
only be a parenthetical remark—this must be done by ex-
ploring in depth Christianity's constitutive role and positive
constitution in the birth of modern Western civilization.
This is the direction explored by Weber with his analysis
of capitalism and the Protestant ethic, although one must
move far beyond this specific feature. The point is that the
various processes of secularization occurring throughout
modernity need not be seen as a leave-taking from the religious source—as is argued by Hans Blumenberg, for example, and by much historiography inspired by the Enlightenment, and also by Catholicism (the Italian Augusto
Del Noce). Rather, these can be seen as processes of secularization, application, enrichment, and specification of
that source.

One of these "positive" processes of secularization of
the Christian message is precisely what Heidegger calls
the advent of the end of metaphysics in modern techno-
science, and the unfolding of the ontological difference be-

tween Being and particular beings—the same process leading up to the discovery that interpretation is productive. It is not easy—though possible—to show, precisely by retracing the paths explored by Weber, the extent to which the Christian message contributed to the development of modern science, out of which, finally, comes the end of the metaphysics of presence. However, we can easily recall along Weberian lines the significance of monotheism for the development of the scientific vision of the world as well as the conception of the human task of mastering the earth, which God, according to Scripture, assigned to humanity. What can be more easily illustrated is that the outcome of the process—the dissolution of the metaphysics of presence and the reduction of the object to the power of the subject—has come to signify the paving of the way for a sort of global recognition that the truth, including the truth of the hard, experimental sciences, constitutes itself as announcement and interpretation.

The increasingly acute awareness of the historicity of scientific paradigms enables contemporary epistemology to acknowledge that even the natural sciences are connected to the history of interpretation and the history of salvation: there is no truth outside of a horizon disclosed by an announcement, by a word handed over. The transmitted word cannot be set in opposition to the truth of objects that are given as objectively present (the classic distinction between the natural sciences and the sciences of the spirit, between explanation and understanding), since even this self-giving is always made possible by an opening, which is language, and therefore by the word handed over and transmitted—provenance.

Those outlined so far are only the incipient steps on the way toward listening to the sense of the comma linking the two parts of the title. Ontological hermeneutics, which explicitly thematizes the productiveness of interpretation, and the end of the metaphysics of presence as the outcome of modern techno-science spring from the action of the Christian message throughout the history of Western civilization. They are interpretations that "secularize" this message in the constructive, positive sense of the term. It should be added here that *secularization* is not a term in contrast with the essence of the message, but rather is constitutive of it. Jesus' incarnation (the *kenosis*, the self-lowering of God), as an event both salvific and hermeneutical, is already indeed an archetypical occurrence of secularization.

If the relation between the history of salvation and the history of interpretation is understood in this way, will not salvation and interpretation be configured just as processes of drifting, in which there seem to be no limits, no criteria of validity, no risk of defeat, and finally, no space for freedom and responsibility, just as in the relation of productive interpretation with the text? In fact, it is all too obvious that once metaphysics has been liquidated, a good, valid interpretation will no longer be configured absolutely as that which is literally or objectively faithful to the text.

What does a productive interpretation generate? It generates Being, new senses of experience, new ways for the world to announce itself, which are not only other than the ones announced "before." Rather, they join the latter in a sort of *discursus* whose logic (also in the sense of Logos) consists precisely in the continuity. Such a continuity— briefly stated—does not have any objective status; it is reduced (but is it indeed reduction?) to rhetorical persuasion, *ad homines*. But not every secularization is good and positive, and neither is every interpretation valid; it must be valid for a community of interpreters.

With a more explicitly spiritual language, one could say that the only limit of secularization is love, that is, the possibility of communicating with a community of interpreters. It is not paradoxical to assert that the history of modern hermeneutics, in which the Protestant Reforma-

tion has played such an important role, is also a long journey of rediscovery of the Church. It is not without significance for the Church, at least as I intend it here, that this
recognition springs from the end of the metaphysics of
presence and from the advent of ontological hermeneutics.
But this way of conceiving of and experiencing the Church
as a community of reference for the validity and continuity
of the history of interpretation is continuously exposed to
the resurgence of metaphysical temptations, which tend to
fall back on the horizon of presence. For instance, the authoritarianism of the Catholic Church lies in the claim to
return to a text given once and for all, bringing to closure
the process of interpretation not in the name of the continuity of discourse and reception of the community's voice,
but in the name of an overwhelming "foundational truth."
The latter is assumed to be present somewhere (for example, in the dogmatic definition, or at worst—as one
hears more often in the discussions of bioethical issues—
in "nature" and its immutable laws).

Thus the reference to a community as the "criterion"
for the validity of interpretation cannot be set apart from
the recognition that such a criterion is legitimated only by
the dissolution of the metaphysics of presence, and as such
cannot be invoked outside of the horizon of such a dissolution. Ontological hermeneutics replaces the metaphysics
of presence with a concept of Being that is essentially constituted by the feature of dissolution. Being gives itself not
once and for all as a simple presence; rather, it occurs as
announcement and grows into the interpretations that listen and correspond (to Being). Being is also oriented toward spiritualization and lightening, or, which is the same,
toward *kenosis*. It is quite probable that ontological hermeneutics, which is generated from the dissolution of the
metaphysics of presence, is not only a rediscovery of the
Church but also, and mainly, the retrieval of Joachim of
Fiore's dream.

5

~

The West or Christianity

IT IS NOT too difficult to fill with meaning this title, whose intention stimulates curiosity and eventually provokes, because it evokes too many things often in conflict with each other. It is not so much a matter of filling the title with meaning as of emptying it, at least in part, by reducing it to a set of coherent and intelligible terms. The multiple meanings we immediately assign to this linked pair indicate at the very least that we take it as a natural, granted, and unquestionable fact, though we cannot spell out why this is the case, as always happens with preconceptions that are too obvious. To begin with, I ought to clarify that the reference to the essay by Novalis, *Christendom or Europe* (*Christenheit oder Europa*) (1799),[1] is not merely polemical or ironic. Though at the outset that was the sense of the title, when I went back and read the beautiful and intense pages of Novalis's work, I realized that my own relationship to those ideas was much deeper, much more positive, at least in some important aspects, as I hope to show below.

What, then, is the meaning in the title of the equivalence, if not the synonymous identity, of the West and Christianity? Indeed, the "or" immediately excludes another meaning that could be given to the use of the particle, which in part is identical: what we are talking about is a synonymous relation (*sive*) rather than an alternative (*aut aut*) one. It seems to me that this clarification already gives us much to think about. In fact, a large current of opinion in our lay and Catholic world suggests that the "or" be read as an alternative relation, an *aut aut*. Christianity's relationship with the West is an *aut aut*, at least as it is sometimes understood by a kind of neofundamentalist Catholic movement, which has discovered that the West and its way of life are profoundly irreconcilable with the substance of the Christian message—after the end of the Communist threat, which obliged people to stand united against atheistic totalitarianism without looking too closely for acceptable "allies." The West, indeed, is a synonym for consumerism, hedonism, a Babel-like pluralism of cultures, loss of center, and obliviousness to any reference to "natural" law. In espousing this thesis, paradoxically (but not really so), Catholic neofundamentalism agrees with the lay defense of the radical autonomy of modernity with respect to the Christian tradition. One of the most recent and well-known formulations of such a thesis is given by Hans Blumenberg's *The Legitimacy of the Modern Age*.[2]

In his polemic with authors like Karl Löwith, who have—rightly, I think—construed modernity as a "secularizing" drift of the Judeo-Christian heritage (above and beyond the Greek heritage),[3] Blumenberg holds that modernity defines itself on the basis of values that are entirely new with respect to tradition, and that can be summed up as a new disposition of the human being toward the world (a position similar to that of the Enlightenment and of much of nineteenth-century historicism, included Hegel's Phenomenology). This disposition is characterized as the will to organize reality in accordance with a rationality that is entirely independent from any utopia. From this perspective, Copernican man is contrasted with Ptolemaic man: true, Ptolemy placed himself at the center of the universe, but his position was ultimately upheld by the authority of the Creator. Copernican man has rolled away from the center—as Nieztsche writes in a famous fragment—but the center is empty, and there is no authority superior to reason (especially scientific reason), through which man may autonomously make of the world his own home.

There are good reasons to argue that these formulations, which construe the relation of the West (or Europe, or modernity) with Christianity as a polemical alternative, are insufficient and ultimately untenable. The first formulation that comes to mind, which, while superficial, points in the right direction, can be summed up as follows: the radical alternative, as it is conceived of by fundamentalist Catholicism, has a reactionary, or at least a nostalgic and definitively "not realistic," outlet (let us say at the outset that this is not a limitation because values should coincide with factual reality, but rather because it entails more than the risk of remaining an unachievable project)—the exit from modernity by recovering a more authentic, prior condition of morality and religiousness, and so on. Note that the impossibility of the fundamentalist project of "restoration" often paves the way for the most appalling compromises in practice, as we recently witnessed in Italian politics. The thesis concerning the new and autonomous legitimacy of modernity implies, for its part, an excessive dose of confidence in the possibility of the radically new and an overall emphasis on the creativity, originality, and absolute freedom of man: all modern dogmas, or perhaps myths, which belong to the epoch whose origin they are meant to explain, appear less obvious at the moment when many perceive modernity as a completed stage, or at least one whose constitutive values are problematic.

If one tries to go beyond these "superficial" reasons for

the critique of the alternative theses on modernity while still moving in the direction toward which they point, one sees that both versions of the *aut aut* between Christianity and modernity are unsatisfactory or simply untenable, because they believe themselves capable of calling themselves out of history, of their own provenance. This is true not only, as seems obvious, for Blumenberg's thesis, which conceives of modernity as a "beginning" in some absolute sense. It holds also for the fundamentalist Catholic version of the thesis, which reasons also as if modernity did not have precedents and roots in the Judeo-Christian tradition. According to this perspective, the Judeo-Christian tradition is a complete denial of modernity. In turn, this view believes itself capable of judging modernity from the outside while remaining immune to the effects of the latter's decline. In sum: both theses make a "panoramic" claim. While one does not grasp the links between modernity and Christianity, the other does not grasp the fact of its own belonging to both.[4]

We could further develop this discussion. I shall only note here that at the core of hermeneutics is precisely the awareness of this provenance, and belonging, and the critique of any "panoramic" claim with respect to history. This core of hermeneutics is still far from having shown all its fecundity and its implications for theoretical and moral philosophy, and for the very concept of religion.

It is hermeneutics, in the end, that with all its philosophical implications shows the basic insufficiency of the two theses of the *aut aut*, and that directs us instead toward a preference of the secularization thesis—*secularization* understood not as abandonment and alternative but rather as continuation and, ultimately, destiny. Indeed, the thesis of secularization retains all the elements present in the other theses (here too one can see, perhaps, a sign of its validity: it "encompasses" opposing theses), but situates them in a historical and existential framework that is not abstractly rationalist and therefore not panoramic. It is true that modernity can be represented also as a defense of the autonomy of man with respect to the sacred, as the gaze's turn toward earthly reality. From this perspective, it can be represented as a position that separates itself from an earlier religious consciousness. However, these phenomena are not intelligible as radical abandonment nor as absolute novelty, because understanding them in this way would amount to ignoring what in other contexts is called the hermeneutic circle, which we can refer to as belonging and provenance.

What is the meaning, then, and what are the theoretical and eventually "practical" consequences (in the sense of a judgment about historical behavior, political options, moral choices, and so on) of the thesis that the West is secularized Christianity? Let me point out that if what I have said about the validity that must be recognized in the two alternative theses of the *aut aut* is true, then this affirmation means also that the West is secularized Christianity and nothing else. In other words, if we want to talk about the West, Europe, modernity—which, in my argument, are held to be synonymous—as recognizable and clearly defined historical-cultural entities, the only notion we can use is precisely that of the secularization of the Judeo-Christian heritage. At a time when the West can no longer define itself only as an alternative to the evil empire of communist totalitarianism and when it is making an effort to recover autonomously and positively its own physiognomy, it encounters precisely its own Christian origin, in the form of a heritage that is certainly changed and "shifting" but nevertheless constitutes its sole identifying element.

Thus, the thesis concerning the "equivalence" between Christianity and the West means above all that secularization is not a radical abandonment or break, since this would imply the possibility of an absolutely new beginning, of the kind conceptualized by Blumenberg (from the fundamentalist perspective, this would be a "demonic" event). This view, I argue, ignores the hermeneutic circularity into which every existence is *de facto* thrown. However, from this immediately follows that to speak of secularization cannot mean invoking in fundamentalist fashion a return to the authentic origins, to the sacral condition that was erroneously abandoned (we shall see that this is not Novalis's project, as one might believe), and it does not mean acknowledging the specific, autonomous, and original vocation of modernity with respect to the Judeo-Christian tradition.

Rather, the point is to grasp more radically that the equivalence of the West and Christianity means two things: a) the West, feeling the exigency of affirming its own cultural identity—due above all to the political events mentioned above, the fall of the communist enemy, and at the same time to the economic and political push to build a unified Europe—does not find unifying and identifying elements other than, in a secularized form, a shared Christian origin, which is reflected in the thesis concerning the *aut aut* (which therefore is right about the content it intends to uphold, though it is wrong in the overall meaning conferred upon modernity, i.e. a radical alternative to Christianity); and b) the renewed vitality of Christianity, which manifests itself in the actual religious revival of our epoch, can be nothing else but the recovery of Christianity as the West.

I shall now try to show the validity of these theses, warning that often the arguments in both cases will be the same, though weighed and appraised from different perspectives, one more political-cultural and the other more religious, or if I may say so, theological.

Novalis, in the essay alluded to in this chapter's title, clearly demonstrated that the unity of Europe is constituted essentially by the Christian tradition. The belief that in Novalis's view Christian Europe consists of national states is a misunderstanding that has to do with our conception of Romanticism. Rather, for Novalis, Europe and its divisions are the children of the epoch of Reformation, since then "in a most irreligious manner religion was confined within national borders."[5]

Novalis's intuition is confirmed today at a time when at the political level there is an effort to overcome precisely the Europe of national borders. Evidence of this position's validity is the decisive role the current pope had in the liberation of Eastern Europe from communist domination, which is certainly one of the conditions for the "recovery of the West." At a time when people think again of a unified Europe, Christianity—and Catholic Christianity in particular, which has historically constituted its unifying element—has gained a renewed currency. The decisive presence of the pope in the recovery and in the liberation of Europe in these years is just a symptom of a broader and more general phenomenon. While trying to recover their identity, Europe and the West encounter their own secularized, Christian origins as the only foundational element.

Indeed, what are Europe, the West, or modernity, if not above all the civilization of scientific, economic, and technological rationality? This rationality, however, as Weber taught us and is repeated *ad infinitum*, has not been realized in any other culture of the planet, even when all the same material conditions have been present, because the Judeo-Christian tradition was "at work" only in the West.[6] Monotheism (to speak in very rough approximations) is the condition in which nature can be conceived of from the unitary perspective of a physical science, which is the indispensable basis of the technological domination over nature. Christian ethics, above all Protestant ethics, is the condition in which labor, saving, and economic success can be thought of as religious imperatives, and therefore are capable of generating a deep and total engagement. Moreover, a theory has been advanced recently beyond

Weber's thesis, though not necessarily against him, that modern consumerism—which hardly fits within the "austere" Weberian view of capitalism as the effect of Calvinist ethics—is the outcome of the secularization of the Christian kernel. In Colin Campbell's book, *Romantic Ethics and the Spirit of Modern Consumerism*,[7] the relationship between consumerism and Christianity is stated clearly, though not as explicitly as here. Campbell shows that the inclination for consumption cannot be sufficiently explained with the argument of the manipulation of tastes and expectations through advertising, which allegedly reflects the expansive demands placed on the market by an industry that has intensified to the extreme its productive capacities. Instead, in order to explain consumerism, it is necessary to explore the deeper transformation of the European mentality, which may be characterized as the development of a curiosity about alternative worlds and the tendency toward fantasy, and therefore an intense desire of novelty. These traits of the European mentality, which, according to Campbell, were explicitly affirmed in Romanticism, are themselves, similarly to the ethics of Weber's capitalist, effects of the secularization of Christian religiosity. The beginning of modernity and the shake-up of the Reformation weakened the "literal" faith in Christian truths, leaving in their place an inclination toward other worlds, which might not be otherworldly but in any case are not identical with visible everyday reality. Hence, through a series of phases, the birth of "Romantic" mentality in the common, even banal sense of the term, to which modern and late-modern capitalist consumption must be traced.

It is pointless here to try to decide whether and to what extent Campbell's thesis—which in any case is documented and argued rigorously—must be accepted or not. Instead, this thesis—formulated in the late-modern condition in which we live, and which Weber had not experienced—indicates more than Weber's the direction in which we must move to develop the idea of the coincidence of the West with (secularized) Christianity. What I intend to argue is that the West is essentially Christian to the extent that the meaning of its own history appears as the "twilight of Being," that is, the diminishment of reality's solidity through all the procedures of dissolution of objectivity brought about by modernity.

Indeed, today if we attempt to give substance to the idea of the West, we do not find, only or mainly, capitalist and technological rationality "next to" a series of ideal themes that are linked though ultimately independent and often in conflict, as, for example, Enlightenment rationalism and Christian dogma, which in turn is divided into Protestant, Catholic, and so on. More than at any other time, all these ingredients (along with others that we could list) appear to be mixed into a whole that is neither organic nor rigorous, but from which elements of strict differentiation are missing. For example, the popularity of the pope in today's world corresponds not only to his lively presence in the political arena or to the recovery of religious faith, of Catholic Orthodoxy and so on. It is probably linked more to the general disappearance of strict differentiations, which has been brought about especially by the spread of mass media. What is often deplored as confusion—always from excessively strict and dogmatic perspectives, whether lay or religious—and as the commodification of all values produced by the media is instead the condition for establishing a tolerance that, as it is easy to see, can only point to the weakening of the idea of truth, and ultimately of reality. (Let me use this terminology without further illustrations: it is the theme of a theory I have proposed under the name of "weak thought"[8]). It is above all for these reasons that today the West can be characterized in many interrelated senses as the land of the twilight, or also of secularization, which is the same thing. Here I outline only some of the traits that in my view allow me to speak in these terms: secularization appears, above all in its Weberian sense, as the application of ethics and of the monotheistic, Judeo-Christian world view to the constitution of capitalism, natural science, and modern technology. Furthermore, the secularization of Christianity is also that opening to other worlds that, as I have mentioned with respect to Campbell, is the foundation of consumerism. Secularization is then the weakening of the sense of reality brought about by science, which studies entities that are increasingly incomparable with those we encounter in our everyday experience. Such a weakening is produced, too, at another level: the world of the "natural" need no longer function as foundation-reality, since we no longer know what it actually is, subjected as we are by the world of production (merchandise), advertising, and so on to the manipulation, or better, to the transformation of our imagination. The same holds true for history and information: historians are more and more aware that knowledge of the past is made possible but also irretrievably conditioned by the application of rhetorical narrative conventions that prevent its objective representation. These conventions serve the same culture that produces them; thus, since the end of Eurocentrism, of Western imperialism, etc., we no longer can speak of a universal history as the ground of specific histories. In the end, then, there is no such thing as history. The same can be said for common knowledge: there is a pluralism of sources of information that no longer "mirror" but rather interpret. It is obvious that these sources never really "mirrored" events, but today the novelty is the fact that everybody is aware of their interpretive nature (everybody knows that the TV lies).

Does it make sense to place all these phenomena under the sign of secularization? It seems that for Weber and the idea of capitalism as the secularizing development of monotheism, there are no doubts about it. Rather, what might be a problem is so labeling the postmodern development of the drift, described by Weber, toward a weakening of the sense of reality and of the notion of truth itself, which I mentioned above. I shall not attempt to put forth an exhaustive argument for this "extension" of the term *secularization*—I intend to attempt this elsewhere. I just want to clarify the meaning of the hypothesis advanced here, which seems worthy of discussion and corroboration. The hypothesis, briefly, is the following: if the West seeks its own identity, it must principally reckon with the phenomena indicated above, namely a Weberian capitalist rationalization plus the world of information and of proliferating interpretations without a center, which tends to weaken the sense of the terms *being* and *reality*. Now this set of phenomena may well be grasped as a whole only if it is seen as a major process of the secularization of the Judeo-Christian tradition. Just as Weber, in trying to find the "distinctive" element for understanding why modern capitalism was born in the West, encountered monotheism and the Protestant ethic, so too today the phenomena alluded to above in a cursory fashion seem comprehensible only in light of the Christian tradition. Let me repeat that here I shall not provide a proper demonstration for this statement; however, one may understand its reasonableness and plausibility by calling to mind arguments such as that made by Campbell on consumerism, and above all by not understanding the reference to Weber as merely an analogy. I mean that, as far as they are connected to the spread of information technologies, the phenomena of weakening mentioned above are linked to secularization in the sense in which Weber intended, precisely via techno-science, which began as the mechanical science of motors and assembly lines and became the science of electronics—TV, computers. Another, more important way of legitimating the use of the term *secularization* for these phenomena of weakening is that which seeks not merely to bring them back to their origin (that is, to that without which they cannot be explained, for then one would proceed along the way paved by Weber, and underline that the society of communication and limitless interpretation is shaped by the logical continuation of a world that has Scripture as its foundation and that develops above all as exegesis). Rather, this approach emphasizes that the weakening of Being is one possible meaning—if not the absolute meaning—of the Christian message, through the radical reading of incarnation as *kenosis*. This message speaks of a God who incarnates himself, lowers himself, and confuses all the powers of this world.[9]

For this part of my argument too, I believe, one might recall the essay by Novalis mentioned above, where he says that "true anarchy is the fertile element of religion."[10] The context clearly shows that the term *anarchy* here indicates the Babel-like confusion and the loss of center in favor of the multiple, irreducible "pictures" of the world that I have suggested one might call a "weakening of the sense of reality."

However, as I mentioned at the outset, we must draw on Novalis especially for the conclusion to his text, to suggest, at least schematically, the argument for the plausibility of the second thesis mentioned earlier. According to this thesis, not only is the West today only definable as a unified entity as secularized Christianity, but also, Christianity today rediscovers itself authentically only if it identifies itself as Western. In other and more provocative words: I mean that today the West, understood as the land of the sunset and of weakening, is Christianity's truth. Two passages by Novalis are worth mentioning here: first, where Novalis defends the "Catholic esoterization of the Bible," the "sacred violence of the Councils and of the supreme spiritual leader," against Luther's *sola scriptura*, because in this way Catholicism ensured that "the absolutely popular character of the Bible, its miserable content, and the roughly abstract outline of religion" that it contained would not become an obstacle to faith. In other words, the Bible is merely the kernel, which by itself, in contrast with the living tradition and faith of the community, cannot be held to be authentic revelation.

The second passage is at the end of the essay. For Novalis, the living faith of the community that gives us hope for the renewal of Christianity has the quality of "indifferentiation" that I used earlier to characterize the contemporary situation. Novalis writes: "Christianity has three forms. One is the generative element of religion, namely joy in all religion. One is the notion of mediation itself, namely faith in the omnipotence of all earthly things to be bread and wine of eternal life. One is the faith in Christ, his mother and the saints. Choose whichever you will, choose all three, it is all the same, you will become Christians thereby and members of one single, eternal, inexpressibly happy community."[11] There is no point in analyzing further the meaning of these three forms as Novalis himself thought of them. He certainly opposed the idea of retrieving the authenticity of revelation by returning to the Bible—to the idea of a "broad" Christianity, somewhat vague, not dogmatically defined—which tends to coincide with the religious spirit theorized by Schleiermacher in the *Speeches on Religion*, which Novalis explicitly cites in his essay. Catholicism always taught that the sources of revelation are both Scripture and tradition, and therefore always acknowledged, at least in principle, that revelation continues and is enriched in the living faith of community (though only up to a point); *de facto*, it always has greatly restricted community boundaries by identifying the Church as a hierarchical organization led by the pope and bishops and defined by the respect for Scripture. Today, in the name of this vision of community, the Catholic Church is far from acknowledging the elements of "lay" religiousness that announce themselves in Western culture. On the contrary, it meets them with skepticism, manifested in an unnecessary emphasis on a strictly disciplinary conception of Christian practice (I am thinking, obviously, of sexual morality, which claims to be based on "natural law"). But if, as I believe, we acknowledge (for example, along with Novalis) that the truth of revelation is contained *in nuce* in the Scriptures, and that it grows and increases in the experience of community, we probably will have to follow the same path as Novalis: the Christian community cannot be too arbitrarily limited by references to the letter of Scripture. The experience of modernity—which I have suggested must be interpreted as the weakening of reality's peremptoriness, and in a related sense, of authoritarianism in politics, of the strict hierarchical conception of the individual subject, and of direct violence that is consumed and attenuated in the mechanisms of the modern right-based state—must be considered in effect a Christian event. Better still, it is the Christian event *par excellence*, as attestation that the seed of divine Word has borne fruit in a broad field and has not allowed itself to be enclosed and hardened within the authoritarian boundaries of dogma.

To conclude in a provisional way, it is certain that we cannot say that "everything goes." If it does not have the strict boundaries of dogma and of hierarchical authority, a "vague" Christianity that we have seen theorized by Novalis has charity and love as its distinctive characteristics. The importance that notions like communication, community, dialogue, consensus, democracy, etc. have assumed in a broad area of contemporary philosophy appears not to be accidental but rather to indicate a "conclusion" of modern thought, which tends in multiple philosophical formulations very different among themselves to conceive of truth more as consensus—we might say as charity, too—than as "objectivity." To grasp and develop the meaning of these signs is the task that today presents itself to those who profess to be openly Christian, and to the many who, outside of any respect for hierarchy, have understood that "they cannot not call themselves Christians."[12]

6

~

The Death or Transfiguration of Religion

TWO SETS OF facts seem obvious in contemporary culture, and they do not have the same meaning. Indeed, as I hope to demonstrate, the task of critical thought is elaborating the difference between them. Let me begin with the most visible phenomena surrounding the renewal of religion, which are also the most vaguely defined. This is what we might call, following the title of a book published in France a few years ago, the triumph of God. The current Catholic pope has an extraordinary audience among non-Catholics and nonbelievers, in part because of his contribution to the collapse of the regimes of "real socialism." The revival of the Catholic Church's presence in social and cultural domains—I ignore to what extent it is manifested in an increased participation in Mass and the sacraments, but it is certainly visible as a general social phenomenon—has been accompanied by the intensification of more or less heterodox religious experiences. These have their inspiration in Christian roots as well as in the Muslim tradition, but also in Eastern religious traditions, Buddhism first among them. My aim here is not to carry out an accurate sociological analysis, for which I possess neither the competence nor the analytical tools. Instead, I want to call attention to these "facts," which need no demonstration since we are all aware of them, to counter the description of ours as a "post-Christian" or "postreligious" epoch given by thinkers such as Richard Rorty.

The reasons for the renewed vitality of religion are many, but some are especially clear. One is, insofar as the Catholic Church is concerned, the contribution of the pope to the collapse of communism in the eastern bloc countries. Another is that, at least in Italy, there is less direct involvement in politics by the Catholic religious hierarchy—though I wonder if something similar is not happening, too, in Spain after Franco. As a result, religious commitment now appears in a more authentic light, no longer confused with the alternatives of reactionary and progressive, or Marxist atheist and Christian democrat. In a broader perspective, the gravity of the problems facing our societies in the wake of recent developments in science and technology gives weight to the voice and presence of religion—in the West, Christianity and specifically Catholicism. I am thinking, of course, of problems linked to bioethics and ecology. In particular, the field of bioethics, where the emerging questions appear far too big to be resolved solely by rational argument and involve life and death (a kind of Columns of Hercules), freedom and self-determination—that is, the destiny of humanity. It is a terrain where one inevitably draws near the sacred. Nietzsche prophesied that modern science (grounded as it is on specialized and collective labor, with every scientist working on very specific and limited topics) would usher in a new model of thought, both moderate and generous. Rather than seeking ultimate truths on which the salvation of the soul would depend, such thought would live in the proximal. "Who cares about me?" This is, for Nietzsche, the motto of the future thinker. Now the limits reached in many fields by experimental science seem a denial of Nietzsche's prophecy: scientists are more often than not those who face ultimate questions. A strict doctrine, elaborated across the centuries by orthodox discipline—like that of the Catholic Church—can be very appealing to people who are busy applying the results of inquiry to concrete cases. The dogmatic thought of the Church seems to provide criteria that are both rigorous and certain, and not defined with the same degree of veracity and clarity in lay philosophy, permeated as it is by the critical spirit.

A number of reasons could be given for the renewed attention paid to religion in our present world, and especially to the voice of the churches. One kind of justification should not be forgotten here: the meaning of religion for social groups looking for an identity by which to save themselves from a situation of *anomie* (the term coined by Durkheim) in which the late-industrial world has thrown them. This need for identity, together with the magnitude of the new moral problems mentioned above, is a powerful factor behind the revival of religion in our societies. This need, like the moral problems, tends to confer on this revival the sense of a return to a foundation, that is, a renewed acceptance of strict discipline and doctrines. Consequently, there is a clear risk of lapsing into fanaticism and intolerance.

And here let us recall the second set of phenomena to which I alluded at the outset. The death of religion of which this chapter's title speaks appears to have been taking place for a long time within and for philosophy, in the sense that perhaps only for philosophers is Nietzsche's sentence about the death of God true. For a long time the main trend of contemporary philosophy—which has developed into two parallel lines of thought that today we tend to call Continental philosophy and analytical philosophy—had no place for theology. It was not a militant atheistic philosophy; that is, it did not theorize explicitly the falseness of religion but rather kept silent about it. It acknowledged

that there are religious experiences radically other than rational thought, a matter of pure feeling, or as in Wittgen-
stein's famous statement, belonging to the realm of things
that, since they cannot be spoken about, should be passed
over in silence. Even recent philosophies—I am thinking
of that of Lévinas, but also of Ricoeur—that seem to escape
this characterization in the end fall within the picture I have
drawn at least in the sense that they articulate a purely
negative "theology." They do grant a space to religious experience, or (in Lévinas's case) they even speak of God,
but only as an alterity and an emptiness that it is impossible
not to acknowledge. However, God (through the Bible)
does not address philosophy in a positive manner, and
philosophy in turn does not speak about God. Consequently, in Lévinas at least, the name of God merely evokes
the finitude of human existence. Yet today the silence of
philosophy with respect to God has no basis in any philosophically relevant principle. For the most part, philosophers profess by force of habit to be atheists or nonreligious, almost out of inertia. The fact is that the decline of
the great metanarratives—i.e., of the systematic philosophies that had claimed to grasp the true structure of reality,
the laws of history, and the method for acquiring knowledge about the only "truth"—has put an end, too, to the
strong reasons for philosophical atheism. If the metanarrative of positivism no longer holds, one can no longer
think that God does not exist because his existence cannot
be established scientifically. If the metanarrative of Hegelian or Marxist historicism no longer holds, one cannot
argue that God does not exist because faith in God belongs
to an earlier stage within the history of human evolution,
or because God is just an ideological representation at the
service of domination. True, Nietzsche, whose contribution was decisive in dissolving the metanarratives, is also
the philosopher who announced the death of God. Yet this
is the main paradox of Nietzsche's philosophy: his an-

nouncement of the death of God, really the announcement of the end of all metanarratives, does not preclude the possibility that many gods might be born. Perhaps we have not meditated sufficiently on the explicit assertion by Nietzsche that "it is the moral God who is denied," that is, God as ground, the pure act in Aristotle, the supreme watchmaker and architect of the universe in Enlightenment rationalism.

Here, then, is my preliminary understanding of the two "facts" characteristic of our epoch upon which I intend to reflect—though it is vague and imprecise, like all preliminary understandings within which our interpretative appropriation of the world unfolds. On the one hand is the return of religion in our common culture, in the form of a renewed attention to the teaching of the Church, of a need for ultimate truth, and of a desire to recover one's own identity, especially with reference to transcendence. On the other hand is the collapse of the philosophical principles of atheism, to which philosophy has not yet paid attention but with which it should begin to come to terms, especially considering the first phenomenon mentioned above. The rebirth of religion in the common culture must pose a problem for a philosophy that is accustomed to considering the question of God irrelevant. After all, this same philosophy has seen disappear with the end of metanarratives the very reasons for its traditional atheism or agnosticism. Yet it is almost fate that in this situation a philosophy attentive to the reasons of the present—that is, ultimately preoccupied with "saving the phenomena," with giving experience its due—will have to recognize the rebirth of religion in our common culture and the good reasons for this rebirth.

With the end of metanarratives and hence the end of metaphysics, can a philosophy that is aware of the absence of strong reasons for atheism ally itself with the new popular religious consciousness—imbued as it is with fundamentalism, communitarianism, anxiety over ethnic identity, and paternalistic reassurances at the cost of sacrificing freedom? My argument is that, if philosophy recognizes that it can no longer be atheistic because of the collapse of the metanarratives of metaphysics, it can find in this awareness the basis for a critical position on the turn to religion and its dangerous fundamentalist features. As long as contemporary philosophy continues to consider itself atheistic or agnostic, thus repeating its prior metaphysical position out of inertia, it separates itself from common consciousness, placing itself in an "esoteric" site. This is precisely the move effectively criticized by Hegel in the preface to *Phenomenology of Spirit*, which coincides with its failure as a philosophy. Today, much specialized philosophy is practiced in enclosed university departments that focus almost exclusively on epistemological, historical, and logical topics, and is exposed to the risk of becoming irrelevant, again to use a Hegelian notion. Philosophy can no longer see the social vitality of religion as a phenomenon of cultural backwardness promoted by cunning priests, or as the expression of ideological alienation to be overcome through revolution and through the abolition of the division of labor. Rather, it must grasp within the historical process the principles for critically appraising its outcome, recognizing that philosophy itself belongs to the same process that promotes the return to religion.

To sum up: since philosophy no longer has reasons for justifying atheism, it must grant some legitimacy to religious experience, though only insofar as it recognizes the end of metaphysics. The idea of demythification has been demythified as well, because critical reason has discovered (following Nietzsche) the mythical and ideological nature of claiming a truth that would be free from ideology and myth. However, this does not mean that reason might return to myth, thereby legitimating any ideological lie. The varieties of religious and ethnic fundamentalism pervading our world often find philosophical legitimacy in the appeal to the end of global metanarratives. Relativist fundamentalism, which has communitarianism as its political form, is widespread today. According to this position, there are only forms of belonging after the end of metanarratives, and the judgment of truth is based only on its correspondence with the paradigms upheld by one's own specific community. The renewal of religion is often accompanied by these attitudes, which are its very strength and supporting horizon.

The question of relativism, which many justifiably find totally marginal as a theoretical problem, acquires meaning only in relation to its implications for fundamentalism and communitarianism. Philosophy cannot avoid posing the following question: Is the newly acquired legitimacy of returning to myth and to communitarian forms of belonging the only logical outcome of the end of metaphysics? Should we give way to a local concept of truth, in which there can be no dialogue but only precarious tolerance or at worst some forms of apartheid, since there is no universal truth?

The thread of the dissolution of metaphysics—which, I believe, makes philosophy more open to the possibility of religion by dismissing the strong reasons for atheism—can supply criteria for avoiding these irrational outcomes. Metaphysics (in the sense Heidegger gives to this term, as the thought of Being understood as objectivity and ground) does not end because one discovers a better truth, which would refute the current one. This would be just another kind of fundamentalism held to be truer than what preceded it. Metaphysics and metanarratives end because they are no longer necessary or credible, like the moral God who, in Nietzsche, dies because the faithful themselves recognize that he is a superfluous lie. The same dissolution of metaphysics has brought about both modernity and late modernity: technology facilitates existence, thereby reducing our anxiety about questions concerning the ultimate. Experimental science, on which technological progress is based, spawns a moderate thought that is more attentive to proximity than to first principles. Increasingly, the outcomes of science are irreducible to the unity of a ground, making metaphysics implausible. The structures of society have become more flexible, replacing the natural community with a more heterogeneous and divided society where the single individual is less identifiable. Political power is evolving toward democratic forms, taking a less direct and centralized physiognomy. Since Freud, individual subjectivity appears as a composite ensemble in which every ultimate is provisional, and thus precludes the possibility of being interpreted in relation to a stable ground.

These processes, which comprise the content of modernity and are the true basis for the dissolution of metaphysics, can be described as processes of weakening. Only within this framework is it possible to realize that there are no strong reasons for atheism and to open thought to the possibility of religious experience. However, what is recovered has nothing to do with the hard discipline and strict antimodernism of dogmatic religion, which is expressed in varied forms of fundamentalism and above all in the Catholicism of Pope Jean Paul II. The recovery of religion is not a return to metaphysics but an outcome of metaphysics' dissolution. To come back to Pope Wojtyla's Catholicism, it is not the naturalist or essentialist ethics he has preached on matters of sexual and family morality, going to the extreme of forbidding the use of condoms in the epoch of the spread of AIDS, that can be recovered. To be faithful to the end of metaphysics, which makes its renewal possible, the religion that presents itself anew in our culture must abandon the project of grounding religious ethics upon knowledge of natural essences that are taken as norms, observing instead the freedom of dialogic mediation. This is realized not in the vacuum of individual wills but by claiming reasons that are less absolute and more historically defined. It is a process forged through the mobilization of a shared culture and of its critique on the basis of criteria inherent within it. The main thread of weakening—of the peremptoriness of ultimate truths; of certainty in the evidence of consciousness; of the sacrality of power, including that of the pope; and so on—can operate as an internal criterion that reveals itself in modernity as the logic for the dissolution of metaphysics, to which critical thought is committed to conform itself.

To what extent, though, does the adoption of this guiding principle for ethical choices and for a general interpretation of modernity also represent a return to religion? I can only mention this issue in passing here, but it is not unlikely that by taking up this main thread Western thought will recover its profound continuity with the Christian tradition, albeit one freed of its metaphysical masks, or—what amounts to the same—institutional (Church) and disciplinary masks. Will a concept of the course of history as driven toward emancipation by diminishing strong structures (in thought, individual consciousness, political power, social relations, and religion) not be a transcription of the Christian message of the incarnation of God, which Saint Paul also calls *kenosis*—that is, the abasement, humiliation, and weakening of God? This is not a new idea: it was articulated by Hegel more or less in these terms; it is also found in the nineteenth century, in Wilhelm Dilthey's reconstruction of the history of the dissolution of Western metaphysics, in which, according to him, Christianity had a determinant role.[1]

Despite its limits, this vision might well define the horizon for resuming the dialogue between philosophy and religion in the Western world, thereby also inspiring the philosophical critique of fundamentalist superstitions that too often threaten to destroy this dialogue in our society.

7

Christianity and Cultural Conflicts in Europe

THERE ARE MANY indications that the relationship of Christianity to the potential hardening or exacerbation of cultural conflicts is not a peaceful one. I mean that today it would be difficult for anyone at first to take this title, "Christianity and Cultural Conflicts in Europe," as a reference to Christianity as a means of resolving or mitigating cultural conflicts. At first blush, Christianity would appear to be, if not a specific source of conflict, at least one of the terms involved. In other words: the presence in the Western world of a Christian tradition as a continuous background, albeit a vaguely defined one without a univocal meaning, is not an element for leveling out conflicts; on the contrary, it is (or has become) a constitutive factor in promoting them, and can exacerbate them. What happens here is similar to what happens in the interpretation of the relationship between religion and politics, as can be observed in several recent debates, where this relationship is almost naturally felt to be a risk for the autonomy of politics. Rarely or never has religion been seen as a potentially positive contributing factor to the enrichment and improvement of politics. It seems clear that here we are facing the outcome of specific historical experiences. For instance, in Italy the reason for a defensive approach to the relationship between religion and politics lies in the long history of interference on the part of the Catholic Church in the electoral process. But, in much more general terms, the notion that the Christian tradition might take part in or promote cultural conflicts arises at the end of Eurocentrism: European civilization is no longer seen as representing the natural, normal development of all human cultures, which it has the legitimacy to bring together under its aegis. Thus Christianity no longer appears as the revelation of truth, which sheds light on the darkness of "other" cultures and frees them of errors and limitations. Rather, it is a religion—and a culture—that confronts other traditions as one of the terms involved in cultural conflicts, rather than as the solution to those conflicts.

After all, not even within the Western world does Christianity appear to operate as a unifying factor. Here, too, are the more remote—and less obvious—origins of the suspiciousness of politics toward religion: even in the West, Christianity has promoted conflict more often than unity and peace. In eliminating religious themes from the lay realm, Western societies have tried to solve the problem of Christianity's transformation from element of cohesion to element of conflict. This transformation coincides with the beginning of European modernity itself, the Protestant Reformation, and the wars of religion, and extends into our epoch. Liberalism has meant the reduction of religion to the private sphere, or at most to the realm of civil society. Once excluded from the areas of struggle for political power and distribution of economic resources, religious choice and belonging cease to represent a threat to social peace. But is the liberal solution to this issue still viable when new religious subjects, that is, "other" cultures that in the meantime have settled among us, are involved? Can

we take it as a model for dealing with intercultural conflicts?

The answer is probably negative. Rather, the situation
seems to be the following: the lay space of politics, which
seems to be well established in Western liberal societies,
does not succeed with equal certainty in peacefully including other cultures present in our societies, or at least some
of them. These tend to see the very secularity of the political as a threat to their authenticity, and therefore take it
less as a condition of liberty than as a negative limitation
that must be overcome. An emblematic example is the story
surrounding the prohibition of the *chador* in French public
schools. The ban on wearing very visible uniforms and distinctive signs, which as affirmative markers of cultural identity might generate conflicts, was motivated by the aim of
establishing a secular condition wherein religious freedoms, or even nonreligious ones, were guaranteed. However, the cultural identity that would be affirmed explicitly
here is other—that of a relatively alien minority with respect to a more established local tradition. If we compare
the prohibition of the *chador* with the widely accepted presence in European schools of Christian symbols (the crucifix
hanging on the school wall in many countries is no longer
even contested, except in a few cases), we grasp the salient
traits of our situation. European society is on average lay
and secularized, but in terms of a fairly explicit Christian
heritage. This becomes clear when confronting persons or
groups rooted in different traditions, who perceive our secularity as deeply marked by a specific religious origin. Liberalism believed that religion could be set aside by rele-
gating it to the private sphere of feeling and faith, which
does not "interfere" with political choices and the normal
dialectic of power. Yet this separation succeeded only because it was realized on the solid, if unacknowledged, basis
of a common religious heritage.

The lay space where religion has ceased to be a factor

of conflict was carved out in Western modernity within a broader, though less acknowledged, religious space of Christian, Judeo-Christian, or biblical origin. All this can be stated in different ways: for example, through the glib saying (which I continue to find very significant), "Thank God I am an atheist"; or, in less paradoxical terms, through the recognition that the secularization characteristic of modernity (the rationalization of capitalism associated by Weber with the Protestant ethic and biblical monotheism) is a typical phenomenon of the Christian world; or through another paradox, namely the acknowledgment that the very idea of a cultural pluralism exists and developed within a specific culture, the Western one.

To be sure, Eurocentrism is the classic form taken by the idea of cultural pluralism in Western modernity, and it is no longer tenable because it placed cultures on an evolutionary trajectory whose highest point was the Christian civilization of the West. Pagan peoples were to be converted to Christianity and primitive societies were to become modern, meaning that they had to model themselves on Western ones, which were understood to be secular, liberal, and democratic. This evolutionary vision of human history, led by the ideal of emancipation as Westernization, modernization, and Christianization, was undermined not only, or primarily, by theoretical reasons. Rather, this image of the meaning of universal history became untenable because of the fall of colonialism and of the many forms of imperialism.

If today we can acknowledge that Christianity no longer presents itself as an obvious means of overcoming intercultural conflicts, this is due primarily to the erosion of the universalizing certainty of modern Western reason, which translated and secularized the Judeo-Christian faith in a divine plan of salvation—albeit unconsciously. Today, the aspect of Christian thought that always saw in this secular translation a betrayal and abandonment of the truth takes pleasure in the floundering of Western "rationalism." However, the main consequence of this floundering is that Christianity tends to present itself more as involved in conflict than as a factor of reconciliation. The issue is all the more urgent since when we speak of Christianity we also speak of liberal society, of the West, and of modern democracy. True, the claim to universalism made by Christian civilization was clouded by and mixed up with the aims of colonialism and imperialism. But must all forms of universalism—the dream of a universal human civilization—come to an end, along with colonialism and imperialism? My argument is the following: (a) there are indications today that many Christian communities (various churches and confessions) share the widespread temptation to oppose universalism, which in modernity was complicit with the Eurocentrism of Western politics, with forms of closure ranging from various types of communitarianism (with their implication of a kind of cultural apartheid) to fundamentalism proper and its often violent outcomes; (b) in the belief that it can thus escape the perverse outcomes of modern rationalism, secularization, and so on, Christianity renounces its civilizing mission. Christianity can retrieve this mission, though no longer in its evolutionary and imperialist forms, only if it recovers its profound solidarity with the destiny of modernization.

Today, the choice facing Christianity (and I am quite aware of the generic meaning of this term: do I mean the Catholic Church? Christian churches? the thought of believers? The answer is all of the above, to some extent) is the following: either it embraces the destiny of modernity (and of its crisis, its transition to postmodernity), or, on the contrary, it claims to be outside it. If the latter option is chosen—and there are signs that this is a temptation— Christianity renounces being a world and a civilization, to become what perhaps it originally was, a sect among other sects and an objective factor of social disruption among others.

To embrace the destiny of modernity and of the West means mainly to recognize the profoundly Christian meaning of secularization. I return to the observation made earlier, namely that the lay space of modern liberalism is far more religious than liberalism and Christian thought are willing to recognize. One of the first consequences of this observation is that it does not make sense for Christianity to situate itself in the new space of intercultural conflicts by assuming a strong identity. Rather, Christianity's vocation consists in deepening its own physiognomy as source and condition for the possibility of secularity.

What I am trying to argue (though with difficulty, since the problem is not a linear one) is that the postmodern dissolution of metanarratives (to use Lyotard's expression)—the idea that the universality of reason characteristic of modernity has been discredited—leads Christianity to see itself as merely an internal element in the conflict among cultures, religions, and world views. It seems to me that a religiously inspired communitarianism, and fundamentalisms in their different forms (including that which sometimes appears in the official teachings of the Catholic Church), correspond to this new attitude, which is legitimized by the fact that it no longer needs to reckon with the imperialist and colonial legacies of Enlightenment universalism and rationalism. As contemporary hermeneutics, along with the existentialism that inspired it (from Heidegger to Gadamer and Pareyson), teaches, the condition for any authentic dialogue is that every interlocutor assume explicitly his own involvement by acknowledging to himself and to the other interlocutor his own prejudices, or more generally his own identity, without assuming at the outset that he knows more about the subject matter or that he might lead the dialogue toward predictable outcomes that he knows in advance to be "true" (this is why, for example, many hermeneutic philosophers are suspicious of a certain concept of the psychoanalytic dialogue that does not presuppose a perfect symmetry between the two interlocutors). In placing itself as an interlocutor with equal rights with respect to other cultures, Christianity should not forget that among the features of its heritage there is also universalism, namely the awareness of a plurality of cultures and of a lay space where these can confront one another. To become an authentic interlocutor in a cultural dialogue, Christianity cannot put aside this essential feature of its heritage and identity; it must present itself as a bearer of the idea of secularity for the sake of its own specific authenticity. This is the very idea of the universalism of reason, emptied of its contingent—though weighty and deeply rooted—complicity with modern colonialism and imperialism. However, this means that instead of "identifying itself" as a religion among others, thereby strengthening its distinctive character in dogma, moral preaching, and disciplinary cohesion, Christianity should develop its lay vocation, which is already visible in that in European modernity it made possible, and promoted, the birth of the lay orientation. Here it is less a matter of acknowledging an accidental, secularized character of Christianity than of acknowledging one of its essential traits that distinguishes Christianity from other religions: that from the outset it was deeply marked by a missionary element, explicit in Jesus' summon to the apostles to preach the Gospel to all creatures. In modernity, the form of this missionary ideal was an alliance with European imperialism, often not experienced as a tragic necessity. At the same time, Christian universalism, in the wake of the terrifying experience of the European religious wars, led to the discovery of the idea of tolerance and to the invention of a "lay" space, where different religious and nonreligious positions that came to the surface in modern society could freely confront one another. The point was, and still is, to grasp the Christian proclamation—based on Jesus' sayings, "give unto Caesar" and "my kingdom is not of this world"—less, or not exclusively, as the end of all (other) false and lying gods than as a legitimate space for different religious experiences. Indeed, it is not rare to find among thinkers who profess to be Christian without reservations an interpretation of Christ's incarnation that legitimates all the purely natural symbols of divinity. If God is incarnate in Jesus, it means that he is not so radically far apart from the natural, human world, and that truth may thus be found in the idolatry of many pagan religions as well.

Christianity frees itself from complicity with the imperialist ideals of European modernity in the wake of a series of historical experiences in which the former colonized nations turned against their "Christian" dominators in the name, too, of a more authentic interpretation of the biblical message. Christianity was forced to recover its lay inclination—to present itself as the promoter of a free dialogical space for religions, world views, ideal dispositions, and other cultures—because in its missionary vocation it had to confront new, unheard of historical experiences. Christianity cannot realize its missionary vocation within the new order of relations among nations and different peoples and cultures by stressing its own doctrinal, moral, and disciplinary specificity. Instead, it can take part in a conflictual or comparative dialogue with other cultures and religions by appealing to its specific lay orientation (since the same stress is not found in those other cultures and religions). This proposal could be summed up with the slogan "from universality to hospitality." Indeed, the diffusion of fundamentalist positions or of forms of communitarian apartheid shows clearly that in the Babel-like world of pluralism, cultural and religious identities are destined to move toward fanaticism unless they explicitly develop in a spirit of weakness. Hospitality (I am thinking here of a beautiful recent lecture by Jacques Derrida) is not realized if not as a placement of oneself in the hands of one's guest, that is, an entrustment of oneself to him. In intercultural or interreligious dialogue, this signifies acknowledging that the other might be right. If Christian identity, applying the principle of charity, takes the shape of hospitality in the dialogue between religions and cultures, it must limit itself almost entirely to listening, and thus giving voice to the guests.

I am aware that the thesis I am putting forth here is controversial and has many implications. Nevertheless, the task facing the Christian world (the West) today is the recovery of its universalizing function without any colonial, imperialist, or Eurocentric implications. It is difficult to imagine that this task might be accomplished by stressing its dogmatic, ethical, and disciplinary specificity. One might reasonably argue that this stress does not correspond to the content of Christian doctrine, but depends rather on a certain historical inertia of the churches insofar as they are worldly institutions. The other path open to Christianity is to recover its universalizing function by stressing its missionary inclination as hospitality, and as the religious foundation (paradoxical as this might be) of the laity (i.e., institutions, civil society, and religious individuals). To return to the example mentioned a moment ago, Christians cannot claim the right to expose the crucifix in public schools and at the same time adopt it as a sign of a particular, highly dogmatic religion. Or, Christmas can continue to be celebrated in Western societies as a holiday for all, but then it makes no sense to complain that it has become too lay, too mundane, that is, that it has been deprived of its original, authentic meaning. In the end, also, the prohibition of the *chador* in French public schools can be justified precisely because in that context it is an affirmation of a strong identity, a kind of profession of fundamentalism. By contrast, in our society the crucifix has become an almost obvious—and hence unobtrusive—sign, which allows for the continued existence of a lay orientation of which it only underscores the religious origin within the context of a development toward secularization. It is precisely by appealing to this generic meaning—one that offers openings and possibilities—that the crucifix can claim its right to be accepted as a universal symbol in a lay society. If world religions, primarily Christianity, are determined to present themselves as strong identities, the only option for liberal society will be to manifest its secularity by further reducing the visibility of all religious symbols in civic life, so as to not arouse reactions from this or that minority or from "other" religions and cultures. Among other things, this would ultimately force us to close most Western museums and to renounce the very cultural traditions of the West, which are so thick with—and inseparable from—religious symbols. By contrast, we should promote a free and intense coexistence of multiple symbolic universes in a spirit of hospitality that well expresses the lay orientation of Western culture, and its deeply religious origin—perhaps taking the museum, with its juxtaposition of different styles, tastes, and cultures, as a symbolic model of democracy. Yet to reach this goal, it is necessary that the world religions, and Christianity in the first place, no longer take the dogmatic and fundamentalist forms that have characterized them to date. In this sense, too, one might say, against all narrowly lay expectations, that the renewal of civic life in the Western world in the epoch of multiculturalism is mainly a problem of the renewal of the religious life.

8

~

The Christian Message and the Dissolution
of Metaphysics

IT MAY BE possible to say that, in a very broad perspective, the two thousand years that separate us from the mysterious event to which our calendars refer can be understood as the progressive diminishing of the validity of a famous saying, "*Amicus Plato sed magis amica veritas*" (attributed by ancient biographers to Aristotle). We might recall that this expression is found in Dostoyevsky, too. When evoking the choice between Christ and truth (*The Demons*, part II, chapter VII), Satov assigns it to Stavrogin. However, in a letter, Dostoyevsky pronounces it in his own name. The sentence cannot be denied or overturned only in the name of love for Christ. Indeed, Dostoyevsky represents a paradoxical case, since beginning with Jesus' words "*ego sum via, veritas et vita*," the inclination of Christian thought has been to identify Christ with truth (in the classical sense of truth as the accurate and objective description of reality), thus denying the possibility that there might be any difference between the two terms. This might be the reason why Dostoyevsky has an exceptional place in

Christian thought.[1] Apart from him, the classical tendency of Christian thought has been to identify truth with Christ. If truth has the power to free us, it is only because knowledge of the real would enable us to free ourselves (but from what? surely not from truth-reality, no matter how burdensome or disagreeable that might be). Redemption (a prayer of the Roman breviary recites, "*Redimisti nos Domine, Deus Veritatis*") would consist in seeing Being itself: *Amor dei intellectualis*, to use a term of Spinoza. Indeed, the traditional idea of eternal life as the (face to face) contemplation of God has been developed in the Spinozan sense, identifying the blessed life with the perfect knowledge of geometry. Was this the reason the second person of the Holy Trinity incarnated and sacrificed himself on the cross?

It seems clear enough from these observations that Dostoyevsky, with his paradoxical choice for Christ, even at the price of truth, is the Christian thinker who is most faithful to the meaning of the gospel. Even more than in Dostoyevsky, though, faithfulness to the gospel should be sought in Nietzsche, and especially in his announcement of the death of God. The God who has been killed by his followers is only—and rightly—the moral God (the supreme guarantor of the world's [geometrical] order who made Socrates say that the righteous man has nothing to fear in this life or in the life after death). Nietzsche's announcement, therefore, is not merely a repetition, in a literal sense, of the biblical story of the crucifixion; it is also the most radical expression of Dostoyevsky's paradox.

Nietzsche does not formulate this paradox as a moral choice to which every individual exposes himself on the way to salvation. Rather, he sees it—and this is the point I wish to stress here—as the very meaning of the history of Europe, of the West, or of "Christian modernity." The death of the moral God marks the impossibility of preferring truth to friendship, because the meaning of that death is that there is no "objective," ontological truth that might be upheld as anything other than friendship, will to power, or subjective bond. Those who pronounce *"magis amica veritas"* do so out of love for another, or perhaps for themselves, for the tradition that speaks in them or for the *"human, all too human"* reasons that Nietzsche so meticulously analyzed, following in the footsteps of the French moralists. These are: friendship and will, or, to speak in Pascal's terms, "the reasons of the heart."

If *European nihilism* (which is the title of a famous fragment written in lenzer Heide in the summer of 1887) means the impossibility of believing in an objective world order, which would justify faithfulness to truth above and beyond friendship and hostility, then Nietzsche does not see (does not want to see, or perhaps cannot see because of his own hostilities: he was the son of a pastor and grew up in the shadows of the Church, as one of his autobiographical fragments says) that nihilism is not confined to his own understanding of the death of God. It comprises also the death of Jesus narrated by the Gospels, or what Heidegger calls the end of metaphysics. This end, as we know, comes to completion in Nietzsche's nihilism and in the historical phenomenon that the Nietzschean doctrine acknowledges, describes, and announces. From the Nietzschean-Heideggerian perspective in which I place myself, nihilism is the loss of credence in an objective truth in favor of a perspective that conceives of truth as an effect of power in the manifold senses of this expression: as a scientific experiment that realizes the *principium reddendae rationis*, its foundation the active will of the subjects who set up the experiment and of those who within a historical paradigm, which is not necessarily arbitrary, adhere to its validity; as an ideology that members of a social class hold to be true; and as a lie invented by monks in order to justify power and social discipline.

To what extent can one consider the consummation of

objective truth in different manifestations of friendship, and therefore of the reasons of the heart, to be an effect of the death of Christ, that is, as a result of the mysterious event that lies at the basis of our civilization and of modern calculation of time?

The author who can best help us answer this question, or one to whom we should refer, is Wilhelm Dilthey. He clearly took over Hegel's legacy, though he updated it in order to soften the most strict and systematic aspects of Hegel's philosophy of history. In the second volume of his uncompleted book, *Einleitung in die Geisteswissenschaften*, Dilthey retraces two stages within the history of European metaphysics: that of the ancients and that of the moderns. The latter was destined to end with the dissolution of metaphysics accomplished by the Kantian critique and its developments up to Dilthey's historicism.

Now, what distinguishes ancient metaphysics from modern metaphysics is the "turning" accomplished by Christianity's advent, which shifted the interest of philosophy from the natural world to the inwardness of man. For Dilthey, Platonism is the emblem of ancient metaphysics, even though it is not naturalism in the strict sense of the word. Its distinctive value lies in Plato's concept of Being (as Heidegger would say later on, since his vision of the history of metaphysics is deeply influenced by Dilthey) as a visible form—*idea, eidos*—and thus as an external "phenomenon," placed as an objective form before the mind's eye. In contrast, Christianity shifts the attention of thought inward, putting at the center the will rather than the intellect. The *Einleitung* says:

> For the Greek mind, knowing was mirroring an objective thing in the intelligence. Now [i.e., in Christianity], experience becomes the focal point of all the interests of the new communities; but this is just simple awareness of what is given in person-

ality and in consciousness of the self. . . . With the enormous interest they generate, experiences of the will and of the heart swallow up every other object of knowledge. . . . If this community faith had immediately developed a science perfectly appropriate to it, that science would have to rest on a foundation ultimately resting on inner experience.[2]

To sum up, briefly: Christianity is the condition that paved the way for the dissolution of metaphysics and for its replacement by gnoseology—in Dilthey's terms, by Kantianism. The principles that inspired Descartes and Kant—the emphasis on the subject, the foundation of knowledge on a self-certain interiority—are the same ones that hold sway in modern philosophy. The latter remained, for a long time, a kind of metaphysics dominated by an objectivistic vision of interiority itself, because the new principle of subjectivity introduced by Christianity did not immediately succeed. "But this inner structure which, with respect to scientific grounding, occupies a place between Christianity and knowledge that grows out of inner experience, did not produce a corresponding scientific grounding in the Middle Ages. The reason for this was the preponderant power of ancient culture, within which Christianity now began to assert itself gradually."[3]

Saint Augustine clearly represents the conflict between the novelty of Christian interiority and the hegemony of Greek aesthetic or "visual" objectivism. He combines the self-assurance of the soul's relation to God with a theory of the *veritates aeternae* derived from Platonism and neo-Platonism: "the soul sees truth through its own self, not by means of the body and its sense organs. We are right back in the middle of Plato's metaphysics again, which we thought we had left behind us."[4] "*On the other hand,*" writes Dilthey, "there are *elements* in Augustine's inner experience which *transcend this Platonizing connection* between man's intellect, the world, and God—namely, in the *veritates aeternae* . . . a component . . . going beyond the thought of antiquity."[5] (Let me point out that this is not the traditional opposition, in Christian thought, between Platonism and Aristotelianism; rather, it is an opposition between the remnants of Greek thought that also happened to be Platonic and the "Kantian" novelty of Christianity.) What takes place in Augustine's thought occurs at different stages of development in the whole history of Christianity from the Middle Ages to modernity. A struggle between Christianity's offering of a new possibility to thought and metaphysics' endurance goes on up to Kant, who draws the antimetaphysical implications of the inaugural move of the Christian message. The reasons for the endurance of metaphysics are manifold and intricate. Sometimes Dilthey attributes them, with respect to Augustine, to the latter's personal history, which is marked by the influence of neo-Platonism. But the endurance of metaphysics in Augustine, as in all the Church fathers and medieval thinkers, may be understood above all in light of the social and political responsibility the Church had to take over after the fall of the Roman Empire. Indeed, the remnants of the ancient social institutions, and the culture they expressed, rested on the shoulders of the Church. Furthermore, the Church developed into a rigid structure, which was unavoidably grounded on an objectivistic metaphysics and on scientific knowledge's claims about the natural world—as Galileo's case shows.

This view of the history of European thought as a struggle between the principles of metaphysics—inwardness, will, certitude of the *cogito*—which Christianity introduced into the world and the naturalist-visual (aesthetic) objectivism of Greek culture deeply marks Heidegger's vision of metaphysics' survival and dissolution. Let me stress that—more explicitly for Heidegger, but also for Dilthey—

there is no question of a struggle between the "natural" (or, paradoxically, "objective") truth of Christian subjectivism and a metaphysics that would reveal itself by falsifying this authentic truth. The substance of the Christian announcement is not Christ's revelation of an eternal truth but rather an actual historical event. It is, then, a struggle between two historical possibilities, or perhaps between two versions of "friendship."

Beginning again with Dilthey is, in my view, essential in order to understand how Christianity could be taken as the starting point of the modern dissolution of metaphysics. It will be sufficient to acknowledge—and this is the meaning of Heidegger's existentialism in *Being and Time*—that Kantianism is still a kind of Augustinianism, namely a claim to trace the inner certitude back to an ahistorical, "natural," and therefore objective structure (the Kantian transcendental, which was already criticized by Dilthey). Hence, the Nietzsche of the death of God and the Heidegger of *Ereignis* are the most radical heirs of the anti-metaphysical principle that Christ brought into the world. Note also that there is a deeply Christian element in Dilthey's concluding remarks on the history and dissolution of metaphysics. Indeed, Dilthey writes that whereas metaphysics as a science has become impossible, "the metaphysical [sic] element of our *life* as personal experience, that is, as moral-religious truth, remains. . . . But experiences of a person's will are exempt from a universally valid presentation, which would be coercive and obligatory for every other intellect."[6] "But," Dilthey goes on, "whatever they will turn up, wherever a man by his will breaks through the structure of perception, desire, impulse, and pleasure, and is no longer self-interested, here we have the meta-physical [sic] element, which the history of metaphysics we have described has merely reflected in countless images. For metaphysical science is a historically limited phenomenon, but the meta-physical [sic] consciousness of the person is eternal."[7] It would be difficult, though not impossible, to read this passage as a critical reference to metaphysical objectivism's survival in Schopenhauer's negation of the will. Yet the passage is quite ambiguous. On the one hand, one might conjecture that the negation of the self and of the will is a radical mode of showing preference for the object rather than the subject (indeed, this is Adorno's criticism of Heidegger in the *Negative Dialectics*). On the other hand, the tone of the passage indicates that Dilthey sees this "eternal metaphysics," which manifests itself in every overcoming of the will to live, as a positive element, that is, as a metaphysical remnant in an eminent sense, which cannot be overcome by our post-Kantian modernity. It was a spirit of negation of will that inspired also Heidegger's notion of *Gelassenheit* (abandonment or serenity). The same ambiguity, though, can be seen in Heidegger's view of the end of metaphysics as the triumph of modern subjectivism and voluntarism, which is the last stage of the forgetting of Being, though it is at the same time the first *Aufblitzen* of *Ereignis*, the first illumination of the event of Being, as Heidegger says in *Identity and Difference*.[8]

Why, then, *Amicus Plato?* Why prefer friendship to truth? We find here the last manifestation of the struggle between the enduring force of the objective residue of Greek metaphysics and the power of Christian novelty. Briefly, we could say that Nietzschean nihilism and Heideggerian ontologism (as expressed by Lévinas's critique of Heidegger) blend Christianity with Greek Platonism. This is the same kind of blend that Dilthey saw in Augustine. (We could ask whether, in different manners, both thinkers express similar personal and psychological elements. Nietzsche, the son of a pastor, rebelled against his father's authority, his sister's, and so on; Heidegger distanced himself from the Catholic Church at the very beginning of his academic career. All this is mixed with issues of politics and power: I am referring to Nietzsche's last writings and to Heidegger's involvement in Nazism.) To a different degree and for reasons that are only vaguely similar to Augustine's, Nietzsche and Heidegger remain captive to Greek objectivism and refuse to develop fully the implications of Christianity's antimetaphysical revolution. These cannot be fully developed without recourse to charity. In other words, only friendship, explicitly recognized as the decisive truth factor, can prevent the thought of the end of metaphysics from lapsing into a reactive—and often reactionary—nihilism, to use Nietzsche's expression.

Here I shall limit myself to a simple sketch—which, I hope, is suggestive enough, though in need of clarification. In my view, the central role of the Other (here we touch on the theological objectivism in Lévinas's thought) in the different theories of Lévinas, Habermas's philosophy of communication, and Davidson's use of the very term *charity* confirms my hypothesis concerning the central role of the Christian *caritas*.

Why, then, should we not prefer Lévinas, Habermas, and Davidson to the dubious authority of controversial thinkers such as Nietzsche and Heidegger? One might answer that only Nietzsche and Heidegger have offered a more rigorous philosophical foundation—by reconstructing the history and dissolution of metaphysics (which can be found also in Nietzsche's chapter, "How the Real World Became a Fable," in *Twilight of the Idols*)—than that advanced by Habermas and Lévinas, who are also well disposed to charity. To put it more explicitly: friendship can become the principle and factor of truth only if thought leaves behind any claim to an objective, universal, and apodictic foundation. Outside of an authentic opening of Being as event, the Lévinasian other is always exposed to the risk of being dethroned by the Other (with a capital letter). Once again, it is a truth that justifies friendship for Plato only by eliminating him as a historical individual. A similar argument holds for Habermas, for his "nonopaque" communication, which operates as a normative horizon, is not grounded on respect for the other as such. Rather, it reduces the other and the self to an idea of rational "transparence." Yet even if Habermas's philosophy is not modeled on a Kantian type of rationalist metaphysics, or precisely because it claims not to be, it is only in the last resort a colonization of the life-world by strategic rationality, which holds sway in techno-science.

Christian preaching on charity is not exclusively an ethical or edifying consequence of the "objective" truth of revelation about our nature as children of God. Rather, it is a call that arises from the historical event of incarnation (it is historical not in the sense that it is a "real" phenomenon but rather insofar as, in its *Wirkungsgeschichte* [effective history], it is constitutive of our existence) and that speaks of the nihilistic vocation of Being. It is a teleology in which every ontic structure is weakened in favor of ontological Being, namely the *Verbum*, Logos, Word shared in the Dialogue (*Gespräch*) that constitutes us as historical beings.

Truth as charity and Being as event (*Ereignis*) are closely related. The central role of the Other in contemporary philosophy acquires its full meaning only if it is placed in the context of the dissolution of metaphysics. Only this condition prevents thought from lapsing into a mere edifying or pragmatic moralism. Notwithstanding the impreciseness of this provisional conclusion, I believe, one should begin here a reflection on what remains to be recollected and undertaken of the mysterious event that took place two thousand years ago.

9

Violence, Metaphysics, and Christianity

IT IS THE paradox of our epoch that we are called to reflect on the link between violence and metaphysics, and on its presence in the history of Christianity, precisely when war is being waged to eradicate war and violence employed to eliminate violence (e.g., of Serbs against Kosovars, or vice versa). The idea that violence might put an end to violence (since every war is supposedly the last) shows that violence ultimately draws from the need, the resolve, and the desire to reach and be taken up into the first principle. I do not know whether this might be the original sin. Yet it seems certain that the almost innate need, which metaphysics addresses, to grasp the origin (*arche*) is deeply linked to *hubris*, that is, to the desire to own one's existence completely. Hence the predominance in humans of laws of survival that "justify" violence where evil dwells. From this perspective, the contemporary interpretation of original sin (which is also found in the Church fathers) as a violation linked to the sphere of sexuality seems plausible. However, this is only because the will of affirmation and the will to survive reveal themselves here in their most elemental sense: in how sexuality is lived immediately and psychologically, and in its place in the reproduction of biological life. A number of corollaries can be drawn here, for example, the "blessing" of sexuality in marriage, which grants that institution the same legitimacy as a just war. It is a justice that can be called into question, that conceals violence—in the case of sex, the will of affirmation and the desire of fulfilling life—with the principle "one must live on," always invoked to justify the perpetration of the worst foul deeds. Furthermore, from this perspective, could the purely ludic use of sexuality be the principal way in which culture tried to diminish the original violence of the law of survival, as if to displace the instincts of self-affirmation and supremacy from war to sport? In any case, the sexual morality long preached by the (Catholic) Church, which sees sexuality mainly, or exclusively, as a means of reproduction, involves considerably less respect and attention for the other than the ludic, seductive, and aesthetic sexuality of Don Juan.

These are just a few possible examples of how, through an intricate, long, and often complex chain of influences—which needs to be reexamined—metaphysical violence affects deeply many of the most controversial aspects of "Christian morality." Metaphysical violence is, generally, all identification between law and nature, which has dominated the traditional teaching of the Church. The command to love one's neighbor, above all one's enemy, appears so barely reasonable as to require a metaphysical grounding in the more natural feeling of fraternal love, of love for one's own—those who are bound to us by virtue of birth. Any morality that ignores Hume's Law tends to be violent. Hume's Law, recall, refers to the observation made by the British philosopher that it is not possible to move from the description of a natural behavior to the assertion of a norm without presupposing another thesis (i.e., that what happens in nature is good in itself).

It is true that the great tradition of natural legal thought always saw itself as reason's struggle against arbitrary violence, and that the Church's concern with the *preambula fidei* was experienced mostly as a preoccupation with dialogue, a way of drawing closer to nonbelievers that did not presuppose their adherence to Christ's message. It was a way of making the Christian message acceptable. However, it is equally true that the tradition of natural legal thought was conceived and practiced as a way of legitimating the "reasonable" use of force, for example to authorize rebellion against a tyrant. And the reasonableness of the *preambula fidei* often has justified coercing people to believe on the ground that human reason itself demands the acceptance of faith. Contemporary Catholic teaching is in line with this when it demands that the laws of the state must conform to the laws that the Church claims to be "natural."

The point, however, is not to discuss the advantages or disadvantages of the tradition of natural law. Perhaps the idea of natural rights had the historical function of diminishing violence in times of extreme cultural fragmentation, hence the idea of a "natural" brotherhood of men. It would be interesting to ask when and how the idea of natural rights, and that of loving one's neighbor on the ground of a natural "brotherhood" of men, fell into crisis and began to reveal their violent foundations. In all likelihood, we would discover that this transformation is bound up with the same principle that, according to Heidegger, has put an end to metaphysics: the fact of its becoming, from the ideal prefigurations of reality's rationalization, an effective law for the functioning of the rational world of technology—and the power grounded in it.

Therefore, violence in Christianity maintains itself and rules as long as it maintains its multiple links to metaphysics. Wilhelm Dilthey, in *Introduction to the Human Sciences* (1883), had argued already that the beginning of the end of metaphysics (understood as the identification of Being with the objectivity of the visible form, that is, as the intellectual vision of ideas with the stability of reality's essential structures) coincided with the advent of Christianity. According to Dilthey, metaphysics lasted well after Kant because the philosophical meaning of the new Christian concern with interiority, subjectivity, and, ultimately, freedom emerged only after a long period during which the metaphysical objectivism of antiquity continued to prevail. This was because the Church inherited the historical structures of antiquity, and in order to ensure its survival had to preserve that culture. Thus Saint Augustine is at once the philosopher of the *Confessions* and the bishop who exercises historical and political power. What Dilthey advances as a purely factual explanation for the survival of metaphysics in Christianity (which lasts more or less as long as the temporal power of the Church and of the churches does) should be broadened and radicalized in the direction suggested by Rene Girard. According to him, it is the survival of the victim-based mechanism, albeit in attenuated form, that explains the recurrence of violence in the history of Christianity. To complete Girard's argument, we learn from Heidegger that what Girard calls the victim-based mechanism is metaphysical objectivism. While Girard sees its nature in the deep-rooted presence of mimetic violence within individuals and human societies (the original sin?), for Heidegger it is the impossibility of overcoming metaphysics. Metaphysics cannot be overcome by a human decision until Being addresses humanity in a different manner (only a God can save us?). What should not be lost in these intersecting interpretations (victim-based mechanism and metaphysics) is, too, the relationship with structures of power.

In my opinion, it is relevant to note here that the hardening of the Church's position on metaphysical-natural ethics manifests itself in the form of a struggle to uphold certain principles in the laws of states. My argument is not that the Church's defense of (what it believes to be natural) law in matters of family ethics and, more recently, of bioethics is an expression of its will to retain the temporal power that over the centuries it has seen erode. Instead, I want to call attention to the fact that the defense of these principles and the manner of their justification (as natural principles, rather than as explicitly Christian theses) correspond to a specific conception of the Church in the world. This is the figure of a structure organized hierarchically and vertically that is ultimately authoritarian. The pope's encyclical *Fides et Ratio* (1998) bears witness to this conception: it invites philosophy to put trust in a reason that is free to search for the truth. Could anyone read *Fides et Ratio* in a different manner? The encyclical's novelty lies in its explicitly stated purpose of "recruiting" in defense of Christian naturalist metaphysics the same philosophy that in the past few centuries, by practicing free inquiry, has increasingly moved away from metaphysics.

To return to the main argument, violence found its way into Christianity when Christianity made an alliance with metaphysics as the "science of Being as being," that is, as the knowledge of first principles. The reasons for this alliance and the circumstances behind it are many, beginning with the responsibilities the Church inherited from the dissolution of the Roman Empire, as the only remaining temporal power. Another reason is the classical identification of Christian existence with the philosophical existence: the human being can realize humanity fully by rising to the knowledge of the first principle (following the model of Plato and Plotinus), to be taken up into it. In this view, the commandment of charity appears totally inconsequential. What ultimately matters is knowledge of the truth, which involves detachment from the sensible good so that struggle for survival and conflict with others may be reduced. However, the positive meaning of forgoing violence is not an (ethical) openness to the other.

The idea that morality has to do with the respect of natural law belongs to the same tradition. It claims that perfection lies in conforming to the first principle and is persuaded, without question or explanation, of the first principle's force. Here *hubris* and submission are inextricably blended and in contradiction, to reveal the neurotic mindset of metaphysics—as Nietzsche correctly pointed out. We are aware that whenever we reflect on the possibility of overcoming metaphysics we encounter a number of theoretical, ethical, and existential difficulties that deeply involve us. The analysis of the metaphysical and violent roots of our culture could put in question even the "*factum*" of the categorical imperative that, according to Kant, speaks within us.

How shall we rethink Christian ethics and metaphysics if we concede that (a) the idea of perfection—as a movement of ascendance toward and mystic identification with the first principle (Plotinus)—is the manifestation of *hubris*, as well as a source of further violence (through the imposition of the natural law against the will of men); and (b) the idea that the moral law can be grounded only upon nature as *factum*—a given beyond which questions cannot be asked—is a contradictory and radically violent thought? (Why should I no longer ask why? And if nature is the law, of necessity it must realize itself, thus making the imposition of a command utterly meaningless.)

Even just posing these hypotheses and the questions arising from them destabilizes many of the most firmly rooted structures of our mindset. How to think of perfection if not as the identification with Being itself, God, the supreme principle? And how to think of metaphysics, or in any case essential knowledge, if not as the theoretical appropriation of first principles? How to ground the law if

not in an incontrovertible, unquestionable, and given structure, which as such can also legitimate the use of force?

For Heidegger, the difficulty of formulating answers to
these kinds of questions makes clear the impossibility of
going beyond metaphysics. Metaphysics cannot be overcome but only *verwunden*—accepted, distorted, and continued in ironic directions that are known to be provisional.
The same may be said of Girard's thesis, according to
which sacrifice cannot not be repeated, even in the purely
symbolic forms of ritual like the Mass, precisely because
otherwise mimetic violence risks unleashing itself again in
unmediated forms of bloody conflict. This recognition, in
its Heideggerian and in its Girardian form, does not exempt us from the effort to understand how we can or must
continue the saving act of revelation, which manifests the
violent nature of the victim-based mechanism and of metaphysics, thus reducing anew the violence of institutions,
including ecclesiastical ones. The difference between Girard and Heidegger, or even between Heidegger and his
hermeneutic followers, can be explained by their different
conceptions of the symbolization of sacrifice, or the meaning of *Verwindung*. This argument can be reasonably developed in reference to secularization. Even Weber's interpretation of Christian ethics as a rationally organized
economy is perhaps a means of symbolizing sacrifice.
Above all, the establishment of liberal principles in a liberal
society and in the political organization (do anything you
will as long as it does not infringe upon the freedom of all
others) is a secular symbolizing of the Christian message.

If we accept Girard's thesis that the natural sacred is
violence, and that sacrifice is the victimization of a scape-
goat against whom all the bloody expressions of the mimetic crisis are unleashed, then it seems difficult to escape
from the logic of secularization as the continuation of the
Christian revelation's saving action. Someone has leveled
the objection—I am referring to debates in which I have

recently participated, but it would be equally possible to cite authoritative printed sources in support of this position—that the idea of sacrifice as violence excludes the possibility of self-sacrifice. Jesus is at the same time victim and priest; therefore, so the argument runs, he is not subjected to violence by another. Rather, he inflicts violence upon himself, thereby escaping from the victim-based logic described by Girard. To this objection, we can reply that: (a) one can understand that Jesus had to sacrifice himself for the love of humanity, even as an act of free choice, only if one grants that a sacrifice was required of him. If the remission of sins requires sacrifice, it confirms the logic of the victim-based mechanism, for the God who demands the satisfaction of "justice" is still conceived of as the violent God of natural religions; (b) if Jesus' free sacrifice was inspired by something other than the victim-based logic, then we must take seriously the idea that it demands to be understood as kenotic salvation. This does not imply salvation by means of kenosis, for if glory had to be reached through humiliation and suffering we would act in full accordance with the victim-based logic. Kenosis is not a means of ransom but ransom itself. To me, this appears the most reasonable reading of the message of incarnation. It might be considered a "nihilist" reading, but only by those who still want to conceive of Being metaphysically in terms of imposition, stability, and the full evidence of the present. These are precisely the attributes found in Aristotle's pure act or in Parmenides' Being, which stand radically opposed to the idea of Being as a creation of a free and loving God. The metaphysical God, whom Christian theology thought necessary to acknowledge as its "natural" foundation, also poses problems, such as the idea of predestination, that are ultimately unresolvable. This requires a theodicy that is always vulnerable to the irony of Voltaire's Candide, and that to this day inspires the naturalist—authoritarian and inefficient—ethics found in the teaching of the pope.

Does this mean then that if we seek to follow Christian revelation more radically against the logic of metaphysics and of the victim-based mechanism, there are no limits or rational guides? Perhaps yes, we might answer. One remains at the mercy of the event, that is, one is entrusted to positivity as an occurrence of creation and revelation, rather than as an expression of natural structures. Why should we place our trust in the certainty of metaphysical evidence rather than in the interpretation of the divine Word, given by the community of believers and freely by each individual believer, which changes in accordance with the becoming of history? This question can have only two answers. Either God is immutable—but then this is the God of metaphysics to whom one cannot attribute the creation of the world in time, much less the loving creation of free beings—or metaphysical evidence is safe from the possibility of freedom, since it all is entrusted to the hands of an authority once and for all, and this authority must grant it legitimacy even when rationally free inquiry discovers that it is baseless. These are not two alternative replies. Indeed, in the Church's ancient and recent history, these answers are inseparable. For this reason, too, their prevalence in our contemporary world cannot be attributed to the perverse cunning of priests. Rather, it must be seen as inevitable, similarly to the persistence of the victim-based logic in Girard or of the impossibility of overcoming metaphysics in Heidegger. However, this does not mean that we should not prepare anew, through a radical critique, for the possible overcoming of metaphysics, even if only in the form of *Verwindung*. Salvation is not positively in our hands. Rather, we are called to be vigilant, so that we might not be fooled by the Antichrist.

10

~

Heidegger and Christian Existence

HEIDEGGER'S RELATIONSHIP TO the Christian, and
specifically Catholic, tradition is still to be thoroughly explored. Heidegger was steeped in Catholicism to the extent
that his bishop subsidized his studies, and he was considered the bright promise of German Catholic thought at the
beginning of his career. Perhaps this relationship to Christianity will appear in a new light after the release of more
unpublished works in addition to those that have appeared
in recent years. Among the latter, the "Einleitung in die
Phenomenologie der Religion" (Introduction to the Phenomenology of Religion)[1] has a central place. This is a
transcript of the course Heidegger taught at the University
of Freiburg during the winter semester 1920, which appeared in 1995 in the *Gesamtausgabe*. As often happens with
his lecture courses, Heidegger is much more comprehensible here than in the "written" texts. The importance of
this "Einleitung" is not only that it anticipates clearly and
effectively many themes of *Being and Time*, which thus appear in the subsequent elaboration of Heidegger's thought.
What is more significant and striking is that the theme of

Being and Time is linked here *essentially* to a meditation on Christian experience, along with the idea of metaphysics as the forgetting of Being, which Heidegger would develop later. This Christian link is essential, especially if one keeps in mind the meaning Heidegger's writings give to the word *Wesen*. By this I mean that the main concepts of *Being and Time* appear unthinkable without reference to the Christian *Event*. Hence this link is of a historical and destinal character, and cannot be deduced analytically from the "concept" of Christianity.

The fundamental nature of the link must be emphasized, because it is precisely the historical (existential) character of the nexus between *Being and Time* and Christian experience that I want to address here. It becomes clear in the "Einleitung"—especially in the first part where Heidegger explores the question of the philosophical and phenomenological analysis of religious experience—that Christian experience is not one among other religious experiences from which the general meaning of religion might be abstracted. What distinguishes Heidegger's conception of phenomenology from that of his teacher, Husserl, is the idea that no knowledge of essences is given outside of the existential relation of the "subject" with its "object." This is already clear as well in another essay (a review of Karl Jaspers's *Psychologie der Weltanschauungen*) of the same period, which was published only in the third edition of the *Wegmarken*, released prior to Heidegger's death. In his review of the *Psychologie der Weltanschauungen*, Heidegger's main objection is that by limiting himself to a panoramic or "aesthetic" vision and to a typological classification of world views, Jaspers has forgotten the genuine philosophical aim stated at the beginning of his book, namely that of analyzing the world views in order to question his own, thereby involving himself thematically in the analysis. It is precisely on the basis of this methodological principle that Heidegger turns to the question of a phenomenology of religion.

The apparently unjustified transition from the first part of the lecture course might be explained by assuming that Heidegger wants to remain faithful to the idea of philosophy that inspires him. There is an abrupt shift between the first part, punctuated by general and methodological observations that lead Heidegger to discuss contemporary theories of religion (from the perspective of an existential phenomenology), and the second part, where two Letters of Paul to the Thessalonians are analyzed in depth. This is a philosophy that does not approach its theme from an external angle but rather subsumes it within the framework of factic life-experience (*faktische Lebenserfahrung*),[2] which phenomenology cannot do without. Consider the following passages from Heidegger's review of Jaspers: "The path that leads to the 'things themselves' . . . is a genuine confrontation with the history that we ourselves 'are.'"[3] It is difficult to say whether this approach is a kind of neutral methodological presupposition, imposed by the concern that phenomenology should be more radically or authentically scientific in a broad sense. This approach would then be applicable to all philosophical analysis, including of religion. By contrast, the very concept of factic life-experience might not be derived from the assumption of religious—and specifically Christian—experience as a model of an authentically radical philosophy. (Religious experience is above all one that cannot take place without a personal commitment, a response that may not be confined in its constitutive form to the objective grasping of a content.) After all, Heidegger seems to confirm such a hypothesis when he argues in the lecture course that the early Christian experience recovered through Paul consists of the experience of authentic temporality. We could say that here it is a matter of logical circles. But it is such circles that make up factic reflection, which after all later will be theorized explicitly as the "hermeneutic circle."

These few remarks already threaten to lead into a vortex, like the abysses of which the later Heidegger speaks. They suggest that it is not only the conceptual framework of *Being and Time* that is inseparable from the reflection on Christian experience but also Heidegger's philosophical attitude as a whole. A phenomenologist like Husserl, or like one of his faithful disciples, easily understands that the concept of science invented by the Greeks has by now become an essential patrimony of humanity, as *The Crisis of the European Sciences* argues. They may think this without further analyzing the relationship between the historicity of this "invention" and the human essence from which it is said to have gradually become indistinguishable. This is a specific movement of thought typical of all Eurocentric philosophy of the West, which always has identified its own culture, in its historical becoming, with humanity—a humanity that supposedly revealed itself most completely in the West. This is the meaning of humanism, to which Heidegger turned in his 1946 "Letter on Humanism." A close reading of the 1920 lectures suggests that, in Heidegger's view, we cannot avoid conceiving of philosophy in Christian terms, while maintaining a clear knowledge that Christianity is an event—that is, fully embracing our concrete historicity instead of leaving it behind in order to turn to the vision of essence. Instead, we are to elaborate the factic life-experience into a critique of metaphysics and the later theme of the "history of Being." Perhaps Heidegger's insistence on terms like *"egheneto"* and *"eghenestai"* (I Thessalonians 1:5–7) in reading Paul refers to the possibility of such an "essential" dimension, understood as destiny and not as a universality in the sense of metaphysical abstractions. Such an insistence can be taken as a justification of the logical "leap" from the first to the second part of the course. If indeed Christian religious experience is recognizable as (definitely more than) the model of an authentic experience of temporality—which insofar as it is our destiny (*Wesentlich*), we cannot avoid recognizing as the *only* authentic experience of temporality—it is because we, those who are set to study religious experience phenomenologically, have already "become," that is, we have already come to know it (*oidate*) because we have received the announcement. We can express this observation in different ways: for example, by recognizing as a constitutive characteristic of religious experience—the one accessible to us—the fact that we can never begin by choosing among different religions, but must find ourselves already in a tradition, in a faith that we can certainly criticize or refute but not decide from scratch to accept or not. Perhaps this is a feature of all religious experience, but it is certain that in the case of Christianity, this has to do with the historicity of revelation and ultimately with the creation narrated in the Bible rather than with the anthropological data that see religion taught within the family, together with a mother tongue and the first rules of behavior. True, the having become of which Paul speaks consists of the transformation that has already taken place among the Thessalonians in response to his preaching; they learn from Paul what they already know. However, it is also clear that in Heidegger this has a broader meaning—insofar as authentic temporality is manifested as a tension between the "already" and the "not yet," which is the structure of Christian eschatology. To reduce *egheneto* to the recent memory of Paul's preaching implies a literal reading that Paul himself refutes (and that we, as interpreters, cannot ignore), since his first preaching to the Thessalonians is the announcement of what they already are by virtue of Christ's redemption.

In what sense, then, does "recognizing oneself in what one already is" constitute the basis of an authentic experience of temporality? Recall that in the first part of the lecture course, Heidegger often evokes historicism as the characteristic feature of our epoch, which manifests itself in a false mode of approaching reflections on religion (because it reduces religion to the historical reconstruction of religions, and of their histories). Historicism espouses a linear conception of time as the succession of instants within which events and things stand as objects that can be approached with an attitude of detachment, that is, "objectively," because our historicity in turn consists of belonging again and again to always different instants along the trajectory of time ("Einleitung" 31ff). However, lived historicity is what Heidegger seeks to grasp with factic life-experience, and it is different than standing inside the flow of time. The authentic temporality of Christian experience appears as the solution to the problem, or at least as an alternative model to standing as simple presence inside the linear flow of time. *Egheneto*, the already that constitutes the background against which Paul's preaching is set in the Letters, is the having already happened of salvation through the death and resurrection of Christ. This salvation is not a "past" event in the horizontal-objective meaning of the term, in the sense that it is not completed and must be awaited as the eschatological event of the *parousia*. Let me point out that the difficulty in thinking through this experience of Christian temporality is not at all different from that encountered in reading passages of *Being and Time* on this theme, though in the latter there is no longer any reference to the biblical texts. The fact is that there is no true description, or positive definition, of the authentic experience of temporality. What does it mean to stand as an object among separate objects along the irreversible and continuous flow of time? As the "Letter on Humanism" says, it was precisely in the effort to reflect on authenticity that Heidegger discovered the "impossibility of overcoming" metaphysics and the lack of a language that prevented him from concluding *Being and Time*, and that constitutes the theme of his reflection later on. Anyhow, the mode in which Paul relates to the faithful in Salonicco, to whom he writes, exemplifies a non-"objective" mode of relating to history. "You are our glory and our joy" (I Thessalonians 2:20) is not merely a rhetorical expression. Paul is aware that his mission's success, and his very salvation, are bound up with the faithfulness to the gospel that the Thessalonians will preserve till the *parousia* ("Einleitung" 97–98). It is also true that neither *Being and Time* nor this lecture course gives clear or positive indications of authentic temporality. At least, we have no more indications than those concerning the overcoming of metaphysics—which in the lecture course is not called in this manner, though it is clearly anticipated in the Pauline (and Heideggerian) analysis of the modes of Christian experience and of its diversions. Paul insists above all on the significance of *thlipsis*, the affliction characteristic of the Christian life, starting with the "thorn in the flesh" of which the second Letter to the Corinthians speaks (II Corinthians 12:2–10), which prevents him, who once was "snatched up to heaven," from boasting about his feeling of superiority to his Thessalonian audience. *Thlipsis* is not so much a specific kind of temptation that Christians should resist (the tradition often alludes to the temptation of the senses) or a suggestion of the saving function of suffering (here too, how much Christian tradition of "pain"!). Rather, it is watchfulness, as the *parousia* is seen not as an "objectively" announced fact but as the "thief in the night" who comes when we least expect him, because it is impossible to know the day or the hour:

> II Cor. 12:2–10 gave us a glimpse of the self-world of Paul. The extraordinary plays no role in his life. Only when he is weak, when he endures the afflictions of his life, he can enter into close relationship with God. What is decisive is not mystic contemplation and its specific strains, but the endurance of weakness throughout his life.[3]

Here the reference to mysticism and the extraordinary experience expressed in the Letter to the Corinthians are decisive: the rest of the commentary and the observations concerning the meaning of the term *parousia* itself suggest that it is a matter of remaining faithful to the idea of Christ's return. This return is understood not as an objective or past event of which we would be certain once and for all (although Heidegger does not make this point explicitly, one might think that faith is not faith in the certainty of historical events, whose verified extraordinariness might ground belief in the announcement), nor as the given presence of mystical experience, nor as a predictable future occurrence located within the flow of time. The Christian language has changed the literal meaning of *parousia*, which in Greek means "presence." "The transformation of the concept, though, discloses another Christian life-experience. . . . For Christians, *parousia* means the reappearance of the Messiah who has appeared once before; a meaning that is not literally in the words."[4] Waiting for the *parousia* does not entail waiting for a future event within linear time: "We never move in the pure analysis of consciousness from a future event to the sense of reference of the *parousia*."[5]

Here we glimpse, if you will, the effort to grasp in concepts the pure historicity of existence, which is not given naturally; instead, it must be conceptualized clearly in opposition to the metaphysical banality in which existence is always already thrown, as *Being and Time* says. Let me cite a few passages to illustrate these concepts: "The characteristic of the Christian life (which means, as we know, the authentic experience of temporality) is that it does not know the day or the hour of the *parousia*."[6] "For the Christian life there is no certainty; constant uncertainty is the basic meaning of the factic life. The uncertain is not accidental, but rather necessary. . . . Those who say, 'Peace and Security!' are taken up by what life offers; they are in the dark in terms of knowledge of themselves."[7] And a bit further: "The meaning of temporality is basic to factic life-experience, just as much as it is basic to problems such as the eternity of God."[8] It is not too difficult to recognize in the inauthentic experience of time the objectifying thought that forgets Being for the sake of beings, which later Heidegger will blame on metaphysics. In the 1920 lecture, the links to metaphysics are visible in the argument that Christianity has forgotten the original meaning of eschatology. "The present analysis has dealt with the core of the Christian life: the eschatological problem. Soon after the end of the first centuries the eschatological problem was concealed. Afterward, the original meaning of Christian concepts was not recognized. In contemporary philosophy too, the Christian formations of concepts are concealed behind the Greek attitude."[9] Concealment (*Verdeckung*) and forgetfulness (*Vergessenheit*) are terms that the later Heidegger employs to speak of metaphysics as the forgetting of Being. Here they are merely a foreshadowing, which is sufficient to pose the question of how the forgetting of Christian eschatology and the forgetting of Being have been conjoined in the course of metaphysics, and of the extent to which they may be the same thing.

If we take literally, as I believe we should, these last passages from Heidegger's text, they lead not only to renewed questioning of Heideggerian philosophy's essential link to the Christian tradition but also to rethinking that tradition on the basis of the vision of metaphysics as the history of (the forgetting of) Being. The commentary to the Second Letter to the Thessalonians provides important indications to this effect, as it focuses on the Christian duty to wait for the *parousia* without mistaking the Antichrist in its multiple forms for the Messiah. These multiple forms may be traced back to the claim that the *parousia* cannot be identified with an "objective" historical event, a fact placed at a determinable instant of time. What in the end becomes clear is that after its origins, the history of Christianity forgot the authentic meaning of eschatological waiting, and therefore can be taken as the history of the Antichrist. It is a history in the course of which the authenticity of the Christian message has been misunderstood, and that runs parallel to the history of the metaphysical forgetting of Being (perhaps not so much parallel to as intertwined with it; by the same token, onto-theology is only another name for metaphysics).

We can begin here an examination of the meaning of this link for Christianity, despite the synthetic way in which it has been studied so far, leaving for a future project the further analysis of its fundamental links to Heidegger's mature thought (from *Being and Time* to the writings following the "turning"). True, Heidegger's hypothesis that the history of Christianity is a "metaphysical" misunderstanding of the original meaning of the New Testament message is not in itself an original thesis. We might ask whether and to what extent it is not the pure and simple retrieval of modernist themes that were circulating in those years within Catholic thought and were condemned by Pope Pius X's *Encyclica Pascendi* in 1907. Here we can see, more in line with Heidegger's changing attitudes toward Catholicism, the basis of his polemical break from the scholastic tradition and from the "classical" metaphysics that this tradition intended to retrieve. This break was motivated by faithfulness to the original Christian experience, and was expressed in analogous terms to what was taking place in Catholic modernism.

Whatever the links that may be verified historically, even at the price of reducing considerably the originality of Heidegger's position, it is interesting to stress some of the implications of his commentary to the two epistles of Paul for a conception of faith and of Christian ethics. The insistence on the meaning of the "affliction" that must be endured without expecting to know the day or the hour has a theoretical significance that takes precedence over the

ethical, and touches the very meaning of faith and the theology in which it finds its inspiration. The Antichrist who
continually tests the faithful and drives them to idolatrously
identify the Messiah with figures who falsify his meaning
refers to representational, objectifying thought (which
Heidegger later on calls metaphysical thought), which,
once it asserted itself in the Christian tradition, pushed
into oblivion Christianity's authentic, original content. If
Heidegger's reading of Paul is legitimate, these texts
should tend not to pay excessive attention to the "theoretical" and descriptive content of biblical revelation.
Every attempt to read revelation as a teaching on the nature
and attributes of God falls into the same error of representational thought—the sin of objectifying metaphysics—
against which we are called to recover the hearing of Being.
The effort to conceive of Christianity and to live the Christian faith in the direction intended by Heidegger should
probably start here, where it makes sense only if one understands that the Christian tradition is the main and most
constant source of Heidegger's ontology, which one can do
on the basis of writings such as the 1920 lecture course. In
other words, if, as I believe, we must hypothesize (or, better, acknowledge) that Heidegger's philosophy is inseparable from its original reflection on the biblical message,
this hypothesis does not merely clarify the historical (*histo-
risch!*) sources of his philosophy or lead it back to Christianity as though in an ultimately reassuring conversion (as
if to say that we may be Heideggerians without necessarily
being against Christianity). Rather, we require an effect of
reciprocity: not only does Paul help us clarify Heidegger,
but Heidegger also proposes observations that, if taken seriously, guide us in a reinterpretation of the Christian tradition.

The separation of the early Christian faith from representational thought (the Antichrist)—cursorily elaborated by Heidegger in the context of his critique of onto-

theology—discloses the task of thinking of faith without "substance," perhaps without dogma, and without a theology as a science. Heidegger's polemical allusions to mysticism in the lecture course appear to take the same direction, for mysticism is viewed as yielding to the need for an "object" wherein to lose oneself (*Versenkung*), thus finding freedom from the weakness of existence, from *thlipsis*— which is the only authentic mode of waiting for the *parousia*.[10] This is, too, the way in which we should read the links established in paragraph 28 between the Antichrist and the history of Christian dogmatic thought (110–112): "It is a profound problem for the history of spirit that the very concept of philosophy has to measure itself against the history of dogmatic thought, which has taken the perspective of representational thought criticized earlier."[11]

Regarding the ethics that might develop out of this kind of faith, the stress on weakness seems illuminating insofar as it discloses the meaning of authentic existence in relation to Being-toward-death (*Sein zum tode*)—of which *Being and Time* speaks. The meaning of Being-toward-death has been seen often (by myself, among others) as a key to authentic existence, in relation to the constitution of existence as a continuous texture of meaning and referrals: existence (*Dasein*) constitutes itself, albeit paradoxically, as an authentic totality only with a view to the possible impossibility of all possibility of life, which is constituted by the impending possibility of death. It is only by facing up to the possibility of death that the various, concrete possibilities of life appear in their true meaning as possibilities rather than hardening in their finality, and therefore let existence constitute itself as a dis-cursus endowed with meaning.

Heidegger's reference to the weakness of life endured with faith, in contrast with mystic *Versenkung*, seems to allude to a vision that is so different as to make us suspicious of this interpretation of authentic existence. Perhaps the authenticity made possible by the anticipatory decision for death cannot really be understood as an experience of meaning. Rather, *Dasein*'s authentic existence has the character of lack and affliction, similarly to the Christian existence in Paul. In other words, *Dasein*'s existence is predicated on the constant renunciation of the belief that existence is meaningful (*Sinnvoll*), and therefore is the weakness endured in waiting for the *parousia*. A few pages on in his text, Heidegger remarks that "In the Christian life, though, there is also an unbroken sense of life with spirituality that has nothing to do with the harmony of a life."[12] (Note that in *Being and Time* there is no mention of anything that could compare to the *parousia*. And yet Heidegger's insistence in his later writings on listening to Being has something to say on this matter.)

Heidegger's last word in his commentary to Paul can be placed in the framework I have outlined so far, namely the reference to the passage from the first Letter to the Corinthians, where Paul defines Christian existence in "negative" terms by means of the famous expression "*os mé*." If Christian existence is so careful not to allow itself to be defined by any positive content on the plane of faith or by any positive obligation on the moral plane (this too would be a form of idolatry, of Antichrist), it appears to resist all definition. Yet one attains an image of Christian existence that is faithful to Paul's teaching precisely by "leaving aside the substantive elements" of revelation.[13] A Christian's life is radically historical, and therefore is determined by the cultural and vital frameworks into which he is thrown. However, while remaining totally immersed in his historical condition, the Christian remains faithful and waits for the Lord's return. This is how Heidegger understands the text of I Corinthians 7:29:

> What I mean, my brothers, is this: time is short, and from now on married men should live as though

they were not married; those who weep, as though they were not sad; those who laugh, as though they were not happy; those who buy, as though they did not have possessions; those who deal in material goods, as though they were not fully occupied with them.

There is no alternative model of Christian life apart from the historical and always contingent involvement required of all the faithful; equally, there is no arcane knowledge of the mysteries that might be foreclosed to nonbelievers. There is no analogy with the mystery religions and initiation rites of the Greek tradition. "The initiate is to be removed from the context of life by means of manipulation. In a condition of rapture, God and the All are had in the present. The Christian knows no such 'enthusiasm,' but rather says 'let us be awake and sober.'"[14] Although it does not appear explicitly here, Heidegger clearly has Husserl's term *epoché* in mind; on the following page he speaks of "phenomenological destruction," and soon afterward he alludes to Augustine and Luther, to suggest perhaps that, for himself, the idea that salvation might come from works rather than from faith is "Antichristian."

Is it possible to link to a profession of Lutheran Protestantism Heidegger's observations about the mode of conceiving and living Christian experience? We should at least keep in mind that in the subsequent elaborations of his thought Heidegger did not explicitly go in this direction. Moreover, his polemics against the Christian tradition and the history of dogmatic thought after the apostolic period increasingly blurred with the effort to overcome metaphysics and the onto-theology that always accompanies it. All this probably means that we would be led astray if we were to read these Heideggerian passages as a giving in to the motifs of Catholic modernism or as signs of the philosopher's transition from one Christian confession to another. It would seem to be more accurate historically, and therefore more faithful to the development of Heidegger's thought, to ask whether here there are meaningful indications for more positive and productive links between the philosophical effort to overcome metaphysical objectivism and the search for a vision of Christianity. This vision would be capable finally of reflecting its own ecumenical sense on the planes of both dogma and ethics, as a way of listening to the new—postmodern—age of Being.

~

Notes

Introduction

1. G.Vattimo, *Belief*, trans. Luca D'Isanto and David Webb (Cambridge: Polity Press, 1999).

1. The God Who Is Dead

1. See Schlechta, III, 853.

2. See for instance my *Il soggetto e la maschera. Nietzsche e il problema della liberazione*, 3rd ed. (Milan: Bompiani, 1999); *Dialogo con Nietzsche* (Milan: Garzanti, 2000); *Introduzione a Heidegger*, 14th ed. (Roma-bari: Laterza, 2000).

3. Martin Heidegger, *The Principle of Reason*, trans. Reginald Lilly (Bloomington: Indiana University Press), 94–102.

2. The Teachings of Joachim of Fiore

1. E. Trias, *La edad del espiritu* (Barcelona: Destino, 1994), 374.

2. See *Concordia Novi ac Veteris Testamenti*, 5:112b–c; and *Expositio in Apocalysm*, f. 5b–c. These two works were edited in Venice in 1519 (*Concordia*) and 1527 (*Expositio*); both reprinted (photo. reprod.) by Minerva Verlag (Frankfurt, 1964).

3. H. De Lubac, *La posterité spirituelle de Joachim de Flore* (Paris: Lethielleux, 1979–1981).

4. Novalis, "Christendom or Europe," in *Philosophical Writings*, trans. M. M. Stoljar (Binghamton: State University of New York Press, 1997), 141.

3. God the Ornament

1. See chapter 10.

2. See the lecture on "Das Ding" in M. Heidegger, *Vortraege und Aufsaetze* (Pfullingen: Neske, 1954), esp. 178–81.

4. History of Salvation, History of Interpretation

1. To illustrate what I am trying to express, even though it may not serve as clarification, I can refer to a page of Heidegger's *Unterwegs zur Sprache* where he employs the colon with the same complex but not obscure sense: "Das Wesen der Sprache: Die Sprache des Wesens."

5. The West or Christianity

1. Novalis, "Christendom or Europe," in *Philosophical Writings*, trans. M. M. Stoljar (Binghamton: State University of New York Press, 1997).

2. Hans Blumenberg, *Die Legitimität der Neuezeit* (Suhrkampf: Frankfurt am Main, 1974).

3. Karl Löwith, *Meaning in History: The Theological Implications of the Philosophy of History* (Chicago: University of Chicago Press, 1957).

4. See the discussion between Karl Löwith and Hans Blumenberg published in *aut aut* 22 (Nov.–Dec. 1987).

5. Novalis, "Christendom or Europe," 141.

6. Max Weber, *The Protestant Ethic and the Spirit of Capitalism*, trans. T. Parsons (New York, Scribner, 1958).

7. Colin Campbell, *Romantic Ethics and Modern Consumerism* (Oxford: Blackwell, 1987).

8. A collection of essays by several authors, edited by myself and Pier Aldo Rovatti, under the title *Il pensiero debole*, was published in Milan by Feltrinelli (1983).

9. On these themes, I refer the reader to my book *The Transparent Society*, trans. David Webb (Baltimore: Johns Hopkins University Press, 1992).

10. HEIDEGGER AND CHRISTIAN EXISTENCE
10. Novalis, "Christendom or Europe."

11. Ibid., 151.

12. "Perché non possiamo non dirci cristiani" is the title of a famous short essay by Benedetto Croce, published for the first time in 1942 and reedited in *Discorsi di varia filosofia*, vol. 1 (Bari: Laterza, 1945).

6. The Death or Transfiguration of Religion

1. For an illustration of the thesis of Dilthey, see chapter 10.

8. The Christian Message and the Dissolution of Metaphysics

1. Most recently, a philosophical reinterpretation of Dostoyevsky from a Christian point of view has been proposed by Luigi Pareyson (*Dostoievskij, Filosofia, romanzo ed esperienza religiosa* [Torino: Einaudi, 1993]).

2. Wilhelm Dilthey, *Introduction to the Human Sciences. An Attempt to Lay the Foundation for the Study of Society and History*, trans. Ramon J. Betanzos (Detroit: Wayne State University Press), 229.

3. Ibid.

4. Ibid., 236.

5. Ibid.

6. Ibid., 308.

7. Ibid., 309.

8. Martin Heidegger, *Identität und Differenz* (Neske: Pfullingen, 1957); *Identity and Difference*, trans. J. Stambaugh (New York: Harper & Row, 1969).

10. Heidegger and Christian Existence

1. M. Heidegger, "Einleitung in die Phaenomenologie der Religion," in *Phänomenologie des religiösen Lebens, Gesamtausgabe*, II, vol. 60 (Frankfurt: Klostermann, 1995), 100. From now on cited in the text as "Einleitung," followed by the page number. *(Translations are mine — Tr.)*

2. Martin Heidegger, *Wegmarken* (Frankfurt am Main: Vittorio Klostermann, 1976), 10.

3. M. Heidegger, "Karl Jaspers's Psychology of the World-

views," in *Pathmarks*, ed. W. McNeal (Cambridge: Cambridge University Press, 1998), 4.

4. "[II Cor. 12:2–10] gab uns einen Vorblick in die Selbstwelt des Paulus. Das Auserordentliche in seinem Leben spielt fuer ihn keiner Rolle. Nur, when er schwach ist, wenn er die Noete seines Lebens durchhaelt, kenn er in einen engen Zusammenhang mit Gott treten. . . . Nicht die mystische versenkung und besondere Anstrengung, sondern das Durchhalten der Schwachkeit des Lebens wird entscheidend." Heidegger, "Einleitung," 100.

5. "An diesem Begriffswandel zeigt sich die andersartige christliche Lebenserfahrung. . . . Für den Christen aber heisst parousia: 'das Wiedererscheinen des schon erschienen Messias,' was zunächst im wörtlichen Ausdrück nicht liegt." Ibid., 102.

6. "Wir kommens niemals durch die blosse Analyse des Bewusstseins von einen zukuenftigen Ereignis auf den Bezugsinn der parousia." Ibid.

7. "Fuer das christliche Leben gibt es keine Sicherheit; die staendige Unsicherheit ist auch das Charakteristische fuer die Grundbedeutendheiten des faktischen Lebens. Das Unsichere ist nicht zufaellig, sondern notwendig. . . . Die 'welche Friede und Sicherheit sagen' (5,3) . . . sind aufgegangen von dem, was das Leben bietet; sie sind im Dunkel, angesehen auf das Wissen um sich selbst." Ibid., 105.

8. "Der Sinn dieser Zeitlichkeit ist auch fuer die faktische Lebenserfahrung grundlegend, ebenso fuer Probleme wie etwa das der Ewigkeit Gottes." Ibid., 104.

9. "Die jetzige Betrachtung behandelt das Zentrum des christlichen Lebens:das eschatologische Problem. Schon zu Ende des ersten Jahrhunderts wurde das Eschatologische im Christentum verdeckt. Man verkennt in spaeterer Zeit alle urpruenglich christliche Begriffe. Auch in der heutigen Philosophie sind noch hinter der griechischen Einstellung die christliche Begriffsbildungen verborgen." Ibid., 104.

10. Ibid., 100.

11. "Es ist ein tiefes problem für die Geschichte des Geistes, das in der Begriff der Philosophie selbst sehr nahe angeht, aufzu-

hellen, die eben kritisierte vorstellungsmässige Einstellung genommen hat." Ibid., 111.

12. "Es gibt allerdings im Christlichen Leben auch ein ungebrochenen Lebenszusammenhang auf einer Stufe der Geistigkeit, was Nichts zu tun hat mit der Harmonie eines Lebens." Ibid., 120.

13. "das Inhaltliche beiseite lassen." Ibid., 116.

14. "Lasst uns wach sein und nüchtern." Ibid., 124.

Index

Adorno, Theodor, 4, 14, 110
Aeltestes Systemprogramm des Deutschen Idealismus (Schelling),
    32–33
Aesthetic: and Greek culture, 108; and Joachim of Fiore, 33; and
    spiritualization, 54–55
Altizer, Thomas, 37
Ancient Greek culture, 62, 108; Platonism, 106–7, 110–11, 117
Aristotle, 103, 120
Atheism, collapse of: and Nietzschian death of God, 3, 5, 13, 17;
    and renewal of religion, 86, 87–88
Augustine, Saint, 48, 107–8, 109, 116
Authoritarianism, 82, 117

Barth, Karl, 36, 38, 43
Being and Time (Heidegger), 13, 14, 109; and "Introduction to the
    Phenomenology of Religion," 123–24, 126, 128, 129, 134–35
Being as event, 21–24, 110; and charity, 112; and creation, 6; and
    history of salvation, 31, 43–44; and humanitarianism, 23–24;
    and scientific paradigms, 6–7; and secularization, 34–35; and
    weakening of Being, 22–23

ture, 28–30; progressivism, 29, 31, 41–42; and radical tran-
scendence, 38; and secularization, 25; and weakening of
Being, 52–53; *see also* Spiritualization
Hospitality, 100–102
Hubris, 118
Humanism, 2–3, 4
Humanitarianism, 23–24, 46
Hume's Law, 114
Husserl, Edmund, 124, 126

Idealism, 53–54
Identity and Difference (Heidegger), 110
Immortality, 53
Imperialism, 99
Incarnation: and assimilibility, 27; and charity, 112; and humanitarianism, 24; Joachim of Fiore on, 28, 43; and radical transcendence, 39, 43; and secularization, 67; and universalism,
100; and violence, 120; and weakening of Being, 80; *see also*
Kenosis
Integral Humanism (Maritain), 2
Interpretation, 57–68; and Christianity in cultural conflicts, 98–
99; and community of believers, 67–68; and end of metaphysics, 63–67; and historicity, 60–61; and history of salvation, 57–59; Jesus as, 59–60, 61; and pluralism, 78;
productive, 62–63, 67; and Western culture/Christianity
equivalence, 61–62, 72; *see also* Spiritualization
Introduction to the Human Sciences (Dilthey), 115–16
"Introduction to the Phenomenology of Religion" (Heidegger),
123–37; and *Being and Time*, 123–24, 126, 128, 129, 134–35;
and Jaspers, 124–25; on *parousia*, 129–33; on temporality,
126–28, 129, 131, 135–36
Italian politics, 94

Jaspers, Karl, 11, 27, 124–25
Joachim of Fiore, 26–27; on Being as event, 31, 43–44; influence
on European thought, 32–34; on multiple senses of